ELVIE

GIRL UNDER GLASS

BY ELVIRA CORDILEONE

Renaissance
Diverse Canadian Voices

First edition 2023

Cover and interior design by Nathan Fréchette. Edited by Drew Gilvary, Evan McKinley, and Allyson Hope.

Legal deposit, Library and Archives Canada, December 2023.

Paperback ISBN: 978-1-990086-51-9 - Ebook ISBN: 978-1-990086-62-5

Renaissance - pressesrenaissancepress.ca

Renaissance acknowledges that it is hosted on the traditional, unceded land of the Anishinabek, the Kanien'kehá:ka, and the Omàmìwininìwag. We acknowledge the privileges and comforts that colonialism has granted us and vow to use this privilege to disrupt colonialism by lifting up the voices of marginalized humans who continue to suffer the effects of ongoing colonialism.

Printed in Gatineau by
Imprimerie Gauvin - Depuis 1892
gauvin.ca

Renaissance acknowledges the support of the Canada Council for the Arts.

Conseil des Arts du Canada

Canada Council for the Arts

*To my sister, Teri, who can't bring herself to read this memoir,
and to Dr. Rose Dymetryszyn for guiding me out of the darkness*

PROLOGUE

She was twelve years old when the recurring dream began: a girl standing behind a plate glass window with her hands pressed up against it, gazing out. The girl observed the activity beyond her, watched the people go by, living their lives. From time to time, she wished she could go out and walk alongside them, laugh with them. But, of course, she couldn't. Her room had no door.

She didn't mind, though. She had everything she needed. Besides, safety lay on the inside.

As the living girl grew to womanhood, the dream girl did not. Although her dream self didn't age, her long isolation in the end caused her great anguish and she longed to escape. Now when the real woman woke from the dream she felt as though her heart would break and asked herself how much longer she could endure such pain.

One night as the dream girl stood with her hands pressed against the glass, a woman with short dark hair and a round face walked up to the window and smiled. It made the girl rear back in fright. No one had ever looked in her direction before, let alone approach the window, as though she'd been invisible.

The woman spoke but the girl couldn't hear her through the thick glass, and she shook her head.

The woman rummaged inside her purse and brought out a notebook and a pen. She scribbled something, tore out the page and held it up for the girl to read.

The woman had written, "Dream it."

The girl knew right away what the women meant and soon she dreamed a door for herself.

CHAPTER ONE

I was born in Italy, a village called Campochiaro, meaning "clear field." The picturesque village clings to the slope of a mountain in the Apennine Mountain range some 800 metres above sea level in the south-central region known today as Molise, caught between the Adriatic and Tyrrhenian Seas, south of Rome and north of Naples.

Although born in Italy, my ancestral lineage is not Roman but Samnite, one of a number of Indo-Europeans who settled the Italian peninsula during the Iron Age. Samnites, a confederation of four, self-governing tribes that came together to fight Roman expansion, occupied what are today the provinces of Abruzzo, Molise and Campania along the Apennine mountains, which form Italy's spine. Not much is known about these Samnites except what later Roman historians wrote about the many wars between them, a hundred years or more after their subjugation.

In 90 BCE a rebellion by Italic tribes, including former Roman allies, fought for independence against Roman autocracy. The rebels had some successes and Rome, rather than fight on all fronts, offered political concessions, which pacified many of the tribes. But not the Samnites, who fought on and only ceding in 88 BCE when Sulla, the Roman general who headed the last Roman campaign, crushed them to near extinction. Ancient historian Strabo noted Sulla said he had realized from experience that a Roman could never live in peace so long as the Samnites held together as a separate people. What Sulla ordered was on the scale of genocide, including razing their cities to the ground.

Today archeologists have begun to excavate what Rome buried more than two thousand years ago, hoping to learn more about how they lived and what they believed in. Temple and theater complexes have been unearthed in former Samnite territory, including a fourth century BCE compound dedicated to Hercules high above Campochiaro where I was born. Bronze tablets have come to light, written in Oscan—a language spoken by the Italic tribes of southern Italy similar to Latin—which lay out sacred rituals and municipal laws. Such artefacts begin to tell the story of a vanished culture.

The emerging story of the Samnites, however, doesn't suggest a culture rich in fine arts and literature. Not only were they physically and culturally isolated from the rest of the Mediterranean world, they were forced to devote their energies to the backbreaking work of: coaxing food out of the rocky soil, caring for the animals to clothe and feed themselves, scouring the mountainsides for wood with which to cook and keep warm and making preserves for winter.

They did have, however, have a rich oral storytelling tradition. Maybe that was why I heard so many wonderful stories as a child. All the adults had a roster of them, from fairy stories to the supernatural to stories of heroic brigands who roamed the mountains fighting for justice against evil feudal lords.

What traits have I inherited from such people? Stubborn pride? Suspicion of strangers? Blind resistance to authority? Love of a good story? Practicality? Maybe all of them.

My mother, Adelina Donata Carmina, nee Pittarelli, told me her labour started one hot morning, a month premature, as she worked in the fields. I came into the world the following afternoon, July 6, 1949. A midwife delivered me in my parents' stone-clad house.

This early arrival, as though I wouldn't endure one more minute of confinement, characterized the rest of my life.

"*Dio mio*, she doesn't look human," Mamma recalled saying to the midwife when she first held me in her arms. What should she make of this bag of bones, her first-born child?

"Don't worry," the midwife replied. "She'll fill out nicely. Before you know it, you'll have the prettiest baby in the village."

While Mamma dealt with the pangs of childbirth, my father, Erminio Liberato Vincenze, had made himself scarce. "Probably lying somewhere up the mountain smoking a cigarette, dreaming his big dreams. He should have been working in the fields like everybody else—but then he always was a lazy sort," Nonna recalled.

My father had reason to dream. He had already applied to immigrate to Canada and only waited for the day he could head out. In the mid-20th century, the village had a population of 1,500 souls, down from a high of 2,500 citizens in the mid-1800s. The devastation left by the Second World War, the hardscrabble existence of eking a livelihood out of a stingy mountainside gradually drained the population to the remaining six hundred today. Most left for Canada or the United States.

As for me, I did fill out rapidly. Mamma produced prodigious quantities of breast milk, so much so she wet-nursed other babies whose mothers didn't have enough. Mamma loved having a baby at her breast, and I loved suckling, and the two of us kept at it for three years.

Both my parents were born in Campochiaro, as were their parents and their parents' parents and many, many generations before them. Everyone born in Campochiaro had a close or distant blood relationship to everyone else. For the same reason, they shared a small number of family names, they had to identify each other by their clan names to distinguish people who had the same legal name. *Paesani* knew Mamma, Adelina Pittarelli, as Adelina Catarina, of the Catarina clan.

I know my parents' fierce sense of loyalty has been bred in the bone; a function of tribal hard-won survival: immediate family first, extended family second, fellow villagers, *paesani,* third, people from their region,

Abruzzo fourth, and other Italians last. As Southerners, they scorned Northern Italians for their arrogance while Northerners looked down on Southerners as scruffy, uneducated peasants.

I was born in Campochiaro but I was plucked from its soil and raised in a world where everything was different, from the weather to the language spoken. We immigrated to Montreal, Canada, when I was 3 years old. I grew up a hybrid, schooled in English, surrounded by a French-language culture, and prohibited by my family from fully participating in either.

They had come to Canada for economic opportunities but they wanted to hang on to their old ways. They still expected me to grow up to be like them and, as a girl, they tried their damnedest to make me live a medieval way of life.

I wouldn't.

CHAPTER TWO

An image flickers in my mind's eye of myself as a very young child, something between two and three, sitting alone on a stone step warmed by an Italian sun. Holding a comb in one hand, I lustily mimic the sound of thundering church bells. It is my first memory, during the summer of 1952 before Mamma and I left Italy to join my father in Montreal. He'd gone ahead the previous year, as so many young village men had since the end of the Second World War. They left to find work and put some money aside before sending for their families.

My Canadian journey started in October 1952, three years, three months and 11 days after my birth. Between 1951 and 1961, almost 220,000 Italians settled in Canada. Most went to Ontario; Mamma and I numbered among the 55,000 of them who made our homes in Québec.

I had turned three when we went to Naples to board the T.S.S. Nea Hellas, a small ship that carried nearly four hundred passengers to Halifax, Nova Scotia.

How did Mamma feel when she left for a place she couldn't even imagine? When she left the village and her friends. Her sisters. Her parents and grandparents. Her beloved aunts? She never spoke of her feelings. I think she believed that as a woman and as a wife her wishes had no relevance. She did what her husband needed and what her family expected her to do.

The crossing, which took 11 days, remains a blank in my mind except for fragmentary images of wandering through the ship looking for amusement. Mamma, suffering from seasickness, spent most of the trip lying down. Even then I ignored her feeble entreaties to stay in her sight.

We docked at Pier 21 in Halifax on October 28, 1952 and stood for hours to get through Canadian immigration. We boarded a train for Montreal, sitting on wooden benches for two days as the train clattered and swayed westward.

Montreal's Central Station teemed with people, which excited me. Mamma must have asked herself if she'd ever adapt to such crowding, to the noise and languages she didn't understand. She was only twenty-five, a mountain girl who had no experience beyond her home in Campochiaro.

We waited in the cavernous hall, Mamma's weary grey eyes searching the crowd for her husband. All at once she smiled, waving at a man pushing his way to us through the throng. My father.

Did the sight of his pale-faced wife and dark-haired daughter, cranky from lack of sleep, please him when he caught sight of us? Or did he regret his loss of freedom?

"Look, there's your father!"

The word "father" meant little to me, for I had no memory of him.

Suddenly he stood before us, a short, stocky man wearing a baggy pair of trousers, a matching jacket, and a coat over one shoulder. I scooted behind Mamma's skirt, shy and a little frightened by the square-jawed face and the flash of dark eyes. My parents hugged and kissed, then my father turned his attention to me.

"Elvie," he said, softly, causing me to bury myself deeper into the folds of Mamma's skirt. He got down on one knee. "Let me see, Elvie. I've waited such a long time to look into your sweet face."

I didn't budge, despite Mamma's encouraging words. She had talked to me about seeing my Papà and I'd mimicked her eagerness to see him. But now when he stood within touching distance, I was afraid. My father reached into the pocket of his coat and took out a small brown bag. "I brought you something," he said.

I peeked from behind the skirt, saw the bag, and looked up at Mamma, who nodded and smiled. Without leaving the sanctuary of her body, my arm reached out to take the small bag, which I hoped contained candy.

"Brava," he said. We left the station.

My father had rented and furnished a flat prior to our arrival in Montreal's downtown, downmarket east side. Until then, he'd boarded with his cousin, Guilio, who'd sponsored his application to live in Canada. At the time, Montreal was the nation's economic centre, and growing. Employers were hungry for labourers, and my father soon found work.

I stared in wonder as a car, maybe a taxi, drove us along broad city streets crowded with other cars and the odd horse-drawn wagon. And oh, how very tall the buildings were, so high above the car I couldn't see their tops.

We moved into a cold-water flat on the second and top floor of a row house on Rue Saint-Christophe. No gardens or patches of lawn led up to them to relieve the expanse of red-brick surfaces. We climbed half a dozen steps from the sidewalk to a verandah with four doors painted forest green. My father opened the second door on the right and led us up a steep interior staircase. I have a vague memory of darkness, of extreme narrowness leading to the top floor.

We reached a small landing with doors to either side. My father unlocked the one on the left and we entered a flat filled with people, *paesani*, ex-pat villagers who'd come to welcome us. Mamma cried with happiness at the sight of friends and distant relatives she hadn't laid eyes on for years. They welcomed us with food and drink, of course, and they ate, drank and talked their fill.

The flat had three rooms which included a small kitchen equipped with a gas cooking stove and an icebox, a good-size living room and a bedroom with a window looking out onto Saint-Christophe. There was also a tiny water closet with a toilet, but no tub or shower. Nevertheless, it was a big step up from the village we'd come from where the toilet was a hole in the ground at the back of the house. The apartment also had running water, another we hadn't had in Campochiaro.

In winter we used an oil burning stove to heat the flat but poor insulation and draughty windows meant the place never, ever got warm. An oilman came regularly to fill a tank in the shed behind the kitchen.

My parents washed in the kitchen using a soapy washcloth and bowl filled with water heated on the kitchen stove. They also concocted a makeshift bidet for personal cleansing by setting a bowl filled with warm water that fit inside the toilet to wash their private parts. For my baths, Mamma used an oval, white-enamelled tub which she placed on the kitchen table and plunked me in it.

Mamma loved the icebox, a big improvement from an earthen cellar. Twice a week, an iceman made deliveries in a horse-drawn wagon. He used a grappling hook to pull out a massive block of ice from the back of his wagon, hoisted it onto his shoulders, hauled it up the stairs and slid it into the top compartment of the icebox. Meanwhile, the horse waited patiently, all the while dropping smelly mounds of poop. In the scorching summer heat, the iceman gave kids ice chips to suck on.

That first night, I had the first unpleasant surprise when we prepared for bed. No longer could I sleep next to Mamma, as I had done ever since I could remember. My parents took the bedroom and expected me to sleep on the couch in the living room, alone in the dark.

"No, you can't sleep in my bed anymore. Besides, I'm just a few feet away," she said, as she made up the couch for me.

"But why can't I?"

Back and forth we went like that as she coaxed me to get between the sheets. Fed up, my father came into the room. "I don't want another word out of you, Elvie. Get into bed right now or else *botte*, blows."

I knew full well what *botte* meant. Mamma, my grandmothers and my aunts had often threatened me with the word when I had misbehaved. Now I looked to Mamma for help when this stranger threatened me but saw no sympathy in her face. Why was she allowing this man to take charge?

Mamma tucked me in and left the room, turning off the light on the way out. I sobbed for hours, convinced she had abandoned me. I sobbed for so long she finally came to me, lay beside me and stayed until I fell asleep. The next night when I cried for Mamma, she did not come. I blamed it on the man in whose bed she now slept—without me—for keeping her from me. That second night I wept until I exhausted myself. The same thing happened the following night.

The next night when I called for Mamma, he came instead. He bent over me, his face a scary black shape While behind him, weak moonlight slipped over him through the windowpane.

"*Shatatte 'zitta*! Keep quiet. Do you hear me? Otherwise, I'll give you something real to cry about." The anger in his voice frightened me.

I whimpered. In Italy adults yelled at kids all the time, I'd earned quite a few slaps myself for misbehaviour but no one had ever terrified me the way this man did.

"I'm warning you. If I have to come back, you'll be sorry."

After that night I stopped counting on Mamma to make the darkness and the unfamiliar sounds of the night less scary. In time, I also accepted I could no longer claim Mamma's full attention. In addition, I had lost all the aunts and cousins and the friends I'd played with in Campochiaro. My world had shrunk to just the three of us, except during weekends when we socialized with our own kind. During those first months my parents enjoyed a busy social life.

By then almost half of Campochiaro had moved to Montreal, using each other as ballast in an alien world. *Paesani* visited us; we visited them. Children always participated. The men played a card game called briscola, playing for beers with the loser paying the shot after each round. Women gathered in another room or outside, weather permitting, to exchange news and gossip about mutual acquaintances. They did not, however, reveal hints of discord in their own families, lest they lose face.

We children were let loose, given our head, as though playing on the streets of Montreal were no different from chasing each other in Campochiaro's piazza. We played until we dropped from exhaustion. I was often the last to give up, the last kid to crawl onto Mamma's lap where I'd fall asleep lulled by the vibration of her voice and warmth from the pillow of her soft, yielding body.

During weekdays at home, however, boredom drew me to the playground where I made friends and acquired enough street French to make myself understood. When November bled into December, appalling cold and snow kept me indoors. I spent hours at my parents' bedroom window, which faced Saint-Christophe, watching the kids come and go from the elementary school the street and marvelling at a whirlwind of snowflakes falling from the sky.

Christmas came and went with loads of food and lots of visiting. But days after we celebrated 1953's arrival came the first of many blows that cracked the fresh foundations of my young life.

CHAPTER THREE

Weeks and months elapsed but I didn't warm to the man who slept in Mamma's bed. A few months after our arrival I witnessed an altercation between my parents, the first of many, only cemented my distrust of the man. When I think of it now, I become a child again, a small, quivering animal whose instincts scream "Danger!" but stands helpless in the face of threat.

The incident happened at home on a Saturday night after we got home from a visit to my father's cousin, Guilio, and his family. Mother had put me to bed and when I heard raised voices coming from my parents' bedroom. I lay in the dark, clamping a corner of the blanket between my teeth, hearing my father's menacing growl, Mamma's frightened, high-pitched responses.

When she cried out in pain I sat up. "Ma!" But the words slipped out too softly for her—or him—to hear. I hadn't forgotten his warning about crying out for her during the night. When she cried out again, I threw my legs over the side of my makeshift bed. My warm feet hit the ice-cold linoleum and, shivering with dread, I tiptoed to my parents' room.

Their door stood ajar. I couldn't see them but now I could hear what they said. I stood out of view, trying to build courage to push open the door. My father scared me at the best of times but now the threat in his voice reaching me from their bedroom had me frozen to the spot. If I showed myself, I knew my presence would infuriate him and he would beat me with his belt as he'd already threatened to do once or twice before when I'd misbehaved.

"You were making eyes at Tony, I saw you. You can't deny it," my father said.

"I didn't! I didn't go near him; I didn't even speak to him."

"You didn't have to. I saw the look that passed between you across the room."

Fear for myself vanished when Mamma let out a scream. I pushed the door and, wailing, I went into the room wanting to crawl on her lap and have her put her arms around me.

I saw Mamma perched on the edge of their bed, arms wrapped around her head for protection, my father standing over her, his right arm raised to strike her with a thin metal rod. Weak incandescent light from the ceiling fixture bathed them in a yellowish glow.

"*Aiutami, tu, Dio mio.* Help me, God," Mamma shouted.

"Mammaaaaa!" Something bitter and hot coated my tongue as the sound left my mouth..

My father, frozen in mid-strike, turned his head towards me but his eyes but his eyes looked strange, as if he didn't see me at all and that scared me more.

I was sobbing now, trembling all over and snot running out of my nose, "Mamma."

Something shifted in my father's eyes, as though a light came on, and all at once he looked like himself again. The rod clattered to the floor. Mamma ran to my side, scooped me up and carried me back to bed. She lay down beside me and drew over us the weighty wool blankets she'd brought from Italy. In the dark we clung to each other.

"Mamma, I want to go home!"

She hugged me closer. "Go to sleep, *pulchinella.*"

I heard my father crying in the other room. Fathers weren't supposed to cry, were they? But he'd been bad, had hurt Mamma, and probably he was afraid Mamma would be mad at him.

Mamma slept next to me all through the night. But the next morning, we went back to our usual ways, as though nothing had happened while I still wanted to go back to Campochiaro. But she had nothing more to say.

Mamma could no more have returned to Italy than I, a 3-year-old, could have moved back on my own. My father controlled all our comings and goings and approved or rejected every cent Mamma wanted to spend. Besides, Mamma's parents wouldn't have welcomed us home since a woman leaving her husband brought shame to the family.

Nevertheless, when my father was out at work and Mamma and I were alone, I badgered her about going home for many months.

As I learned from Mamma years later, domestic violence was nothing new to her. Her father drank, and combined with jealous, controlling nature, she witnessed time and again her own mother trying to protect herself from the blows that came with his bursts of rage. To her, living with an abusive husband, while unpleasant, must have seemed normal.

Neither could Mamma have asked for help from Montreal *paesani*. Wife battering, while ostensibly frowned upon, was not uncommon in the community. But battered women hid the fact, a family's dirty little secret, because a good wife protected the façade of a thriving, happy family. Face trumped everything, even a woman's torment, even her life.

In the days after the occurrence, my father's subdued demeanour carried him as close to an apology as he ever would get.

By soon after, Mamma's sister joined her in Montreal and that brought her a measure of consolation, for a while, at least, until things went awry between Papà and my aunt. Zia Carmelina was the second of four sisters, Mamma the eldest, Zia Maria Teresa—known as Tresa—the third and Zia Antonietta, the youngest. They were born two years apart to a father who'd longed for a son and blamed his wife for not providing one.

Zia Carmela arrived in Montreal in 1953. Antonietta, known as 'Ndunetta, made the crossing the following year and Zia Tresa joined them in 1959.

Zia Carmelina lived with her husband and his parents on the ground floor of a duplex on des Ecores in a newer, nicer part of the city than the one we lived in. The two sisters had always been close but Zia Carmelina and my father despised each other. My father tried his best to prevent Mamma from seeing her sister, including forbidding Zia from crossing our threshold but failed to keep them apart. On this score, Mamma would not budge and one way or another the two sisters managed to visit each other regularly, sometimes in secret.

Decades later when I asked Zia Carmelina what had caused the rift, she told me my father had made a pass at her in our flat one day when she'd come to visit. She threatened to tell Mamma if he ever again even looked at her in a suggestive way—and he never did but he got back at her by accusing *her* husband of molesting Mamma.

My father and my aunt never reconciled.

In February of 1953 Mamma found a job as a sewing machine operator in a garment factory. She didn't mind. Most of the women from Campochiaro worked in factories. A good life in Canada meant owning property and if the women worked, along with making sure they spent no more than absolutely necessary, they could own their own houses in time.

But what to do with me while Mamma was at work? With no friends or relatives close by to make day care feasible, they sent me to board weekdays with a *paesani*. They dropped me off on Sunday nights and picked me up five days later. Every Sunday I clung to Mamma when they took me there. But I'd settled in when they came to pick me up on Fridays after work and I didn't want to leave.

The family took me in for about a year. They had a daughter a year my junior. And while I envied her long blonde hair, blue eyes, angelic face and alabaster skin, her sweet disposition soon won me over.

I'd got quite used to the living arrangement when my parents abruptly stopped taking me there. Nobody told me why. Maybe my father took it into his head that the father had eyes for his wife. Whatever the reason, they next parked me with Giulio's, the relative who'd sponsored my father's application to come to Canada.

Giulio's wife didn't work in a factory as Mamma now did. But the family made extra money by taking in newly-arrived immigrants until they found their feet. Giulio's wife did the cooking and cleaning for her family and two or three boarders while raising their two children, a boy of eleven and an auburn-haired daughter of nine named Filomena. Fil, as I called her was four years my senior, who became a life-long big sister to me. When I moved in with them, not only did Fil have to share her bed with me, she patiently endured me as I followed her around like a tiresome puppy. I loved her and drank in her sweetness and kindness.

CHAPTER FOUR

I stayed with Fil's family until spring, 1955 when, suddenly, my parents once again yanked me away when a free babysitter came on the scene when my father's youngest sister, Vilia, came to live with us in 1955, in the summer before I started school.

Zia Vilia, was a single woman of 27 and she needed to earn a living and soon got a night-shift job in a commercial bakery. Instead of finding a sitter to look after me during the day so Zia Vilia could sleep, to save money they devised a plan whereby Zia Vilia would continue to look after me. After all, they reasoned, she was home all day. So, what if she needed to sleep part of the time? Besides, the arrangement would last only a couple of months until I started school in September.

Zia Vilia was supposed to be home by 7:30 a.m. just in time for my parents to leave.

Things didn't work out as anticipated. Zia Vilia often had to do overtime and didn't get home from work before my parents left in the morning and I had to manage on my own. My father gave me strict instructions to stay inside and not open the door to anyone, not even to somebody I knew, certainly not neighbourhood kids. Mamma mother concocted amusements to keep me busy. A needle with a long piece of coloured thread and a piece of fabric to sew, a pencil and a pile of scrap paper to draw things on or some other doodad. "Be a good girl. And for heaven's sake don't bother your aunt when she's sleeping," she admonished every day on her way out the door.

I did try to play nicely, as Mamma had ordered. I sat down and tried to sew but soon the thread got tangled up and soon the hunt for fresh diversions began. I rooted around in the shed in closets, I climbed on the countertop to get something in one of the kitchen cabinets, I ransacked the drawers, and when I got tired of that, I risked my father's wrath and went outside to play, scooting back indoors when I caught sight of Zia Vilia turning the corner on her way home.

At home I followed her around and kept up a constant chatter as she cleaned herself up. We sat at the table and had something to eat before she went to bed. She put a fresh length of thread on my needle and told me to go play. I did my best to delay the moment when she would lie down on the hard couch, which we both used for a bed, to sleep, exhausted.

Happy with my new length of thread, I'd play in my parents' bedroom—my playroom—but inevitably, the thread would knot again, leaving me again with nothing to do. I wasn't allowed to bother my aunt so I looked around for something interesting to occupy me and one day my eyes fell upon a workbook my father was using to learn English. I went into the kitchen to get pair of scissors and had a wonderful few hours turning the book into tiny perfect squares ,into a shower of confetti. When my father came home and discovered what I'd done, it took both Mamma and Zia to stop him from turning me black and blue with his belt.

Sometimes I dressed up in Mamma's clothes and played princess. She had a glossy, dark green dress with a black geometric pattern in the closet I especially liked. I accessorized it with her high-heeled shoes—the ones with the peep toe—and attached linked bobby pins to each of my earlobes so that they dangled and completed the ensemble with a smear of Mamma's best cherry-red lipstick. Then I paraded in front of the dresser's wide mirror, imagining admiring glances from a pretend audience.

My paternal grandmother died that summer. The news came in a letter from Zia Luisa, my father's second-oldest sister. By the time we got the news, she'd already been buried.

My father's mother died in her early 60s, of what I never learned. Zia Vilia was heartbroken. Mamma took it hard, too. She had liked and respected her mother-in-law. Compared to the tears and lamentations of the women, my father appeared unaffected by Nonna's death. I wondered whether he was mad at his mother for dying.

"Brigitta was a saint, a real saint, a martyr to her husband," Mamma said, wiping her eyes. "She worked like a dog and he never lifted a finger to help. She was well rid of him when he croaked in his 40s."

My father hadn't reached his teens when his father died. I never heard him speak of the man. Years later when I asked people about my paternal grandfather, no one could say how he died. Maybe they preferred not to speak of it. Suicide? Or had he died under suspicious circumstances? My grandfather's clan had a bad reputation, well, the men did. Their clan's name, Cazzotto, meaning "a punch" might offer a clue. Villagers considered them opportunists and not above pulling a con. Then again, my paternal grandfather might have died of an untreated illness. Good quality medical care didn't exist in a mountain village during the mid-1930s and the family wouldn't have had the money to go to the city for treatment.

Following village custom, Mamma and Zia Vilia donned black from head to toe, long-sleeve dresses, stockings, shoes, coats, gloves and hats to signal mourning. The tradition inflicted real hardship on women, especially in the broiling heat of summer. Men did not have such strict requirements. How long a woman wore black depended on the closeness of her relationship to the deceased. As a mere daughter-in-law,

Mamma had a year of black penance; Zia Vilia, her daughter, got two years. My father wore a black suit when he attended the Mass, said in her honour at our parish church, and that was it. Widows were obliged to wear black for life but widowers did not have the same obligation.

For weeks after my grandmother's death, *paesani* came to our flat to pay their respects. They brought consolation gifts, the same sort of offerings commonly given the bereaved in Campochiaro, gifts considered luxuries in an impoverished village. They brought bags of fine coffee, bottles of vermouth, tins of cocoa and other foodstuffs. Close friends and relatives came to cook meals for us, a ritualistic way to leave the family free to grieve.

Throughout the comings and goings after the news of Nonna's death, Mamma kept a mental list of who did their duty towards the family. Those who didn't would be repaid in kind in *their* hour of need. She attached huge importance to duty, to rules and rituals that had evolved over hundreds of years, rules that had kept the community civilized.

In a village like Campochiaro, especially after the Second World War, it had made sense to feed a family coping with death. In Campochiaro if people didn't work at growing their own food—vegetable and animal—they didn't eat. It gave the bereaved a few days to collect themselves before life resumed its rhythm of work. Now living in Canada, their needs had changed but the rituals remained until those who were born in Canada let them drift away. The mourning period for Nonna prohibited any entertainment or celebration for a year. We couldn't listen to the radio, attend weddings or christenings or any other celebration or entertainment. The previous year we'd sometimes escaped the miasma of summer heat at Belmont Park, a huge amusement park on the banks of Riviere des Prairies in the suburb of Cartierville, where we met up with *paesani*. It was a long trek by tram to Belmont Park but I loved the clouds of cotton candy, the merry-go-round and the noise of the games' barkers. Once my father won a small stuffed bear that I cherished because my parents never spent money on toys. In Italy, I'd had few toys, but it hadn't mattered because nobody else did either. But in Canada the French-speaking neighbours' kids had dolls of all sorts big and small, miniature dishes and stuffed bears and other animals. One girl even had a tricycle.

I have a picture taken at Belmont Park of the three of us from one of those outings. Mamma stands to my father's left, her arm linked through his. I lean against his leg on his other side with his palm cupped around my chin.

Sometimes we fled the flat's impossible, suffocating summer heat and sought relief at nearby Parc La Fontaine, 850 acres of relief with grass, plenty of trees and two man-made lakes linked by a bridge. Luckily, we could walk there from our flat. True to its name, the park featured a gorgeous illuminated fountain. At the time it also had a children's theme park, *Le Jardin des Merveilles*, with turtles and rabbits, and for a time, an elephant. We went so often I could have found my way there on my own, wearing a blindfold.

On the heels of heartache due to Nonna's death, life delivered some good news, at least it was good news as far as I was concerned.

CHAPTER FIVE

Mamma's belly began to swell and when I asked her about it, she said I was going to have my very own brother or sister. It was the summer of 1955 and I would soon be starting school.

"I want a sister."

"Well, that's up to God."

"Well, can't you tell him I'd rather have a sister?"

As fall approached, I marvelled at how her belly got bigger and bigger, as big as the watermelons we cracked open all summer. I liked to put my ear against the big balloon of her middle and listen to all the swishing and squeaking.

"When is my sister coming? Is she in there? Can't you just take her out?"

Mamma quit her factory job in August just before I started school. She wanted to keep working a few weeks except that her once-shapely ankles had swelled so much she had trouble walking. As for me, I loved having her at home and I stuck close to her side, peppering her with questions, inserting myself in whatever she did, wanting to participate until, exasperated, she shooed me outside.

During that time, she seemed out of sorts and often snapped at my father. They argued a lot, even in front of Zia Vilia now. I noticed that Zia always took Mamma's side, which made me love her more. I also noticed my father resented Zia for supporting Mamma.

Mamma appeared happiest when immersed in some activity. In spite of the balloon stuck to her belly and her swollen ankles, she never sat idle. After she finished cooking and cleaning, she'd pick up her mending basket or make braided rugs from strips of discarded clothing. At times, she busied her hands with a crochet hook, making doilies, or picked up long, curved knitting needles to make socks.

I started school in September 1955, my sister, whom my father named Teresa Anna, was born one month later, a terrible month for me.

Grade1delivered me into the hands of the nuns who ran Our Lady of Good Counsel, a Catholic, English-language school located on Craig Street East—now rue Saint-Antoine—about a mile from our flat. The sisters of the Congregation of Notre- Dame had built the small, four-storey school, with its grey-stone façade, in 1891 to educate a wave of young Irish girls whose families had fled the Irish famine. Sixty years later, when I showed up, Montreal's massive growth had turned its once-ideal location into a dirty, noisy industrial zone.

In the 1950s, the city's school system at the time was divided along confessional lines: Catholic and Protestant. The Catholic system had two streams, English and French while the Protestant schools taught exclusively English. My father could have enrolled me in the French-language Catholic school, which sat directly across the street from our flat but refused to do so. He scorned our French-Canadian neighbours, considered them a people without ambition.

"English is the language of commerce," he thundered. "If you want to make money you gotta' speak English."

Three quarters of the more than thirty thousand Italian immigrants living in Montreal in those days and those that came in the next two decades sent their children to English schools.

English Catholic Schools were in high demand but in short supply. The immigrants made it clear to their Catholic Church leaders they would convert to Protestantism to get the education they wanted for their kids rather than send them to French Catholic schools. Fearing the loss of their congregations, parishes put pressure on the Montreal School Commission to build more schools, which it did.

The Sunday before the first day of school the nuns asked students and parents to join them for Mass at St. Mary's, the school's parish church. My big-bellied mother took me. We went by tramway, rather than on foot, thanks to her swollen ankles, much as she would have liked to save the tramway fare.

As we stood in front of the church, Mamma took a clean handkerchief from her purse, shook it open and placed it on her head. Inside, I imitated her as she dipped the fingers of one hand into the holy water font and crossed herself before slipping into a pew at the back. The place was full well before Mass started.

Mamma carefully lowered herself on to the hard seat and let out a sigh of relief. I stood on the kneeler to get a good view but as I looked around, I noticed I was the only one bareheaded, while all the other little girls wore hats. It upset and ashamed me, and I turned to Mamma for an explanation.

I leaned close and whispered in her ear, "All the girls have a hat. Why didn't you buy me a hat? Maybe God will get mad at me."

"Don't worry, God understands. He knows you're little and it's not your fault. He'll forgive me too because He knows I don't have the money to buy you a hat."

Her answer didn't placate me and throughout the service I worried God might punish me. Plus, it was embarrassing to be the only one in the church without a hat—well, the only girl. In the row in front of me, one girl wore a pretty, bright red one with a feather on the side. How I longed to grab it and put it on my own head. But why weren't the men or the boys wearing hats? Did God think that was okay?

When the long Mass ended and God hadn't struck me down, I concluded Mamma had prayed to God not to punish me and He'd spared me. But why did God bother having rules when He didn't enforce them?

I looked forward to starting school even though I had no idea what it was about. The first day of school Mamma took me by tram and picked me up in the afternoon. Our Lady of Good Counsel had two Grade 1 classes of 30 boys and girls each. Among my classmates were Eva and Pasquale, children of *paesani* who lived a block from us.

Our teacher was a nun who belonged to the Congregation of Notre Dame. Her voluminous, floor-length black robe, white bib and white-peaked headdress made her look like a giant black-and-white bird. As Big Black Bird yammered on, I didn't understand a word that came out of her mouth. We lived in a French neighbourhood, a poor one, and I'd had no chance to pick up English.

Many of my classmates' families were new immigrants like me, but within a few months most of us managed well enough. However, it took me only a day or two to figure out the teacher didn't like children, especially the immigrants among us.

School came as a big disappointment. I'd hoped for a bit of fun; instead, it delivered hours of excruciating boredom. Big Black Bird made us sit at our desks with our hands clasped on the desktop while she strolled up and down the aisles, the skirt of her robe swishing as she went by, holding a menacing wooden pointer.

"What is 1 plus 3?" she'd ask some hapless, trembling kid.

"5?"

"Wrong!" Down came the pointer across the kid's knuckles.

I had my share of raps that year. It didn't help me to learn. It made me hate the teacher and school, but it terrorized some of my classmates. One unfortunate girl who sat two rows over from me wet herself whenever the Big Black Bird came near her. By the end of the school year a permanent dark circle marred the wood floor around her desk.

Within a week of starting Grade 1, I decided school wasn't for me. I liked finding out about new things but hated the endless repetition. Worse, it caused me agony to sit completely still for hours on end. How many times did Big Black Bird admonish me with "Stop fidgeting, Elvira," followed by a rap on the knuckles with that pointer?

Religious training started immediately as the nun prepared us for the sacrament of our First Holy Communion to take place in the spring the following year. What Big Black Bird told us frightened me to my core, much more than her pointer ever could.

I was born a Catholic and baptized within weeks of my birth. I'd seen many crucifixes, including one hanging on the wall over my parent's bed. Although both my parents were Catholic, their adherence to the faith was cultural rather than mystical. They did what they could when they could, including Mass on Sunday.

"Ma, my teacher says it's a black sin if we don't go to Mass every Sunday. She says we'll go to Hell."

Mamma rolled her eyes. "Easy for her to say. She doesn't have two children, a husband and a house to take care of. Besides, I told you before, God knows if you're doing the best you can. God understands I can go to Mass only now and then."

We belonged to the Italian parish of Madonna del Carmine. Although there were several French-language churches in our neighbourhood but my parents naturally preferred to deal with priests who spoke their own language. Madonna del Carmine sat about a mile away on Dorchester St. Italians built it in 1907 to accommodate the first influx of Italian immigrants, which coincided with many other Europeans arriving in the late 19th century.

My father, like many of the Italian men from Campochiaro hardly ever went to Mass. "God? You have to help yourself," he often said.

The Big Black Bird used religious images of the tortured Jesus Christ in our religious training that gave me nightmares. Blood oozed down

Christ's tormented face from the crown of thorns pressed into his skull; blood dripped from his side his ribs where a Roman soldier had driven his spear; blood flowed from the palms of his hands and the top of his feet where the nails tethered him to the cross.

Our teacher also told us that every time we did something bad—committing a sin, she called it—we made Jesus cry. It. Every time we missed Mass, every time we disobeyed our parents or broke one of the ten commandments, we made his suffering worse. When it sunk in that I had a part in making Jesus suffer and bleed, I'd burst into tears.

The lesson was repeated and reinforced for my next eleven years at Catholic schools.

Just before Christmas, Big Black Bird went on to teach us another unforgettable lesson about Christian charity. She gave her students a sheet of pretty wrapping paper and showed us how to make a cone. That done, she passed out enough candies to fill each cone to the brim. We got all excited, thinking the candies were for us. We were wrong.

Once the cones were full, our teacher had us line up, then led us upstairs to a Grade 2 classroom door. She knocked. Another nun opened the door. They had a few words and then the Grade 2 teacher invited us in.

One by one we were matched up with a Grade 2 pupil. "Now children," said Big Black Bird, "give your partner the present you made and wish them a Blessed Christmas."

I handed mine over with great reluctance. Even after we returned to our classroom, I still hoped our teacher had a few candies set aside for us. Wrong. When she released us for Christmas break at the end of the day, I felt she'd tricked us.

CHAPTER SIX

While I grappled with nightmares of a tortured Jesus on the cross and the boredom of school, my sister came into the world on October, 3, 1955, three months after my sixth birthday. My father looked at the religious calendar hanging on our wall, saw that it was the feast day of Sainte-Therese of Lisieux and named her Teresa.

"What do you think, Elvie? Is it a good name?"

I shrugged.

I'd thought I'd wanted a sister but now that she'd arrived, I had my doubts. The interloper gobbled up all of Mamma's attention, morning, noon and night. And she cried a lot and one day I thought I'd be helpful and pick her up as I'd seen Mamma do. The crib was tall, but I did manage to get hold of her—she was wrapped in swaddling bands like a mummy from the shoulders downs as was customary for a newborn and easy to pick up—but I ran into trouble when I tried to lift her over the crib's protective railing and I dropped her. She fell to the floor with a thump and when Mamma flew into the room I skedaddled and took protection under her bed. Luckily, Teresa sustained no permanent damage.

Nevertheless, once Teresa came into our lives, Mamma changed. Everything I did irritated Mamma. I started to think Mamma didn't care about me anymore and I turned to Zia Vilia for comfort.

"What's wrong with Mamma? She's always mad except when she's holding the baby."

"Don't worry, *picione*, chick, she's not mad at you. She's just a very tired lady."

We didn't celebrate Christmas or New Year that year because the family was still in in mourning for Nonna. I spent as much time as I could outdoors to avoid the baby's endless crying. Somebody had given me a pair of old ice skates and I often went to playground where they'd set up an ice rink to while away the time. But I was poorly dressed for the bitter cold and my fingers and toes soon went numb and drove me home.

Our flat was frigid, too. It was attached on either side, so that helped, but the front and back walls facing the street and the back lane were thin and let the cold in. We had an oil stove for heating but even though the flat only had three rooms, the warmth dissipated the further you got from the stove. On the coldest days I stayed near the stove, otherwise, I walked around the flat wrapped in a blanket and at night I hunkered under a mountain of heavy wool bedding Mamma had brought from Italy.

After the Christmas break when school resumed in January 1956, the cold, ice and snow made the trek there so much harder. Mamma had made arrangements with the parents of my classmates, Eva and Pasquale, who were neighbours, to take me to school with them. Since I was going on seven now and they lived a mere block away, I was allowed walked to their street by myself before we set off.

We trudged to school—on foot or by tram, depending on how bad the weather—weighed down by clunky boots, heavy coats, wool hats and scarves covering our necks and faces. Sometimes the snow reached our knees. Sometimes, the frigid air burned my cheeks.

When spring finally burst on the scene I cheered up. I loved seeing the leaves grow out of the branches of the trees and the sensation of the warming breeze on my face.

Although school remained drudgery, my excitement revved up as the time approached to celebrate my First Holy Communion in May 1956. The pleasure I took in preparing for it went counter to everything the

Big Black Bird had told us about the event's religious significance. My interest had to do with the accouterments accompanying the ritual - the white dress, the gloves, the gifts I'd receive.

Mamma and I had shopped long and hard for an inexpensive white dress — white for purity, the nun had told us. I saw a couple of dresses I begged her to buy, two of which had crinolines so that the skirts puff up like a cloud around me. But she remained deaf to my pleas and to my tears. "Who do you think we are, the Rockefellers?"

Instead, she chose a plain one she could afford. It did have a nice enough skirt and a bit of embroidery on the bodice but no crinoline. Mamma mother saw the profound disappointment on my face but said nothing. A few days later she went out and bought rhinestones and sat down to embellish the bit of embroidery on the bodice and added them one by one so that my chest sparkled, like stars at night, when I tried it on.

The Big Black Bird doubled up on the First Communion preparation as spring approached.   As she explained it, we would partake in the holiest of the Catholic sacraments, the Holy Eucharist, for the first time, which represented the last supper Jesus shared with his disciples before his crucifixion.

It disturbed me no end when she said the consecrated bread, a thin unleavened wafer, which the priest would place on each of our tongues, would be the *real* body and blood of Jesus. I didn't want to eat Jesus.

Part of the preparation included cleansing our souls of sin and so for the first time we first graders participated in the sacrament of Confession in order to purify ourselves to receive Christ. This sacrament had its own set of procedures and prayers, which we had to memorize and practice over and over.

A week before our First Communion, the Big Black Bird led us to nearby St. Mary's, where the ceremony would be held. We sat on the uncomfortable wooden pews, fidgeting, waiting our turn to go into the confessional box to tell the priest all the bad things we'd done. It made me nervous to tell this strange man what I'd done.

The confessional box had three enclosed cubicles, one on each end with the priest seated in the middle. I stepped into the cubicle when my turn came and knelt. The priest slid open the latticed window between us, which gave me my cue to begin. I swallowed, "Bless me Father for I have sinned. This is my first confession."

"Yes, my child. What sins have you committed?"

"Father, I disobeyed my mother."

"How often do you disobey your mother?"

I had to think about it. "Once a day?"

"You must respect your parents, my child. It is your duty."

"Yes, Father."

"Do you have any other sins to confess, my child?"

"I told my father a lie but I only did it so he wouldn't hit me."

"What lie did you tell."

"I told him I did my homework but I didn't do it."

"I see. Well, my child, lying to your father is a sin in the eyes of God. It is better to tell the truth and take your punishment. It is better still to do your homework."

"Yes, Father."

I couldn't think of anything else to tell him. As penance for my sins the priest told me to say two Hail Marys. I recited the Act of Contrition, left the confessional and returned to the pew to say my Hail Marys.

On Holy Communion Day, I slipped on my sparkling white dress, pulled on white stockings and put on new, sparkling white shoes. Mamma placed a white veil on my head and anchored it using a headband embellished with small silk roses. When I checked myself out in the mirror, I thought I'd burst with pleasure.

I went to St. Mary's with Mamma and my godmother, a stylish young cousin of hers, my hands clad in a pair of sheer rayon gloves and carrying a white, basket-shaped purse in the crook of my elbow—gifts from my godmother. Inside the purse she'd placed a children's missal, a book containing an abbreviated version of what's said during Holy Mass, bound in white leather. She'd also given me a rosary made of lovely carved clear crystal.

I'd never owned such beautiful objects and they left me in awe.

The ceremony over, the excitement and the attention I'd enjoyed too soon ended. But I didn't have time for gloom because we were about to move and everything was upside down as we got ready. With three adults and two children living in a one-bedroom flat, we had to have more space.

CHAPTER SEVEN

At that time May 1st was the official moving day in Québec. It was inconvenience for families moving into a different school district because the school term didn't end until the end of June and forced children into a new school at the end of term. I wasn't affected by the relocation since our new flat was only a couple of blocks east.

I didn't mind moving. Change of any kind assuaged my chronic boredom but I regretted moving away from the playground, kitty corner to our flat, where I had spent entire days on Saturdays and Sundays in summer days while Mamma or Zia kept an eye on me while sitting on our balcony.

On moving day, a man showed up with a pickup truck. He and my father loaded our belongings, lashed the pile together with ropes, and minutes later pulled into our new street, St. Timothee, the same street where my classmates, Eva and Pasquale, also lived on the next block, just south of us.

The houses on our new street came with houses in several shapes from duplexes and triplexes with pretty curved wrought iron staircases interspersed with blocks of identical, linked three-storey buildings whose red-brick facades, without staircases or balconies, fell three storeys straight down to the sidewalk. Our new flat was in one of those buildings. serried windows with dark green shutters and entry doors—two per property—inset with bevelled glass windows with a single step leading up to each.

Our building had three storeys and our flat was on the second floor, near rue Robin.

Past the front door, an interior staircase led to a landing and our unit and then carried for a few feet beyond to the third-floor staircase. Mamma inserted the key and we stepped into a spacious kitchen. To my delight, it had two bedrooms—which meant I'd now have my own room and my own bed, which I would share with Zia Vilia. Teresa, now seven months old, would sleep in a crib in my parents' room.

A short hallway off the kitchen led to a bathroom and beyond that, the front parlour with a window facing St. Timothee.

We had no balcony at the front but I loved the wide verandah at the back of the flat accessible from the kitchen via a storage shed and a back verandah almost as wide as the kitchen.

This new place felt downright luxurious compared to the old flat. The bathroom was an actual room, not just a closet with a toilet, with a tub and a sink, and the kitchen had an electric refrigerator and a great big wood-burning stove for cooking and heating.

I longed to explore the neighbourhood and make new friends as my parents and Zia Vilia worked to set things up, washings cupboards, scrubbing the floors before starting to unpack everything for the bathroom, but my Mamma said no. She was busy, and needed me at home to keep an eye on Teresa. That didn't stop me from pestering her to release me, though.

"*Te* juro, Elvie, you're really trying my patience," she warned.

Mamma unlike Papà, could sometimes be talked round. And because she sometimes gave in to my relentless pestering, I kept trying even though I risked she'd get mad enough to stop what she was doing and throw one of her house slippers across the room at me. She missed, mostly.

In the ensuing days, once things were in place and we settled into a routine, I had more freedom. The families above and below us were nice. An Italian family, although not from our region, had the flat above us but their teenaged son didn't advance my search for playmates. However, below us lived a woman and her two boys around my age. They spoke French, just like my St. Christophe playmates.

I made friends with a girl who lived around the corner on Robin—she took ballet lessons, whatever that was—and who lived in one of those flats across the street with the curling staircase. Lucie had a beautiful set of blue-and-white, doll-sized dishes.

I explored the immediate area along Saint-Timothee and Robin on my own. But it was a very long street, all the way down to our school on Craig Street and all the way to Lafontaine Park on Sherbrooke. As well, four other families from Campochiaro and several Italians from other regions also lived nearby, including Eva's and Pasquale's.

We had a convenience store steps from our door at the corner of Robin—tiny but packed to rafters with everything a child could want, from penny candy to toys and games.

From the window in our front parlor, kitty-corner to the convenience store stood a majestic grey-stone church, the French parish of Sainte-Catherine-d'Alexandrie. I loved to look up to its soaring that seemed to reach into the sky. Having a church that close made it easier for Mamma to take me to Mass, but she was always so busy she rarely went.

School let out at the end of June, releasing me from the clutches of the Big Black Bird. Mamma went back to work at the factory after a *paesana*, who lived two doors from us, agreed to look after Teresa and me. Zia Vilia, at last, had peace and quiet and slept when she came home from her night job.

Mamma worked and worked. When she wasn't at the factory she worked at home. Zia helped in every way she could but the brunt of cooking, cleaning, laundry and raising two children rested on Mamma's shoulders. She did all our laundry by hand for a year until they saved enough to buy a wringer washer. In the old flat she had to wash everything, even bedding, in the kitchen sink. Now she had a bathtub for the job. She'd kneel alongside the tub, belly pressed against it, to scour our dirty things against a corrugated glass scrub board. She scoured each item with lye soap—Teresa's diapers, sheets, towels, snot-filled handkerchiefs, my father's trousers and shirts, our dresses and socks— rinse them in cold water, wring them hard and move on to the next item. We had no hot water heater but even if we had had, she would have given the laundry a cold-water rinse to save money. The chore took hours. In frigid winter months, the near-freezing water numbed her hands and turned them deep crimson.

She hung the laundry outside on a clothesline stretching from the verandah to a tall wooden pole at the edge back of the back yard until the worst of winter weather. An unexpected drop in temperature would sometimes freeze clothes solid. How it made me laugh to my father's boxer shorts stand up on their own. During the worst winter weather, she hung wet things to dry in the kitchen on ropes that ran in parallel lines from one end of the room to the other. As the dried, the humidity created an unpleasant miasma of fog in the flat and condensation on the windows which rotted the wood. Once dry, Mamma got busy ironing just about everything. Drip-dry fabrics were rare in those days and she even gave dishcloths and dishtowels a quick pass with the hot iron.

I wondered often why Mamma never stopped working around the house, never took a day off the way my father did. On weekends, he sat at the kitchen table or in the front room reading his Italian newspapers and news magazine while my while Mamma swept or sewed, cooked or ironed clothes and fed or changed Teresa.

It didn't seem fair to me that she did so much and he so little and I asked her about it "That's just the way it is, Elvie," she said.

CHAPTER EIGHT

The summer of 1956 brought a debilitating heat wave when hot air curled up from the pavement like smoke and sunset brought scant relief after the angry sun finally set. Heat collected indoors throughout the day, sneaked in through window frames and closed shutters filled the rooms with soupy air that made it hard to breathe. As my father put it, "This city is one of Hell's furnaces. Why did we ever come here? Sure, it got hot in Campochiaro but we didn't live like prisoners in a few rooms in a city where the air stinks with dirt and noise."

"Well, let's go back, Papà."

As he turned his gaze to me, I was relieved my question hadn't upset him. "Elvie, one day not too far away, you'll discover for yourself that doing what you want isn't always possible."

The summer of 1956 came and went in a flash. I spent most of it outdoors, made friends and played with them on the street where our sitter, a middle-aged woman—whom I liked because she was gentle—with two grown sons living at home, kept an eye on me and fed me. But as the time to start school approached, I began to worry that I'd get the Big Black Bird again as my teacher or somebody like her. The thought of her stalking the aisles between our desks with her pointer poised to strike my knuckles made me cringe with fear.

To my utter delight, not only was my Grade 2 teacher not a Big Black Bird, she was not a nun. Our Lady of Good Counsel Elementary had closed its doors and all its pupils transferred to nearby Edward Murphy

Elementary, a Catholic English-language school on Craig Street. Best of all, Edward Murphy didn't have a single nun on the teaching staff.

In 1956 Edward Murphy had about 100 Grade 2 pupils alone, which they divided into three classes. My teacher, Mrs. Wendt, seemed old but really nice. Although spoke in an irritating, high-pitched whine. Still, she treated us with kind discipline that warmed me and by the end of the year, I loved the woman.

Until the weather turned cold, Eva, Pasquale and I walked to school together, supervised by one of the mothers, who took turns dropping us off and picking us up. I had a feeling Eva's and Pasquale's mothers didn't like me. They never used endearments to address me as they did when they spoke to the other two: "Pasquale! Wait right there, *piccione*, my little pigeon," or "Eva, don't let go of my hand, *bella*." But when they addressed me, their tones hardened and frowns appeared. "Stop racing ahead, you wretched girl!"

Hard as I tried hard to be good, they kept saying I didn't "listen" or that I had ants in my pants. Other than showing more curiosity about the world and asking a lot of questions, I couldn't figure out what I did that was so bad. The mothers' treatment made me feel like an outsider.

Besides, although I liked Eva, a tiny, timid girl with not a drop of meanness in her, I liked Pasquale. He was always showing off, always rubbing my nose in it when he got higher marks than I did and he had a way of getting what he wanted from adults, except for his father who was a strict disciplinarian

My father saw through Pasquale, though. "That kid's a little prick, just like his father. Can't believe a word that comes out of either one of their mouths."

After the first few days of excitement at a new school, my interest waned. Mostly, the days seemed long and boring except when we took turns reading stories out loud or drawing with crayons, both of which we did for a bit every day. Other that that it was the same old boring memorization, including the torture of multiplication tables.

For me, sitting at a desk for long hours remained a real hardship, but what could a kid do? I endured moments when something in me tried to jump out of my skin, to leave my body there and let my mind go outside to play.

I found some distraction creating stories around a boy who sat one row over and one seat down from me. I liked Michel and wanted to befriend him, I liked his small, thin frame, his fine facial features with a smattering of freckles across nose and cheeks, his thick head of straight black hair and navy-blue eyes. Best of all, Michel had a remarkable talent for drawing and could reproduce, freehand, any image from our reader and just about any animal without a picture in front of him.

At night in bed, I made up stories about the two of us living together, like married couples did. I imagined Michel coming home from work to a supper I'd prepared, a supper that included strawberry or raspberry Jell-O for dessert. While he ate the meal I'd prepared, I fed our baby seated in a highchair, using an espresso spoon, just like Mamma fed Teresa, delivering the food into the round, open mouth that made me think of a baby bird.

In my fantasy life, I didn't go out to work in a factory like Mamma. I stayed home to look after the house and the baby the way mothers of non-immigrants did. When those kids got home from school their mothers had snacks ready. Their mothers had time to make sure their school tunics were clean *and* pressed. Their mothers didn't ask daughters to wash dishes, to sweep, to make beds or to look after their baby sister.

I found excuses to speak to Michel in the schoolyard but he never approached me himself. I didn't hold it against him; I thought it was because he was too shy. So, it surprised me to see him walk right up to one of our classmates during recess one day and offer her a piece of candy, which she took. From that day forward he stuck to her side at every opportunity. The girl had a beautiful face and long, undulating waves of flaxen hair reaching down her back. She wore it parted in the middle with barrettes shaped like butterflies on either side.

In fact, Michel wasn't the only boy who sought her attention. The fact that he liked her and not me made me crackle with envy. Why didn't I have long blonde hair instead of this black mop which, worse still, Mamma forced me to keep it very short to make it easier to look after? Why did my arms and legs look like dry sticks while hers had the roundness of ripe fruit? When another classmate with whom I was playing Bollo remarked on the cluster of boys around the beautiful blonde girl during recess, I said, "I wish I looked like her"

My classmate snorted: "She's a nice girl but haven't you noticed she's not too smart. She's always at the bottom of the class."

That made me think. Would I rather be beautiful and have boys pay attention to me or be smart but unnoticed? I didn't want to choose; I wanted both. This business of boys and girls caused me consternation. Why did I like Michel, who paid me no mind, while Réjean, another classmate, annoyed me with his attentions while providing no consolation for Michel's disinterest? I wanted Michel. Réjean was too pushy, too persistent—too much of everything.

Whenever Réjean followed me in the schoolyard, I told him to go away. After school he walked along with Eva, Pasquale and me, part of the way home after school I ignored him. Once, he offered to carry my school bag, but I told him I could carry it perfectly well myself. Unfortunately for him, he made the mistake of saying how much he liked me in front of some other kids, and it embarrassed me so much I never spoke to him again.

The days of fall months moved slowly then winter came, and they picked up speed with the lure of Christmas. A week before the end of term, Mrs. Wendt handed us our report cards to take home and a quick glance told me my father would be furious with me. "Elvira is a very bright child and could be top of the class if she applied herself. Homework is sloppy and she tends to daydream in class," Mrs. Wendt commented.

CHAPTER NINE

A flock of crazed butterflies collided in my chest as I walked home with the report card throbbing in my school bag. I hadn't worked very hard. My marks and ranking—12th in the class.

All the way home I hardly heard Pasquale boast that he'd come third in his class worried about what my father would do to me.

"How did you do," Pasquale wanted to know.

"None of your business!"

"I bet you're saying that because I beat you," he said, grinning. "What about you, Eva?"

"None of your business either," she replied in solidarity. But she'd already told me she'd ranked fifth.

I waited until after supper to give my father the report card. My hand shook when I held it out to him as I stood before him. He noticed and gave me a long stare before taking it. As Mamma cleared the table, he slipped the report card out of its envelope and examined it—he understood enough English by then to make sense of what the report card said— while I waited for his features to take on the familiar hardness that presaged the fall of the axe.

"Nineties in reading and spelling. That's good," he said, impassive. "Sixties and 70s in mathematics, science and geography. Not good. Twelfth in the class. Very bad."

He held the card out to me. "Translate what the teacher wrote here."

I suspected he already knew what it said but wanted to rub my nose in it. I told him and rose from the chair with a long sigh. My body shrank and I turned my head towards Mamma for help, but she stood at the sink with her back to us and hadn't been listening. I tried to make myself small, pulled into myself, preparing for a lashing. But instead of unbuckling his belt, my father pulled a $10 bill, put it on the table and resumed his seat. The unexpected move disoriented me. Was he playing some sort of trick?

"Sit down," he said, in a sombre tone.

I perched on the edge of the chair to his right, the chair I used for homework—when I did any.

He parked his elbows on the tabletop and rested his chin in his palms. "*E così*, and so, what do you have to say for yourself?" He regarded me not with disappointment, not anger, although I would have preferred his anger because I would have known what to expect but this new, kinder treatment confused me.

I lowered my head and stared down at my worn shoes, shoes that needed replacing.

"Nothing to say?"

I shook my head. What would he do with that $10 bill he'd put on the table?

"Well, since you're not interested in school it looks like you should start thinking about going to work. At least you could pay your own way. No point in wasting any more time at school."

My head snapped up in surprise. Could he really make me go to work? I was only 7. I didn't know any kids my age who worked. Besides, what work could I do? Mamma worked at a sewing machine, but I couldn't do that; I didn't *want* to do that. She complained often about bosses who wanted "blood" out of their workers, and I didn't want to give anybody my blood.

"I'm too little to go to work," I said, edging towards defiant.

"That's how much you know. I could send you to work with your mother tomorrow if I wanted to. A big girl like you can sweep floors, if nothing else. I'm your father and I'm in charge. What I say goes. *Capish?*"

My gaze returned to my shoes to prevent him from seeing the mutiny in my eyes. Taking me out of school and sending me to work seemed unfair punishment for coming 12th out of nearly 40 students. The injustice provoked an unfamiliar surge of something hot in my chest, something that made me want to hit him. Instead, I gripped the edges of the chair with both hands and squeezed hard. I promised myself I would never, ever work in a factory. I'd run away if I had to.

My father picked up the $10 bill. "See this?"

When I didn't look, he lifted my chin with his index finger. His eyes, whose shape and colour he'd given me, searched my face. "If you do well in school, Elvie, you won't ever have to work in a factory like your mother and me. You'll be able to earn this," he lay the bill on the table, "without being a slave to ignorant people who look at you with disgust. Do you understand what I'm saying?"

"Yes. If I do better in school you won't make me work in a factory."

He nodded. "See these hands?" he said, holding them out for me to examine. "I have to use these hands, so our family has a place to live, and food to eat, and clothes to wear."

Isn't that what all fathers did, I thought? All my friends had fathers who took care of those things. Besides, Mamma worked, too, didn't she? But I knew not to interrupt.

"I'm saying that for people like your mother and me we have no choice in how we earn a living because we have little education, none in English. In Campochiaro, school only went to Grade 5. After that we worked in the fields to grow the food we ate. See?"

I nodded. I didn't see, though. I had no memory of life in Campochiaro.

"On the other hand, if you're truly not interested in getting a good education, we should start thinking about getting you a trade. At least with a trade, you have something you can always rely on for a living."

"What's a trade?"

"Something practical that pays well."

"Like what?"

"Like hairdressing. Would you like to be a hairdresser?"

I shrugged. I'd never thought about it. Mamma sometimes went to a hairdresser to get her hair cut but she did her own perms. As for my hair, she sent me to a barber because that cost less.

My father's pressed his lips together, his eyes narrowed. "It's one or the other. Study or go to work sooner rather than later. Do you know how much it costs to feed you, clothe you and pay for everything else you need?"

"A lot?"

"In Campochiaro only the children of a few rich people went away to study to be professors or doctors or lawyers. The ones with education didn't have to break their backs working in the fields. It's the same in this country. Except here, instead of working in fields we work in factories. I'd give anything to have had the chance you have to go to school. Don't waste it, Elvie.

"To do well you have to work hard at it. If you can't be bothered, then there was no point in our family coming to Canada."

I didn't think ranking 12th was so bad, but I'd have to do better.

"Okay, Papà. From now on I'll do my homework every day and pay attention in class."

He smiled and patted me on the head. "Good girl. Don't let me down," he said, putting the $10 bill back in his pocket.

Until my father sat me down that day, I'd thought of him as a sort of ghostly figure who came and went, a creature I put up with but who had no real significance in my world. Yes, he had control over my every-day life, and I feared his anger but I felt no visceral tie to him the way I did to Mamma. Now he'd shown me the extent of his power. I didn't like it. If he could yank me out of school and make me go to work what else could he do if I didn't do as he said?

Still, Christmas holidays were starting, and I didn't want to think about what he'd do and I put it out of mind.

CHAPTER TEN

In early December, our class helped Mrs. Wendt assemble a large nativity scene that took pride of place at the front of the classroom next to her desk. Inside the open-faced stable, we'd placed paper-mâché figures of Saviour baby Jesus lying peacefully in his manger, beaming parents Mary and Joseph, on either side of the manger, and the Three Wise Men who'd come to pay their respects. The scene included a couple of lambs, a cow, some chickens as well as the donkey that had carried the Holy Mother to Bethlehem where she gave birth to Jesus. We crowned the setting with two smiling angels who hovered above the infant Jesus.

At home, there was no Christmas tree, wreaths or other decorations. Our celebrations centered on food. Mamma started baking a week before the holidays, with me getting in her way, trying to help.

The flat stayed warm and cozy from the baking, and fragrant smells in the air filled me with comfort and contentment. My eyes grew large as I eyed the goodies: mountains of almond cookies with honey, called *mostaccioli*, *pizza di riso*, a luscious pie of creamy custard mixed with milk-cooked arborio rice, and *scr'pell*, long columns of deep-fried dough dusted with sugar: my favourite. Of the traditional bought sweets, I loved *torrone*, even though this Italian version of nougat had the tensile strength of granite.

We didn't exchange gifts. In Campochiaro, there had been no such tradition. People didn't have the resources to indulge in extravagances. Even now that we lived in Montreal, we had little money left after attending to basic needs. They put aside every extra penny in the quest to buy a house. Owning property meant having an anchor in a new country that welcomed newcomers for their labour yet despised them for their foreign ways, for their refusal to assimilate. Home ownership meant security and independence and a way to thumb their noses at those who disrespected and denigrated them.

Still, even though my parents were practical people who didn't encourage me to believe in fairy tales, it didn't stop me from hoping there was a Santa Claus. Just in case he did exist, I made a list of the many things I wanted and put it under my pillow for two whole weeks prior to Christmas.

At best, my sister and I could expect from *la Befana*—the Italian version of Santa Claus in the guise of an old hag—were new pajamas via our parents. I would have exchanged 10 years' worth of pajamas for a pair of ice skates that fit.

Nevertheless, a couple of weeks before Christmas Mamma took me shopping at Dupuis Frères, Montreal's first department store. She told me a Santa Claus would be at Dupuis that day and promised I could speak to him. Breathless with anticipation, I skipped ahead as we made our way to the Ste-Catherine Street East store.

"Is he really Santa Claus?" I asked.

She laughed. "I don't think so. Probably just an ordinary man dressed like Santa. Every big store has one."

I shut her denial out of my mind. If Santa didn't exist, I'd never get my ice skates. I knew for sure *my parents* would never buy them for me.

We often shopped at Dupuis Freres because it was closer to us. Eaton's, Simpsons and Hudson's Bay department stores lined up one after the other much farther west on Ste-Catherine. Dupuis had opened in 1868, where it stayed until it shut its doors in 1978. The elegant store catered almost exclusively to the French-language bourgeoisie, many of whom lived in Montreal's eastern flank. Its marketing strategy appealed overtly to French pride in heritage. The store openly recruited French-speaking Catholic staff and gave priority to local French-language suppliers.

This fierce pride in heritage and the fear of losing it, as the newsletter implied, presaged Québec's Quiet Revolution of the 1960s. Beyond heralding social and political change, it also hinted at the rise of nationalism that culminated in violence in October 1970.

But on the day, we visited Dupuis Frères, my only thought was getting Santa to deliver ice skates to my house. We entered the store where everything sparkled and twinkled and went straight to the toy section. Hundreds of kids and moms were lined up to talk to the big man with the long white beard. But when Santa's booming voice invited me forward, I stood frozen to the spot with sudden shyness.

Mamma nudged me to go ahead.

"*Tu ne veux rien pour Noël, ma petite?* Don't you want anything for Christmas, little one?" he asked, when I showed reluctance to sit on his knee.

I nodded with vigour. "*Oui, j'veux un cadeau!* Of course, I want a present." I let him help climb on to his knee.

"*Murmure à mon oreille.* Whisper in my ear," he said, leaning in to allow me to reach his ear.

"*Des patins, s'vous plaît.* Ice skates, please." I wanted them so much badly it hurt. Mine were shabby hand-me-downs and too big. When I skated, my ankles knocked together and the blades splayed outward.

Mr. Claus smiled. "*Très bien, ma petite. Ce sera des patins.* Fine, little one, ice skates it will be."

"*Merci!*" I said, my heart swelling. I hopped off his knee, convinced the skates would show up.

Mamma grabbed my hand and hustled me out of the toy department to keep me from pestering her to buy something. She led me, protesting, to housewares but I pulled away and skipped ahead.

"Fine, pout if you want," she said. "It doesn't bother me one bit."

Usually, she let things roll off her back, although lately Mamma had seemed distracted and irritable. Soon enough, the store's brilliant seasonal decorations, blinking Christmas lights, the endless displays of merchandise all captured my attention.

I stopped at a showcase displaying glittering jewels and found myself intrigued by a pair of pendant earrings studded with pale blue stones that winked at me. Unlike many of the Italian girls my age, Mamma hadn't had my ears pierced early on—not that I longed to have someone put a needle through my earlobe—but it meant I couldn't wear the pretty earrings they did.

"Just say the word and I'll pierce them for you," Mamma replied when I brought it up.

"Okay, let's do it right now."

But when she brought out the needle and rubbing alcohol, I'd chicken out. Now as I watched the light play over the blue stones, my cowardice made me mad at myself.

My gaze shifted to a thick necklace with pale yellow stones when I heard a heavy thump behind me. As I turned towards the sound, Mamma lay on the floor. The sight came like a punch to my chest and took my breath. Was she dead? Had she gone to Heaven like the grey-faced old lady in the coffin at the funeral parlour?

"Ma!" I screamed, running to her side.

Her eyelids fluttered open. Patrons and clerks came running. Someone helped her sit up, helped her to her feet and led her to a bench near the elevator with my trailing behind, my breathing fast and quick, terrified Mamma would die.

A couple of decades later I asked Mamma whether she remembered the incident.

"Sure, I remember. I fainted because I was pregnant. It had happened with each of my pregnancies." That day when she fainted in the middle of an aisle in Dupuis Freres, announced she was pregnant with my brother.

When we left the store that day, Mamma seemed fully recovered and I was happy because Santa Claus knew about the ice skates I wanted and I couldn't wait for Christmas Day until he delivered them, which I was convinced he would.

We hadn't put up a Christmas tree nor did we have a fireplace for Santa Claus to use to get into our flat, like the stories Mrs. Wendt had read to us, but I figured he'd find another way in. We spent Christmas Eve eating mountains of food then got together with another family to play Tombola, the Italian version of bingo, until late. Even as I lay in bed, I did my best to stay awake as I listened for sounds of Santa's arrival and my first thought, when I opened my eyes Christmas morning, was to get my hands on the skates.

Everybody was still asleep. I slipped out of bed quietly so as not to wake Zia Vilia and scurried into the kitchen, my bare feet on the cold linoleum floor, expecting to see a box on the table. But there was no box. I tiptoed past my parents' room to the front parlour, where I even checked under the sofa and chair. Still, I didn't give up and told myself he'd probably left the skates in the shed? I headed to the shed where I lifted storage boxes, looked around my father's tools and behind the wood pile, shivering with cold in the unheated, freezing room attached to the kitchen before I gave up. But still I had hope and I ran back into my bedroom to check under the bed, around the bed and inside the clothes closet. Nothing. Nothing at all.

Santa Claus hadn't come. Mamma had been right; Santa Claus was an ordinary man hired by the store. I didn't let myself cry.

CHAPTER ELEVEN

After the holiday break, we dug in for the long, frigid, boring months of winter when the skies darkened so early it seemed as if we lived in the dark all the time. We left for school when it was dark, and we came home as the sky darkened. I wasn't allowed to play outside except for the walk to and from school and on weekends when the weather wasn't too bad, we stayed indoors. Sometimes I did all my homework just to keep busy, played with Teresa and annoyed Mamma, whose belly was growing bigger and bigger, by resisting doing the chores she wanted me to do around the house.

Sometime during that summer of 1956, Zia Vilia got herself a suitor. Her friends and family had long been worried that my aunt, verging on 30, would never get *sistemata*: settled. My aunt did not possess the delicate features and curvy body then much sought after. She had a bony frame, a beak for a nose and the same hard-edged, square face as my father, although softened by the kindliness in her eyes.

Although my aunt and her future husband, Nicola, who had immigrated to Sault Ste. Marie, Ontario, knew each other from Campochiaro, it would be an arranged marriage, two people brought together by their friends. They married in 1957, as soon as her mourning period ended, and she moved to The Soo. It so happened that's where Mamma's youngest sister, Zia 'Ndunetta, had lived since 1954.

Zia Vilia had often interceded on my behalf when I'd misbehaved and my father threatened to use his belt on me. She'd entertained me by playing endless games of cards and sometimes slipped me a nickel when my parents wouldn't. But Zia Vilia was also a relentless nag. With her departure I had one less adult ordering me around and the bedroom to myself—or so I'd imagined. Not so. Teresa, twenty-two months old, became my new bedmate. In the early summer of 1957 Mamma's belly had swollen to gigantic proportions, even bigger than the last time. Her belly grew in tandem with my father's dark moods and the frequency and volume of their fights with him accusing her of betrayal, got scary.

"Who's the father, eh? Who is it? Is it somebody at work? Did you sneak around behind the building during a lunch break?"

She ignored his provocations until she couldn't stand it. "How dare you, *disgraziato*, you miserable wretch! You're the one who slept around with every willing slut in Campochiaro, including Rita, while we were engaged. And you think I haven't heard what you were up to while you boarded with Giulio before I came to this Godforsaken country? This child is yours; God help me."

Sometimes she tried to reason with him but when he'd sunk into those moods it only made things worse, made him meaner. I watched them, sometimes holding Teresa's hand, silent and worried for Mamma, as he heaped accusations on her, as she wept.

I'd noticed my father often complained that people, and not just Mamma, didn't treat him the way with respect, and it made him suspicious.

"You and your family, you act like you're better than me because they own half of Campochiaro and your mother has been getting piles of money from your father since he moved to the United States."

"If I thought that, would I have married you?"

"Why did you marry me? Only to cheat on me?"

And on and on it went.

Often, fights erupted after we were all in bed. Their barbed voices woke me, worried me, and I sat up ready to intervene in case Mamma called for help, each time reliving the trauma of the scene I'd witnessed when we'd lived on Saint-Christophe when I saw him when he was about to strike her with a rod. During one such fight when my fear rose so high in my chest, I thought I would pass out and I cried out for them to stop. "Go the fuck to sleep!" my father shouted. But they stopped fighting, at least that night.

Mamma quit work at the end of June when the school term ended, her ankles and legs as swollen as big as an elephant's. My final Grade 2 report card provided one bright pot almost succeeded in pleasing my father: I had ranked fourth, better but not good enough, he said. Still, it thrilled me so much when he handed me a quarter as a reward that resolved to try harder in Grade 3. But for now, summer freedom stretched ahead like a glass of iced Kool-Aid on a hot afternoon.

Mamma didn't seem too happy about being home even though she often complained about how demanding some of her bosses were and how cheap.

She was among the thousands of immigrant women and French-speaking, who toiled in Montreal's airless, brick clothing factories for a meagre wage. She never complained about having to work—she liked it and enjoyed the camaraderie— but resented the poor hourly wage, the miserable bosses who pushed and pushed for more and more and worst of all, the intolerable summer heat intensified by the machine motors turned the factories into furnaces.

Still, the work was physically hard with long hours on hard chairs, hunched over an industrial machine in a room filled with dozens of machines that buzzed and whirred and screeched: single needle sewing machines, sergers, machines that cut the raw edges of fabric and overcast them with V-shaped stitches, buttonhole makers, double needle and embroidery machines. Mamma learned how to operate many of them. Fabric dust from the textiles they handled seeped into their lungs and made them cough.

When we got off the ship in Halifax in 1952, Mamma stood straight and tall. At 5-feet-5, she was much taller than the average Compochiaro woman, only a couple of inches shorter than my father. In the village, she told me they got their water from communal wells, filled them with huge copper pots, and carried them home balanced on their heads. Now after five years of stooping over sewing machines, the top of her spine had begun to curl forward.

By the time I reached my teens she had developed a humpback.

In the mid-1950s, Montreal garment factories mostly hired women to work the sewing machines while men handled the big machines such as the big blades that cut the textiles the women sewed. Seamstresses earned an average of 99 cents an hour, while the cutters got $1.51. The pay disparity had little to do with skill since operating a serger required as much expertise as cutting patterns out of a stacked pile of fabric.

With Mamma now at home for the summer, I anticipated a carefree summer vacation, but she was grumpy all the time and more demanding of my help around the house or babysitting Teresa. I begged her to let me join my friends and when she allowed it, I rushed out, pretending I didn't hear her telling me to take Teresa along.

The summer vacation took a turn for the better after Lise moved in with her aunt and cousins below us. She was 12 to my 8, the same age as my cousin Fil and we clicked instantly, and I spent all my spare time with her. Eventually, Mamma came out of her fog long enough to notice and tried to put an end to it.

"I don't want you hanging around with someone like her."

"Why? What's wrong with her?"

"They're not like us, Elvie."

"But she's so nice to me, and so is her aunt."

"It's not about being nice or not nice. Why, I wouldn't be surprised if that woman isn't even married and those two boys of hers are bastards. And she doesn't work, pays to feed her family with money the government gives her every month when she could get work tomorrow because they can't get all the operators they need."

"But how could she have children if she isn't married?"

She shook her head. "Listen to what I'm telling you, Elvie. It's for your own good. That family is a bad example."

"Can't you get money from the government and stay home too?"

"They only give it to people who have no money at all. Your Papà has a job, and I work because we want to buy our own house."

I ignored Mamma's directive to stay away from Lise and invited her to come upstairs and play on our verandah when I was forced to take care of Teresa. Mamma got to know Lise. She came to like her and not only relented; she came to rely on her to keep an eye on me.

Lise had stringy, shoulder-length, dirty-blond hair with bangs that covered her brows and tickled her eyelids. Her face had a doughy appearance, and her skin an oily sheen. Although she was only 12, the girl already stood as tall as Mamma, and she had a woman's curves. As Lise and I strolled along neighbourhood streets searching for distraction, her ponderous, bra-free breasts drew relentless catcalls and whistles from men of all ages. Sometimes they stopped to proposition her, which puzzled me.

"Why do they want to give you money?" I asked.

She'd laugh. "They want to touch my boobs."

"But why?"

She shrugged. "Cos they're big and juicy and they like how that feels."

"Have you ever let somebody touch them?"

She shrugged. "Sure. A couple times."

"Do you like it when somebody touches them?"

"I don't mind. But I like the money more."

Lise opened doors to new worlds to me, including typical French-Canadian dishes: shepherd's pie, which she called as *pâté Chinois*; cretons, a pork pâté, and *sucre a la crème*, a fudge made with brown sugar, cream and butter. At home we ate sweets only on special occasions and discovered an intense new pleasure in the extreme sweetness of *sucre a la crème,* the like of which I had never imagined.

Sometimes Lise and I roamed the neighbouring streets at summer but most often we sat on our shared front stoop to watch people go by, skipped rope or played hopscotch or hung out her back yard verandah. I asked her a lot of questions because I wanted to know why Mamma thought her family wasn't like ours.

"How come you don't live with your parents?" I asked Lise one day as we lolled on her aunt's verandah at the back. The packed earth yard before us stretched all the way to the wooden poles that held one end of the clotheslines for the three units in our building.

"I don't have a father. I live with Mom but she works at night now so *ma tante* said I could stay with her."

That Lise, like her cousins, didn't have a father struck me as strange but quite appealing. I wouldn't have minded having my father out of the picture. When he wasn't around, things were nice and quiet at home but the moment he got in, a big wind blew us here and there.

"What work does your mother do?"

We had settled on a blanket on her verandah floor. Directly above us, Mamma's footsteps made creaking sounds on the verandah and Teresa babbled in her barely understandable language. Mamma enjoyed sitting outside to mend or shell peas or crocheted and spent a lot of time sitting as the doctor had told her to put her feet up to help the swelling.

Before answering my question, Lise dug her fingers into a glass jar and, pulled out an impossibly red maraschino cherry, popped it into her mouth and passed the jar to me. I put one in my mouth and sighed in delight.

"Well, my mother is a dancer. She works in a nightclub and nightclubs are only open at night. She and her boyfriend broke up and she didn't want me to be alone by myself all night so here I am."

"A dancer?" I had never imagined people could do such fun things as a job. Everybody I knew worked in a factory.

"I can show you how she dances if you want. I saw her do it once. She didn't want me to see her dance, but she took me to work with her one night. I peeked from the side of the stage when it was her turn on stage. You wouldn't believe how the men watching her cheered and whistled like crazy."

I gave her back the cherries and she tilted back and dropped another one into her wide-open mouth. "I'll show you but not today 'cos I have to have the right costume and music."

A few days later Lisa was ready to put on a show. She used the verandah floor as her stage while her cousins and I watched in rapt attention sitting on chairs we'd plunked on the yard's uneven dirt. She wore a floor-length, shiny, pale blue dress, gloves in a matching colour that reached all the way to her middle upper arms—also blue—and white high heels. She'd borrowed the lot from her aunt. Lise had the record player ready, placed the needle on the record and started moving to the slow rhythm of trumpets and drums, wiggling her hips to the beat of the music as she teased each glove off her arms, hands then each finger, lifted the skirt of her dress and pulled off the garters holding up her nylons before rolling the nylons down her legs and off her feet and dropped them to the floor. Then she turned her back to us. We watched as she unzipped the dress, exposed one shoulder then the other before it slid to the floor and she was left with nothing but her ill-fitting cotton panties and brassiere. When she had almost nothing left, she covered herself with a big feather fan, took off everything else and left the stage. The men clapped like crazy. While we clapped like crazy. Lise turned and took a deep bow before exiting the stage.

"Does your mother ever come here to see you?" I asked after she'd dressed and rejoined me.

"Sure."

I wondered why I'd never seen her though. "Tell me next time she comes. I wanna see if she looks like you."

"Oh, I don't look like her at all. She's pretty," Lise said.

"What about your father? Do you ever see him?"

Lise shrugged. "Don't know who he is. My mother says he's not important."

CHAPTER TWELVE

Mamma went into labour during the night of August 13, 1957. I awoke with a start when Angelina, the neighbour who had looked after us before Mamma had quit work, came into my bedroom and lay down next to me.

"It's okay, sweetie, your mum and dad have gone to the hospital to pick up the baby."

"Ma!" I cried, trying to get out of bed.

"They're not here, Elvie. Your Mamma will have to stay at the hospital a few days, but I'll look after you until Papà gets home. Go back to sleep."

I lay down reluctantly but worried that my father had hurt Mamma, worried she might never come back. Teresa, who lay asleep next to me, hadn't stirred.

Angelina put her arms around me, soothed me until I fell asleep, but I woke up as morning light pushed through the slats of the closed shutters. I found myself in bed alone and I jumped out of bed and hurried into the kitchen looking for Angelina, but there was only my father at the table making toast and Teresa sitting on the floor playing with some spoons.

"Where's mamma?" I asked.

"She's at the hospital with your new brother."

"How come you're home but mamma isn't."

"The doctor wants to make sure the baby is okay and that means Mamma has to stay with him. Don't worry, they'll be home in a few days."

"Why can't she take care of the baby here?"

He sighed. "Why don't you sit down and eat some toast. Look, I made a whole pile."

Throughout the week Mamma was in the hospital and Teresa cried for her. We both tried our best to console her. I took her with me wherever I went while he sat her on his lap to tell her stories or just talk to her.

"What do you think we should name your brother?" he said one day. Teresa looked up at him with wide eyes, not understanding.

"Mamma went to get another baby. A baby like you but only smaller," I said.

"To play? she asked.

"Yes," I said. But I didn't understand why Mamma wanted another baby. It seemed to me Teresa and I should have been enough.

"Elvie, what do you think about calling your brother Riccardo, eh?"

I picked up Teresa from the floor, placed her on the chair with the booster and pushed it close to the edge of the table while he buttered toast, put it on a plate, cut it in two and gave it to her. I buttered my own toast while he heated milk on the big stove.

"Do you know why I thought of that name?"

"Why?"

"There was a very famous English king named Richard the 'Lionheart.' In Italian that translates to Riccardo Cordileone. Maybe an important name will bring him good luck."

"Maybe," I replied. I didn't care what he named this needless new addition to the family.

In Momma's absence I fretted about her. My father visited her every other day, and I begged him to take me along. I wanted to see with my own eyes that she wasn't hurt.

"Listen, will you?" he said, squatting to my level. "Hospitals don't let children go into the rooms of sick people."

"Mamma's sick!" I said, stricken. "Is she going to die?" He patted me on the cheek. "No, she's not sick! But getting a baby is hard work and now the doctor wants her to rest for a bit. But there are other people in the hospital who *are* sick and it's dangerous for kids to get too close. *Capish?*"

I nodded but wasn't convinced. For some reason he took pity on me and the following day he took me with him to the hospital. He did his best to sneak me past the receptionist, a nun, but she saw me and wouldn't let me through, so he went up to see Mamma while I waited for him in the lobby. Riccardo was born at Hôpital Notre Dame on Sherbrooke Street East across the street from my beloved Parc La Fontaine. Mamma came home after a week, looking more rested and rosier than I'd ever seen but she brought home this mewling little creature who, once again like Teresa before him, took her full attention day and night. She was home now, and I stopped worrying about her being hurt but at the same time she seemed different from before as if she didn't see me when I talked to her.

She gave me more chores than ever. On top of the usual sweeping, dusting and babysitting, she showed me how to iron small items like pillowcases and dishtowels. I complained; she yelled, and sometimes a slipper came flying across the room for emphasis.

On the other hand, my father seemed cheerful, even helpful now and then. A couple of weeks after she and Ricky came home—as we now called him—I answered a knock at the door to find a nun standing there.

"*Bonjour, petite demoiselle.*" She spoke softly and had a kind face that seemed to glow. "*Est-ce que ta maman est à la maison?* Is your *maman* at home?"

She didn't look anything like my sour former teacher, the Big Black Bird, and she didn't dress like her either. She was dressed in a pleated grey robe—not the voluminous black my former teacher wore—covered by a short, sleeveless hooded cape and a black bonnet.

"Ma!" I left the sister standing there while I hurried to get Mamma, who was in her bedroom with Ricky, putting him down in the crib vacated by Teresa.

Perplexed, Mamma nevertheless invited in the good sister, who explained that she was a member of the Grey Nuns attached to Notre Dame Hospital who gave new mothers a hand at home to help them get on their feet. She said my father had signed up for it.

The sister came early every morning for the next two weeks. She swept and washed floors, did laundry—including mountains of diapers—hung it up on the clothesline and took it down when it dried and folded it. She made beds, dusted furniture and kept an eye on Teresa and me when Mamma ran errands. She would have made meals too, but Mamma thanked her politely but refused. She was a picky eater—no hard cheese, not even a dusting of Romano or Parmigiano on her pasta; no butter; no beef or lamb—and wanted to make sure she knew what was in the food she ate. For that reason, when we attended banquets of the five or six courses, she stuck to the first: antipasto and bread.

I loved having the nun those couple of weeks. Sometimes, after she'd finished her housework and had time to spare, she'd dandle my sister on her lap, pull up a chair for me and tell us stories. They were religious but more palatable than the blood-drenched ones I'd endured in Grade 1. She also answered all my questions with utmost seriousness.

She was still there when my father came home from work, and I noticed he didn't behave like himself. He was very polite, spoke softly and smiled when he spoke to her. Why didn't he act like that with us?

I told Lise about the kind *religieuse* coming to our house.

"You know the nuns are very rich, eh?" she said.

"They are?"

"That's what my aunt says. Filthy rich, the lot of them."

"She doesn't look rich to me."

"Yeah, well, my aunt says nuns and priests own half of Montreal. Her pockets are probably filled with pennies for poor people like us. If I were you, I'd ask her for a few."

"Are we poor?"

Lise rolled her eyes heavenward. "Weren't you the one complaining about having to walk around with a hole in the soles of your shoes? Why do you think that is?"

The very same afternoon I asked the nun for a few pennies.

"A*h, ma petite*. Your friend, Lise, is quite mistaken. I don't have a single penny in my pocket or to my name. You see, when I became a *religieuse,* I made a promise of poverty to God, which means I own nothing at all. Not even the clothes I wear belong to me but to my community."

How disappointing. How could Lise have gotten it so wrong.

CHAPTER THIRTEEN

When the nun stopped coming, I missed her a lot and fled Mamma, Ricky and Teresa at every opportunity. Mamma had changed and I didn't like being around her. The only time she smiled was when she held my Ricky in her arms, cooing over him, kissing him as though she wanted to eat him up.

The end of August neared, I was bored and looking always for something to do that wasn't housework. If Lise or other playmates weren't around, I wandered the nearby streets, sometimes with Teresa tagging along, to pass the time. On the hottest, most searing afternoons, Mamma might give us a few cents to buy an ice cream.

On one such afternoon as I headed home along Robin when someone called my name. I looked up and waved to a neighbour leaning against the railing of his verandah on the second floor. He and his wife were friends with my parents and from time to time they got together there on hot summer evenings to enjoy a beer or a nice cold soft drink and try to catch a cool breeze.

"What are you doing walking around all by yourself like a lost soul?" he asked, his arms resting on the wrought iron.

"Nothing. I'm looking for my friends but there's nobody around."

"Come up. I'll give you a glass of Coca-Cola."

At home, soft drinks were a rare treat so I ran up the curling staircase eager for the treat. He smiled, pointed to one of the chairs, told me to sit down while he went inside to fetch the Coke.

He and his wife were Italian immigrants, too, but not from Abruzzo like us. They seemed a lot older than my parents with a married daughter who'd just had a baby, living above them and an almost grownup daughter who lived with the couple but seemed to disappear from time to time.

The man held out the tall glass beaded with condensation. I drank it down fast, the bubbles tickling my nose, enjoying the sweetness even as its coldness felt like a burn as it went down my throat. I gave him back the glass and said thank you.

He placed the glass on a small nearby table and picked up a window shutter leaning against the wall. "Terribly hot today, isn't it?" he said.

"What are you going to do with that?" I pointed to the shutter.

"Fix it."

He was tall with a narrow bony face and a head of black wavy hair made glossy by the Brilliantine he used, something my as father used, although my father's hair was thin and straight.

"Is Elena home?" I asked.

"She's away in the country."

Too bad, I thought. She was a lot older than me but fun to talk to. The last time Elena had come back from a visit to the country she'd shown me: picture frames, baskets, ashtrays and all sorts of other things she'd made there. I wished I could go to the country and learn how to make things.

"When is she coming back?"

"Probably in a few months."

"Why does she go to the country so much?"

He sighed but didn't give me an answer. "Here hold on to this side of the wood while I tighten this screw."

I did as he asked. "How come you're not at work like your wife?" I asked. Every other Italian man I knew worked every weekday and sometimes Saturdays, too.

"Aren't you a curious little so-and-so," he replied.

I stayed until he finished repairing the shutter and went home. As soon as I got in, I asked Mamma why Elena went to the country so often.

"Poor girl," she replied. "She's sick."

"Sick how? She doesn't look sick."

"Never you mind."

I had liked visiting with the neighbour, liked spending part of the day with someone to talk to, someone who paid attention to me and who gave me all the Coca Cola I wanted, and I went back whenever I could.

Then one day he invited me in as it began to rain. He asked me whether I wanted to play a game and, of course, I said I wanted to. It involved me sitting on his lap. So I climbed on his lap. He kissed me on the lips and I let him even though it seemed an odd sort of game because it felt nice but when he tried to push his tongue into my mouth it spooked me and I pulled away.

"What's the matter?"

"I don't like that."

"Okay, I wont do that anymore."

He kept his promise at first but soon out came the tongue again, and even worse I felt something hard and uncomfortable under me and I squirmed and pushed against him until he released me.

"I'm going home now."

I expected him to get mad at me for stopping the game, but he didn't look mad.

"Okay," he said, remaining seated as he waved goodbye.

I hadn't told Mamma about my afternoon visits to the neighbour's. I didn't know why but something told me she wouldn't like it. And yet, even after the kissing game, I went back. He hadn't hurt me, and I wasn't afraid of him and besides I had nothing better to do.

My visits with the neighbour came to an abrupt end a few days before school resumed after I told Lise about him.

"You shouldn't go back there. He's a bad man," Lise said.

"No, he's not. Come with me and you'll see. He'll give both of us some Coke."

"I'll come but only because I don't want you to go by yourself."

He wasn't out on the verandah that afternoon. Lise and I climbed the swirling staircase to the second floor and knocked on his door. He frowned when he saw us standing there and stared at Lise so long it seemed he might turn us away but eventually stepped back and let us in. I flounced in, Lise close behind me, as though I owned the place and invited her to take a seat at the kitchen table.

The man didn't look pleased with me and he didn't join us at the table. Instead, he leaned against the counter, eyes narrowed, with his arms crossed at his chest.

"Can we have some Coca-Cola?" I asked.

I could tell he was really mad at me now because his face looked just like my father's did when I did something he didn't like, and it burst my bubble of satisfaction I'd felt at showing Lise I had an adult for a friend.

"Didn't your mother teach you any manners?" he said in Italian. "You have some nerve coming here demanding Coca-Cola? Do you think Coca-Cola pours out of the faucet?"

"What's he saying?" Lise wanted to know.

"He says it's rude to ask for Coke."

Lise got to her feet. "Come on, let's get out of here."

He got like that sometimes when I wouldn't let him kiss me, but he didn't stay mad. Besides, it felt good to get an adult to do what I wanted. "But why? We just got here!"

"I don't like him. Why do you come here anyway?"

I shrugged.

Lise went to the door. Turning to me, she said, "come on, let's go" using the tone of voice an adult would use.

I glanced at the man who looked back at me with the suggestion of a smile on his lips. Lise saw it too and shouted, "If you don't come with me right now, I'll tell your mother you've been coming here."

The man laughed but his face got red. "Tell her what? Tell her mother how much Coca-Cola her kid's being drinking," he replied in thickly-accented French.

"Okay," I said to Lise, who never handed out idle threats, including to the two younger cousins she lived with.

"Yes, go and don't come back!" the man said to me in Italian. "I never invited you here so don't you go telling stories about me because if you do, I'll tell them you're the one who kept coming here, bothering me."

It was true I had gone there without being asked and if my parents found out—especially my father, he would beat me.

"Promise me you won't ever go back there by yourself," Lise said.

"I promise."

As we rounded the corner all at once I felt terribly ashamed I'd let the man kiss me but didn't understand why Lise was making such a fuss. Kissing must be bad, I thought.

I thought my promise to Lise had ended the matter, but Lise told Mamma about my visits to the man behind my back. Mamma confronted me in father's absence. She was so upset she could hardly get the words out. "Tell...me...what...happened! Did he—did he touch you?"

I looked down at my feet wanting to crawl under the table, wanting to hide, to pretend I'd never seen the man and he had never kissed me.

"Come here to me," she said.

I was sure she would she hit me and I moved gingerly towards her where she sat. Instead of striking me, however, she got down on her knees, wrapped her arms around me and sobbed. Her tears unleashed my own avalanche and soon, my sister, who played quietly on the floor, joined in.

"What did he do to you?" she asked when we were all cried out.

"He kissed me," I said, unable to look her in the eyes.

"*O dio, o dio mio, o dio mio....*" She spoke the words in a haunting singsong, her arms wrapped around herself and rocking back and forth.

It pained me to see her so upset and that I had caused the hurt and my insides trembled because of it. I was a bad person and a bad daughter because I kissed the man and surely God would punish me, maybe even take me away and send me straight to Hell.

When she calmed down, she pulled out the handkerchief she kept in her bra and wiped her eyes. "What else did he do?"

"What do you mean?"

"Did he touch your private parts?"

"No!"

"It's okay, you can tell me, *figlia mea.*"

"No!"

"*Sicur?* For sure?"

"*Sicur!*"

Her face relaxed. "Your father can't ever find out about this, *me capish?* He'd go over there and cut his throat."

Relief washed over me. At least I didn't have to worry about how my father would punish me.

Mamma never mentioned the incident again but from then on, she found reasons to refuse the man's wife's invitations.

CHAPTER FOURTEEN

The new school term of September 1957 distracted me from watching my father for signs he'd gotten wind of what I'd done with the man and saw only a gloomy man who hardly spoke to any of us. His euphoria over the birth of Ricky had been replaced by longer bouts of brooding and muttering followed by outbursts of rage. When he wasn't out working, he hid himself away in the front room reading newspapers and magazines. We almost never went out visiting. At mealtimes, he cast sidelong, venomous glances towards Mamma. To my relief, he hardly noticed me at all although I took care to tiptoe around—we all did, even Teresa who was only 2—for fear of provoking him.

The explosion came in the fall during Sunday lunch. Mamma had spent all morning making *cavatelli* for lunch—tiny dumplings I'd help her roll—and slow-simmered tomato sauce with meat balls, braciole rolls, and pork bones to pour over them.

My father hadn't spoken all day when we sat down to eat when all at once he slammed his spoon onto the table and glared at Mamma.

"You need to tell me the name of the man who fathered your latest bastard!"

She flushed deep red. "Why do you poison everything, even the food I put in my mouth?"

"Is it that rich Jew, your boss? Is he the father of the kid you want to pass off as mine?"

I stopped chewing, the softness of tiny dumplings and tangy richness of sauce now bitter on my tongue. It wasn't the first time I'd witnessed a fight between my parents or heard my father say he was not our father. That day, however, the shadows in my father's eyes, the way he held his body, coiled like a cat ready to spring on its prey, turned my body rigid. Teresa, sniffing tension, climbed down from her chair and up onto Mamma's lap. Ricky lay asleep in his crib.

"Answer me, *putana*, you whore."

"It doesn't matter what I say," she said, pulling my sister into her body.

"Well, why bother denying it, I guess?" He reached across the table to spear a plump meatball out of a platter heaped with them.

To my horror, my father turned to me. "Elvie, you know your mother's a whore, eh? Don't grow up to be like her."

He'd called her that many times. I didn't know what *putana* meant, except it had something to do with Mamma and other men. Maybe kissing, like I'd done with that man. Had Mamma let her boss kiss her? Is that why she had my brother? Would I get a baby too because I'd let the man kiss me? I didn't want a baby.

"You're disgusting," she said.

He laughed. "I'm disgusting? You're the whore who's got me breaking my back to raise other men's children." He again turned to me. "Elvie, which one of us is disgusting?"

"Leave her out of this!" Mamma roared. Sliding my sister off her lap, she marched into their bedroom and came back with her coat on and my brother in her arms, wrapped in a blanket.

"Come on kids, let's go," she said to my sister and me.

As I went to stand, my father held me back. "You can go with those two bastards but this one stays here with me to make sure you come back."

I struggled to pull away but that only made him tighten his grip.

Mamma's face had paled to the colour of the milk I poured on corn flakes. "If I'm a whore and these kids bastards, wouldn't you be better off without them?"

He ordered me to sit down. I sat down. Then he drew a pack of cigarettes from his breast pocket, tapped out a smoke, flicked a match and lit it. He took long pulls before speaking.

"You don't seem to understand I *own* you. I own you and I own them—their birth certificates say I'm their father. I have control over your every movement."

"Papà?" I said tentatively.

"Shut up."

I knew tears had gathered in her eyes because they shone too bright, but she didn't cry. "Come, Elvie, come here to me."

But I didn't have the courage to defy my father. He laughed, releasing smoke rings in the air. Mamma stood at the door another minute then her shoulders slumped, and she started across the room. Halfway to their bedroom, holding an infant in the cradle of her arm and with me clutching her skirt, she confronted my father.

"I pray to God he gives you a slow, painful death," she told him.

My father snorted derision. "Pray away. I don't believe in your god."

"I'll pray every night. I'll pray you suffer two days of agony for each one you've given me."

"Can I go, too?" I asked.

"Yeah, you can fuck off, too. You'll probably turn out just like her, anyway. Another whore."

Mamma lay on her bed with my brother tucked next to her on one side and sister on the other. I squeezed in beside my sister. Some time elapsed before I heard the door to the shed open followed by clanging noises as he rifled through the storage area looking for who knew what. After the shed door banged shut, it sounded as if he was moving furniture in the kitchen.

For some reason, that disturbed me. My heart thumped hard. "What's he doing, Ma?" I asked.

Mamma lay unmoving as though asleep except that her eyes were open.

"Ma?" I said, shaking her shoulder.

She squeezed her eyes shut for a second or two then opened them with a sigh. "I'll go and see. You stay here."

The moment she stepped into the kitchen the shouting began. I crept down the hall.

My father was standing on a chair in front of the bedroom door nearby. My sister came up behind me and took my hand.

"They're your children!" she shouted, looking at up him. "You can do blood tests. Will that convince you?"

He didn't reply. Instead, he carried on with what he intended, hammering a big nail into the doorframe's lintel. I feared going past him to get to Mamma, who was crying. Nevertheless, I squeezed my sister's hand and we both hurried to her side. I didn't know what he planned to do but if it had made Mamma cry it was bad. My mouth and throat had dried up. Swallowing hurt.

She put an arm around each of us, and the shaking of her body felt like electricity.

When my father finished hammering the nail, he got off the chair, and went to the table to get a length of thick rope. He returned to the chair and played with the rope. Well, what else could he do with a rope? I asked myself. Then he climbed back on the chair.

He'd made a noose.

He tied one end to the sturdy nail, tested it for strength and stepped off the chair. We all looked up and stared at the noose swinging a bit from side to side.

Mamma let out a wail that raised goose bumps on my body.

"You'd better get ready to die," he told her.

He wanted her to die because she'd kissed somebody? That made no sense. What could I do to stop him? What *should* I do?

Mamma turned to my sister and me. "Don't worry. We're just playing a game. Go back to the bedroom. Take your sister."

I couldn't leave her; the hard thump of my heart, my bones, told me she was in danger.

"See where your betrayals have landed you, bitch?" my father shouted. "I hope you've said your prayers."

"Why are you doing this? I . . ." but before she finished, her words caught on a sob.

He pointed to the chair, to the rope.

"Stop it! Stop it! Stop it!" I screamed in terror. My sister wailed. Neither paid any attention.

Mamma looked up at the rope.

"Get on that chair or I'll drag you up by the hair."

Her face, her lips had turned chalky. "Don't do this! Think of the children. Who's going to look after them?"

"Oh, you mean your bastard children? Don't worry. One of your sisters will take them."

When she didn't move, he shifted in her direction like a black thundercloud.

Standing with my body pressed against hers, I felt her give up. She slackened from the inside, as though her bones had liquefied and no longer held her up. She bowed her head for a moment, made the sign of the cross.

"Elvie, take your sister, go into my bedroom, and shut the door. Do it for me."

I would not leave her. I wasn't capable of movement.

"Death will be a blessing after having had to endure you," she said as she stepped to the chair.

Only when she balanced against the doorframe and put a foot on the chair did I act.

I had never seen someone die but I had an animal's understanding. My mouth opened and let out a deep animal howl, low pitched and enraged. The sound rocketed from below my feet, through two columns of legs, past my torso, out my throat and into the air. I thought God could hear it.

Maybe, maybe not. But as the sound ricocheted against floor, ceilings and walls, somehow it slammed into my father and shattered his enchantment. His body deflated, collapsed inward, as had Mamma's. He fell to the floor in a heap.

"Mother of God, what have I done?" He turned to me, eyes filled with fear and pain.

My mother stepped down from the chair. She pulled a handkerchief from between her breasts and wiped her nose and eyes.

"What have I done?" he repeated over and over, as Mamma walked into the kitchen on quivering legs and sat.

The incident deepened the lesson that men were dangerous. Would my father have kicked the chair out from under her feet? Likely not, but who knows? He might have been playing chicken to wrest a confession of infidelity from her.

My mother never had been the sort of woman to flirt with other men, let alone commit adultery. My father, himself a philanderer, couldn't believe she had no interest in other men.

CHAPTER FIFTEEN

To all appearances, my parents made up after my father tried to get a noose around Mamma's neck. For a long time after that incident, he was subdued and kinder towards us but Mamma's willingness to forget it didn't sit right with me. He'd done a very bad thing and should be punished just as he punished my misbehaviour.

Mamma kept herself busier than ever before and didn't talk much, not to us, not to anybody not even our former babysitter, Angelina, who lived only two doors away, and few people came to our house. When I spoke to Mamma, she took a long time to answer, as though my voice forced her to come back from far away. I thought maybe Mamma sometimes left her body and floated near the ceiling as mine had that time, and that's why it took her a long time to answer.

I worried a lot about her, worried my father might go crazy again and the worry kept me awake when I went to bed at night, I stayed awake as long as I could listening, waiting for the voices to erupt into argument, anxious he might try to hang her again.

Maybe my parents noticed how worried I was because they sent me away to live with Mamma's youngest sister, Antonietta, Zia 'Ndunetta, who'd settled in Sault Ste. Marie after she got married and came to Canada. They had no children.

"But why? What did I do wrong?"

"You didn't do anything wrong, Elvie," Mamma said. "It's just that I'm going back to work and this way I have one less person to take care of."

"But I help you! You don't have to look after me."

"I promise you'll like it in the Soo. Besides, Zia 'Ndunetta has no kids and she wants you so much. It'll only be for a little while."

"But I just started Grade 3. What about school?"

"They have schools in the Soo."

"But I don't wanna go. Why don't you send Teresa?"

"She's too little. Now. *Basta*. No more argument."

The morning of my departure, a Saturday, I came awake with a start remembering this was the day I would be leaving.

"Get up, Elvie!" Mamma called from the kitchen. "The train won't wait for you."

Didn't she realize I *wanted* to miss the train? I pulled the bedclothes over my head but a few minutes later Mamma marched into my room and yanked away the bedclothes.

I sat up and looked up into her face and wondered why she had purple smudges under her eyes. "Don't make me go, Mamma."

"You'll thank me once you're there," she said. I thought maybe she sounded sad. "Come on, get up. I'll make you a beaten egg with hot milk, all right?"

My father was in the bathroom shaving when I pattered into the kitchen in my pyjamas. I plugged in the old toaster, put a slice of bread on each side and kept checking them for doneness. Soon my father joined me at the table bringing with him the fragrance of the Aqua Velva aftershave he liked.

"Looking forward to the trip?" he asked, helping himself to toast.

I shrugged. "No. I don't want to go."

"Come on, it's an adventure."

I buttered my toast and turned to watch Mamma standing at the stove. Who would help her if my father went crazy again when I left?

I finished my breakfast, got dressed and played with Teresa until it was time to leave for the train station. My father would be taking me all the way to the Soo and I hoped he'd be in a good mood.

"Time to go," Mamma said, handing me my coat while my father stood at the door with my suitcase. "*Ne fa la scushtemata, va buon?* Don't be rude over there, okay? Remember you're not at home to do as you please."

"Why do I have to go? I don't want to go."

She crouched down and hugged me close for a long while and then kissed me on both cheeks and on my forehead. She hadn't done that since Teresa was born, and I'd missed her touch. I buried my face against her and cried.

"Go, now. Go," she said.

She watched us from the top of the staircase as we walked down to the street door. "Behave yourself," she called out.

The bus ride to Windsor Station didn't take too long. We sat side by side, but I had little to say as the lump got bigger and bigger in my throat. Why didn't I have parents like Eva's who didn't kick their daughter out of the house? Mamma often called me *cattiva*, a mischief-maker and maybe that was why I had to go. What could I do to make them love me?

Windsor Station awed me with its massive vaulted ceilings almost as high as the sky. We'd arrived early and walked around until a loudspeaker announced our train.

"How long before we get to the Soo?" I asked.

"Twenty hours."

We climbed aboard and my father settled me into the seat next to the window and took the one opposite. He tried to talk to me, but I didn't want to talk to him and answered in monosyllables. He got tired of trying and turned his attention to an attractive woman that had taken the seat next to me. He seemed a different person when he talked to people who he didn't know: the frown disappeared, his eyes twinkled and he smiled wide, showing perfect teeth. I'd like him a lot more, I thought, if he could be like that at home.

I sighed and turned away to look out the window. Trees, so many trees on both sides of the tracks. They grew so close to each other on either side of us it seemed as though we were going through a tunnel. I wondered why all those trees were there taking up so much space when Montreal had only a few trees but a whole lot of apartments and houses and other buildings. What was the point of having all those trees standing there doing nothing?

Our train made a lot of stops, stop after stop until we got off at Sudbury where we waited hours and hours before getting into another train. I slept, ate sandwiches Mamma had packed, and walked up and down the aisle to pass the time.

"Can I have a Coca-Cola?" I asked as a man pushing a food cart rumbled down the aisle. The pretty lady my father had been talking to was gone now, her seat taken by an old man in whom my father took no interest.

"Okay." To my surprise and delight, he also bought me a bag of potato chips.

I ripped open the bag and dug in. "Aren't you going to offer me any? After all, I paid for it."

I held out my arm but only halfway because I didn't want to give him any and he knew it because he chuckled as he reached in and brought out a fistful of chips.

We got to the Soo stiff-limbed and exhausted. Zia 'Ndunetta and her husband, Zio Mike, were there to meet us. Zia wrapped her arms around me in a bear hug and planted kisses all over my face. The youngest of my aunts, she was only 16 when I was born. Since immigrating to Canada in 1954, she'd come to Montreal once a year, sometimes more to celebrate a wedding or a funeral of a close relative.

My aunt and uncle lived in a two-storey, three-bedroom rented house shared with three other adults and a toddler. Zia Carmelina, her husband, Zio Luigi, and their daughter, born a month after Teresa, had moved to the Soo from Montreal, along with Zio Mike's unmarried brother.

"Where am I going to sleep? But Zio told me we'd soon be moving into a brand-new bungalow in a new subdivision which he was building with his own hands." I wasn't the only boarder in their rented home and it was already full. Uncle Mike's unmarried brother, Nick, lived with them. Zia Carmelina, her husband and baby daughter had left Montreal on the promise of better jobs.

"There's no room for me, Zia," I said.

"Don't worry. I have a cot all ready for you in the hallway outside my room."

My father stayed with his sister, Zia Vilia, and went home after a couple of days. It didn't upset me to see him go but it did bother me when I learned Zia 'Ndunetta, unlike Mamma, ran an orderly household with many rules she expected me to follow to the letter.

CHAPTER SIXTEEN

All the sudden changes—banished from home, adjusting to a new household and a new school—ratcheted up my anxiety made me more excitable, which got on everybody's nerves. Reprimands from the five adults in our household came fast and furious. When their rebukes hurt me, and I'd go hide somewhere and feel sorry for myself but nobody took notice.

I started school, a short walk away, and made a friend, another Italian girl, in our neighbourhood. In early December after I had barely settled into the new school, our household pulled up stakes and relocated to the now completed bungalow Zio had built on Estelle Street. For me that meant getting used to yet another new school.

I'd never seen a brand-new house and this one left me in awe. It had large rooms with big windows which bathed the inside with light. I loved the kitchen cabinet doors with their etched glass insets, which had been built by Zio's brother, who was a master carpenter. Best of all, the new house smelled sweet and clean.

Unlike Mamma, Zia 'Ndunetta's enforced a strict 9 o'clock bedtime even after I tried to make her understand it was too early. But she wouldn't listen and I'd go to bed—here too in the hallway since the bungalow only had three bedrooms—and lie awake for a long time, often until they all went to bed and one of them started snoring. When morning came, Zia would have to drag me out of bed to get me to school on time.

My new school, St. Theresa's Elementary, a single storey shoebox, couldn't have been any closer than directly across the street. Zia's urgings were to hurry up, and in spite of that I was slow and sleepy. I raced across the street into the school yard mere seconds before the bell rang. On Estelle Street I made a new best friend, a girl named Silvana, who was the daughter of *paesani.* Her family's bungalow was a few doors away and twice the size of ours, and much more luxurious. When I asked Zia about it, she told me Silvana's father owned a construction company and the family had lots of money, but Silvana wasn't stuck up and she never acted like somebody who had a lot more than I did. Like me, she was the eldest of three.

I spent a lot of time at her house. Silvana had plenty of friends and included me in their activities. Zia gave me an allowance and sometimes extra money, so I go with Silvana on outings with her friends. At home, I'd never had an allowance, only bus fare for school. Every extra penny my parents gave for an ice cream, a candy bar or an activity organized by my school had to be cajoled out of them. Now, for the first time, Zia provided the means to be live like all the other kids and almost as important to me she bought me new clothes, which she made sure were clean and nicely pressed so that I looked neat and tidy.

The Campochiaro ex-pat community in the Soo was much smaller than Montreal's, and for that reason, much tighter. I saw plenty of Zia Vilia at weekend get-togethers as well as spending many weekends at her house. At the ripe old age of 30, she was pregnant with her first child, and she gave birth to a daughter in December the year I was there.

In time I came to like a new life. I even stopped worrying about Mamma and I felt calmer. Even better, when Zia Carmelina and her family didn't make a go of it in the Soo and returned to Montreal, I moved out of the hallway and into my own bedroom.

Suddenly, four months after new life began, Zia told me my parents wanted me to go home.

"But why?"

"Well, *bella*," replied Zia 'Ndunetta, "it's because your Mamma wants to go back to work."

"But why can't I stay even if she goes back to work?"

"Well, you see, Teresa will be coming to stay with me. It's easier that way because you'll be in school, I'll be taking care of your little sister and your momma will pay for a babysitter for Ricky."

"I won't go!"

"I'm so sorry, *bella*."

In January 1958, my father delivered Teresa to Zia and took me home to Montreal. Zia 'Ndunetta wept when she saw me off. "Be a good girl," she said, wiping her eyes with a handkerchief, as Mamma so often did.

During the long ride home to Montreal, my father sat in gloomy silence and I shied away from him. I looked forward to seeing Mamma, though, but once I found myself standing in the familiar kitchen inside our flat, I suddenly felt shy of her. She, like all the things in the flat, looked the same yet felt different and that made me feel odd.

When she held me close, however, the baby-powder smell of her, and pillowy softness of her bosom and belly reassured me. Both Zia 'Ndunetta like Zia Vilia had had little padding on their bones but Mamma had cushioning I could nestle into, when she let me.

In honor of my return, Mamma had made my favourite pasta: rigatoni smothered in slow-cooked, fragrant tomato sauce. She'd also gone to the trouble of baking a sponge cake. Ricky, now five months old seemed to have tripled in size, puffed up like the bread dough Mamma left to rise overnight in a bowl. Nothing else had changed.

We soon fell into our old routine: work for my parents, Edward Murphy Elementary for me—into the same Grande 3 class I'd been in in September—with Angelina babysitting my brother.

As an eight-year-old girl, I was old enough to get to and from school by myself, which I liked and I took pride in the new self-reliance, riding the tram on Amherst, which I boarded a block east of Saint-Timothee or walking when the weather was good.

My teacher that year was Miss Summerfield, whom I worshipped for her beautiful face and a beautiful name. Her pale blondness glowed, and I marvelled at the lovely dresses she wore, dresses I'd only seen in magazines. When she took her turn supervising recess, her pupils vied each other to walk around the school yard at her side, flitting around her like butterflies.

Miss Summerfield, however, was also the teacher responsible for causing great embarrassment near the end of the school year. I'd been having stomach cramps and I put up my hand and asked to go to the toilet and she let me go. But later when I needed to go again, she refused, probably thinking I only wanted to get out of the classroom.

I squirmed in my seat, tightened my sphincter and held on until the final bell rang. As the class lined up, I asked her again to please let me go. Again, she refused.

"Let's not hold everybody up. Surely, you can wait until you get home," she said, frowning.

"Yes, Miss." I couldn't wait but saw no point in saying so because I didn't think she'd let me go anyway.

I had strict instructions from my parents to walk when the weather was good to save the tram fare. It was early June, a brilliant warm afternoon. I started to walk and movement made me more desperate for a toilet. In my hurry to get home, I walked even faster and, to my horror, halfway home nature took its course. I felt warm feces leave my body and drop heavily into my cotton panties. I kept on walking, pretending nothing was amiss in spite of the stink now rising into my nostrils.

On my way, I passed in front of a French elementary school as pupils were coming out. My face grew purple with shame when they caught a whiff of me and pointed fingers as we passed each other. In my desperation I broke into a run, which jiggled the mess in my panties and causing some of it to fall out, splashing my leg before hitting the sidewalk. By the time I got home I was in tears, and glad there was no one home to see my humiliation.

Miss Summerfield lost her special place in my heart and the following day I marched up to her and told her what had happened thanks to her refusing to let me go to the toilet.

I ended Grade 3 with good marks but another lonely summer stretched ahead, although I looked forward to my ninth birthday in July. Not that there would be a celebration because in our family we didn't do anything special for birthdays. No, I wanted the years to pass so I could become an adult, and everybody would stop telling what to do.

The mood in our household remained relatively calm since my return from the Soo, although my father remained glum and moody. Compared to the early years after Mamma and I landed in Montreal; our family's social life had shrunk to almost zero. Even when my father took me along to visit his cousin, Guilio, which I loved because I got to spend time with Fil, Mamma rarely joined us. She turned 13 in August 1959, had loads of friends and let me hang out with them.

We barely see Zia Carmelina at all, the edge of enmity between her and my father only sharpened with time and Mamma, so tired with her job, taking care of Ricky, and the housework, little to no energy was left. Misery was there if she spent time with her sister, although she nevertheless made the rare effort.

After one such visit in the relative calm that had reigned for months came to a sudden end. He berated and verbally abused her well after they went to be, and the old, cold fear that he would kill seeped through until I couldn't stop myself from shouting: "Stop it! Stop it! Stop it!" That night it worked; usually it didn't. Most of the time my father didn't answer my cry and sometimes I wondered whether I actually called out or if I only whispered to myself.

That summer Mamma gave me more and more chores to do. I graduated from ironing dishcloths and pillowcases to learning how to iron my own clothes. I also washed the supper dishes, something I hated because I couldn't reach the tap at the back of the deep kitchen sink and had to kneel on a chair to do the job.

"Why can't we each wash our own dishes?" I asked one day at supper.

"Did you pay for the food you put in your mouth tonight?" my father replied.

"No."

"Did you cook the food you just ate?"

Oh-oh. Another lecture coming. "No."

"So, do you understand each of us contributes to the family as we re able? I earn the money that buys the food. Your mother cooks it. You can do the dishes as your way of helping out."

"But Mamma works, too. How come she also has to cook and look after Ricky and clean the house?"

"Because that's a woman's most important job. That's what women are born to do. Your mother's job helps but I earn most of the money we need."

"That's not fair."

He looked surprised, thought about it a moment replied, "You may be right about that. But that's just how it is."

CHAPTER SEVENTEEN

My sister came home from the Soo in the winter of 1959 after almost a year away. I now had both a warm little body next to me in bed and new and irksome extra babysitting duties. Teresa was far from a difficult kid but what nine-year-old wants to have her three-year-old sister hanging around when she's with her friends?

I was in second term of Grade 4 and had a teacher named Miss Savage who was especially mean to the boys. She punished them by making stand at the back of the class with their knees bent and forced them to stand that way until the pain made them cry.

In March my father announced he'd bought a house and we'd be moving in May. He also decided to surprise us, including Mamma, with the purchase of a television set, a 20-inch Canadian Marconi encased in a nice wood cabinet, which he said was one of the best. It was the pride of the place in a front room already crowded by a sofa and two matching armchairs. Mamma complained about the expense, but I sided with my father about the TV. Lots of my friends had them and often one or another of them would ask me over to watch the programs they talked about. My favourite was Lassie.

The winter seemed especially cold that year, it made my body tremble and my teeth chatter while waiting for the bus—most of the trams had been replaced by buses—to and from school. At home, I didn't go out unless I had to, and I often found myself at the front window when it snowed to watch the mad snowflakes fall to the ground and bury everything.

But as soon as the hint of spring gentled the air, I was out of the house.

On May 1, a Friday, our belongings went into the cargo bed of a hired pickup truck. While my father and the truck owner loaded up, I went door to door to say my sad goodbyes. Lise had gone home to live with her mother the previous September and I'd missed her.

The truck came and went three times, and when the last load went on its way, Mamma was carrying Ricky in her arms, and Teresa holding my hand. We walked along Robin to Amherst to catch the bus to our new place. Mamma insisted it wasn't that far when I complained but it seemed far to me since we also had to make a transfer. When Mamma finally hustled us off the second bus, northward along Saint-Laurent. The upheaval of moving had made Ricky and Teresa unruly and I squabbling with Ricky—in particular—who kept trying to run up and down the aisle.

We rode north along Saint-Laurent and got off on rue Bernard. Our new street, Saint-Dominique, was one street east of Saint-Laurent and we reached it along a short laneway past an oil depot on one side of the mouth of the lane and a two-storey building with pictures of almost naked girls on the other.   As I trailed behind Mamma, I felt a sudden pang at the loss of friends, classmates and even the old playground, although I hadn't used it much lately. Would there be girls my age in this neighbourhood? Would they be nice? When I thought of having to go to a new school on Monday my stomach knotted up. I cheered myself up by thinking about all the new streets to explore and having a bigger house on the ground floor with a backyard all to ourselves.

The lane ended at Saint-Dominique, we turned right and half a dozen doors way there stood our house, 5726 and 5728, a duplex in the middle of long brick wall that took up half the block and each pair of doors had a balcony above it.

My father stood waiting for us with a big smile on his face, and when I stood next to him looking at the entrance of a house that belonged to us, he put his arm around my shoulders. I wished he'd be happy like this all the time because when his mood was good, I wasn't scared he'd go crazy. "You know, Pasquale lives just over there," he said, pointing several doors south.

I shrugged, wishing it had been Eva who'd moved there rather than Pasquale. Why did this boy keep popping up like an annoying mosquito? I crossed my fingers and hoped I wouldn't be put in the same class.

"Go in, have a look at our new house, Elvie."

I climbed the single step into a tiny mudroom, through a second door into wide hallway that narrowed as it moved towards the back. To the left of the hallway was a double room with an arch dividing the space, and a room further up on the right. The hallway opened into a large room with a door to a bedroom to the left and a doorway to the kitchen that extended beyond the rest of the house. I went through the kitchen, opened the back door and liked that it had a verandah and that the dirt back yard went all the way to lane.

He joined me on the verandah. "What do you think?" he asked, a benign expression remained on his face.

"I like it. It's much bigger than Saint-Timothee. What about upstairs? Is that ours too?"

"You bet. And the people who live there pay us rent."

Mamma bustled into the kitchen, looked at all the boxes and sighed. "Take the kids into the yard, Elvie, while I start unpacking this stuff."

I muttered a complaint that infuriated her. "Listen, you!" she said, eyes flashing, hands on her hips. "Who do you think you are, the Queen of England? Do your part and be quick about it."

I wanted to yell, *No, I don't think I'm special. I'm just a kid who doesn't want to look after your kids.*

My mother blew hot at times but usually she cooled down fast. But she could be unpredictable and a small thing could make her explode and before I knew it her slipper would come flying across the room. She seemed in that sort of mood now and I thought it best to shut up.

With Ricky holding one hand and Teresa the other, we strolled along the alley, avoiding greasy patches left by oil trucks that supplied S. Albert & Co. and peered into the neighbours' yards—there were no fences dividing the back yards—on our left side and the backs of the commercial buildings facing Saint-Laurent to the right.

I hoped to catch sight of kids my age until I remembered it was a Friday, a school day for the kids who didn't have to move. I crossed my fingers, hoping more girls than boys lived in the neighbourhood. Boys weren't as much fun. They had their own games, like dodge ball, which I didn't like mainly because I wasn't good at it, I couldn't hit the ball hard and I was always afraid of being hit by the ball.

We reached the end of the alley, turned left into a short laneway, and as we rounded the corner onto Saint-Dominique to head home, I took note of a convenience store with a large candy counter.

This half of the block looked much prettier than our half, I thought, with mostly three-storey buildings with black railings snaking up from the street and up to the second and third floor. Some of the street level flats in these buildings even had small gardens with black fences and gates around them. The opposite side of the street was a different story. It was taken up with a big baseball field on one end, an empty field on the other end and a big black three-storey building between them, the Patronage Jean-Léon Le Prevost, a charitable community centre for boys and home to the Catholic brothers who ran it.

When we got home, Mamma told us to stay outside while she got things better organized. It was a warm, sunny day but I was bored and jittery.

"Ma, can we go buy some candy? There's a store at the corner." I didn't hold out much hope but it didn't hurt to try.

"No. It's almost lunchtime and we'll be eating soon."

Resigned, I'd turned to go my father whom came on the scene. "Wait." He forged into the right-hand pocket of his trousers and held out a quarter.

I took it with a smile. "How much can we spend?"

He returned my smile and patted my head. "It's a special day, spend it all."

I almost liked my father when he was nice to me, although I did wonder what had made him so generous and I hurried out for fear he'd take it back.

Mamma got mad. "You're always undercutting me," she grumbled.

CHAPTER EIGHTEEN

My parents allotted the one enclosed bedroom with a window looking out onto the back yard to Teresa and me. They took the inside half of the double parlour at the front. It was bigger and they needed the extra space for my brother's crib. For privacy Mamma put up pretty, floor-length drapes across the archway to divide the sleeping area from the front room.

It was tight but we ate in the kitchen, and they turned the area at the end of the hallway in front of the kitchen into a family room instead of an eating area, and put the TV, sofa and chair and end tables we'd brought with us in there.

The first night in the new house traumatized me. Sometime in the wee hours, I awoke to what sounded like galloping horses racing across the ceiling. I shot upright, fully awake. Blood thundering in my ears, I held my breath, straining to figure out what was causing the racket. I had closed the shutters on the window, and it made the bedroom so dark I couldn't see my hand in front of my face.

I waited, Teresa never stirring, sitting up and my heart racing, until the noise finally faded away and I lay down again, but like a guard dog, my senses were on high alert and I couldn't go back to sleep. Had I dreamt it?

On the brink of sleep once more the thundering noise overhead returned. Dark as it was, I threw off the covers with trembling hands and I felt my way out of the room, out into the family room and down the hall toward my parents' bedroom.

At the sound of my soft footsteps Mamma came instantly awake and sat up. "What's wrong? What is it?" she whispered. I heard the sheets rustle as she pushed them away and threw her legs over the side of the bed.

"I'm scared. There's something in the ceiling."

My father stirred and soon his bedside lamp came on. We all blinked with the shock of sudden light. "What's happened?" he asked.

"It's the rats," Mamma said. "They woke her up and scared her."

"Come here," he said to me.

I hesitated. Would he smack me for waking him up? Head down, I took slow steps towards him and cringed when he reached for me. But he only took my hand.

"It's only rats," he said, kindly.

Rodents terrified me—mice, squirrels, but rats in particular. I'd seen big rats in our old neighbourhood, rats jumping out of garbage cans, I'd seen their ugly bodies crawling close to the ground at dusk, long tails slithering behind them. They filled me with dread and an indescribable disgust. Even pictures of rats made me shudder.

"Listen," he said, "believe me when I tell you they're much more afraid of you than you are of them. Besides, you're a lot bigger than they are. One good kick and that's the end of the rat."

"There was more than one up there, Papà. Besides, what if they get in while we're asleep? They could make a hole in the wall and sneak in and crawl into our beds and bite us."

"They don't want to bite us, Elvie. Mostly, they're looking for food. But tomorrow we'll check for holes in the walls and if we find any, we'll plug them. We'll set traps, too, okay?

"I guess."

"Now go to bed. I promise they won't come in."

But I was afraid to go back alone. My mother took me by the hand. "Come on. I'll come with you."

"You're too soft. You'll spoil her," my father said to her back.

The next day I parked myself on the front stoop while my parents continued to put the house in order. I kept an eye on Teresa and Ricky who'd both had already found playmates. I hoped I would too, and my prayers were answered when a girl about my age came out of one of the flats like ours at the far end holding a yellow hula hoop. If she noticed me, she made no sign of it. She put the hoop over her had and moved her hips and arms until it whirled around round and round around her waist, round and round it went, as she made it go up from her waist up to her chest, back to her waist, down to her hips and back again.

Impressed, I walked over to her. "*Allo.*"

"*Salut,*" she replied, looking me over with cool, violet eyes, the hoop in constant motion, small hip movements, barely noticeable, kept the thing circling. "*Comment tu t'appelle?* What's your name?"

I told her. "*Pis toi?* And you?"

"Rose Marie. I live just here." She indicated the door behind her, an upstairs flat, with a tip of the head. She lived next door to Pasquale's duplex.

"Can I have a turn with your hula hoop?"

"*Non,*" she replied, matter-of-fact.

That shocked me. In the old neighbourhood kids shared their toys. Besides, somehow, I had imagined that her doll-like appearance, with its porcelain face, rosy cheeks, rounded limbs and long curly hair, suggested a sweet disposition.

The bald refusal embarrassed me and I turned and started back to my own door.

"*Yoo-hoo, attends!* Wait!" someone called out.

I stopped and turned to find the girl belonging to the voice trotting in my direction.

"*Allo,*" she said. She smiled, showing nice even teeth.

"*Allo.*" I returned the greeting but I was wary now. My lips curl up at the corners but I didn't show my teeth; but then I hardly every smiled showing my teeth. I'd become self-conscious about them because two of my teeth, the ones on either side of the front teeth, had grown in crooked.

"You must be the family that moved in yesterday. My name is Renee. I live in the house next to Yellow Sample. *Et toi comment tu t'appelles?* And you, what's your name?"

She spoke a clearer, more precise French than the street patois I'd heard around me and which I spoke. Renee wasn't as pretty as Rose Marie but sure seemed a lot nicer.

" *Viens t'asseoir sur mon perron.* Come sit down on my stoop," I said. "I have to keep an eye on my brother and sister."

Renee lived on the ground floor of her family's duplex, the last on that side of the block next to the Yellow Sample Shoe factory which separated our side of the block from the prettier part. She told me she lived with her parents and two older brothers, while the eldest brother and his wife had the flat above them.

Renee was a year my junior and attended Grade 3 at St.-Georges, a French school on Bernard Street. I'd be going to an English school.

"Are you Italian?" I asked.

"Yes." Renee's family came from Abruzzo, as did mine.

"All the Italians I know go to English school. Why do you go to the French school?"

"Cause my parents were in Belgium before we came to Canada. I was born there so I went to a French school, my brothers, too. When we came to Montreal it was just easier to keep going in French school. My brothers, too."

That explained her French pronunciation. "You don't speak any English at all?"

"No."

That didn't strike me as strange. Plenty of French-speaking kids in my old neighbourhood didn't speak any English.

"*Rose-Marie est pas gentil.* Rose Marie isn't nice." I said it even though I risked alienating Renee if they were friends.

"*Parfois.* Sometimes," she said, sighing. "But don't worry about Rose Marie. You'll get used to her ways."

We'll see, I thought.

"Does Rose Marie go to the same school as you?"

She shook her head. "She goes to Notre-Dame-de-la-Defense. It's a bilingual school."

"Why does she go to a bilingual school?"

She told me she was half-Italian: her father was Italian; her mother, a French Canadian from the Gaspe region, and they wanted her to be fluent in English and French.

"What's a bilingual school?"

"In the morning her subjects are taught in French and in the afternoon her teachers teach in English."

Just then my father came into the mudroom behind us.

"Hi, girls."

"*Bonjour, Monsieur.*"

"Where are going Papà?"

"I'm going out to buy paint for the walls. What colour do you fancy, Elvie?"

"Yellow!"

"For every room?"

"Yes! I like yellow."

"Yellow it is."

We rose from the stoop and moved aside to let him pass. We resumed our conversation once he'd gone, and he found us still sitting there chatting away when he came back in a taxi with half a dozen gallons of paint.

It was almost lunchtime by then and Renee went home while I pulled my siblings away from their new playmates and hurried indoors to check out the shade of yellow in the cans.

"What colours did you get?" Mamma asked.

My father looked at me and grinned. "Yellow," he replied.

"Yellow and what else?"

"All yellow except for the white high-gloss for the kitchen and bathroom."

"You bought yellow paint for the whole house?" Momma said, incredulously.

"I like yellow," he said. "Besides, this awful flat paint only comes in yellow, ugly pink, stinky green or pukey baby blue. I didn't like the other colours."

Mamma rolled her eyes.

We ate sandwiches Mamma had prepared, Ricky and Teresa too hungry to bicker, accompanied by soft drinks after which they shooed us out of the house to begin the arduous task of painting the flat. It took them the better part of a week, although the hardest part for them and for us was working with the oil-based paint used for the kitchen and bathroom walls. The oil paint was not thick and hard to apply. Its vapours burned our eyes, irritated our throats and the smell took a week to disperse. But they liked it because its lustrous sheen repelled water and made it easy to keep clean.

During those first couple of weeks, my father also laid down new flooring. It came in huge sheets--greyish background with borders that had pink and white flowers—which he had to cut with precision to make it fit. He took pride in cutting the material so that you didn't notice any seams.

CHAPTER NINETEEN

Three days after we moved in, I started classes at my new school. Luke Callaghan Memorial was an English-language Catholic school run by the Sisters of Saint Anne and situated two short blocks from home on Clark Street between Bernard and Saint-Viateur.

My father had to take a day off work to take me to school that first day in order to register me. My mother had quit her job downtown because the commute would have been too much but she couldn't take me because she didn't speak a word of English.

Children played in the schoolyard as we climbed the stone steps of the pretty red brick, four-storey school buildings. There were a few others ahead of us as we waited in line outside the office for our turn.

We were second in line when the school bell shattered the quiet at 8:30 a.m. and made me jump. Two minutes later, the children who'd played in the yard started filing in. Two by two, class by class, starting with the youngest, they marched in by the hundreds up the stone stairs and disappearing round the bend towards the upper floors in total silence. Why, I asked myself, were they all girls? Where were the boys? Well, at least it meant I wouldn't be in Pasquale's class.

Our turn came and the school secretary, a nun, invited us into her office. She asked him questions, filled in some papers then handed my father a list of supplies he needed to buy for me at the school store, which was just outside the office and to the right. We lined up and waited our turn and were attended to by the tiny nun, in fact, the tiniest adult person I'd ever seen, barely an inch taller than I was. My father paid for several fresh copybooks and a roll of plain kraft paper—not the expensive vinyl type—with which I had to cover school owned textbooks she handed me but I didn't need nib holders, nibs, pencils, erasers or a ruler because I already had them.

My father left and the tiny nun locked up the little store and escorted me and the others like me to our assigned classrooms. I ended up in 4A, one of three Grade 4 classrooms. She knocked on the window of 4A and opened it without waiting for a reply.

"Good morning, Mrs. Keyes. Good morning, children. We have a new pupil joining the class today." The nun handed Mrs. Keyes a piece of paper, smiled and left.

Mrs. Keyes came from behind her desk to greet me. "Children, says hello to Elvira. Please make her welcome."

"Hello, Elvira," my new classmates said in unison.

My face went tomato red with embarrassment. The attention made me want to crawl under the floorboards, fly out the window, run out the door--anything rather than absorb the heat of 30-plus pairs of eyeballs boring into me. I looked down at the floor so I didn't see them looking at me.

"Take that seat over there, Elvira," Mrs. Keyes said, pointing to an empty desk at the back of the room.

I hurried to the seat but relief evaporated when the teacher said, "We'll rearrange the seating tomorrow. We can't have little Elvira in the back row. She won't be able to see a thing."

Mrs. Keyes picked up where she'd left off. When the bell rang for mid-morning recess, it surprised me how quickly time had passed. Mrs. Keyes knew how to keep our attention.

We lined up, two by two, in the wide aisle along one wall and stayed in formation until the teacher released us to the schoolyard. Mayhem ensued as children chased each other, laughed, and shouted.

Not me. I stood near the chain-link fence and watched. Soon enough one of my new classmates took pity on me and walked over. "You wanna take a turn at hopscotch with me and my friend?"

"Okay." We walked across the yard.

"What's your name?"

"Margaret Bacon." She was plump with short blonde hair and blue eyes.

"Are you Italian, too?"

"Nah. I'm Irish. Lots of Irish kids in the school. And lots of you Italian kids. Mrs. Keyes is Irish, you know. Her daughter, Rosemary, she's is in 4B."

"She has a daughter our age? But she looks old."

How could she have a 9-year-old daughter when she had grey in her hair and lines in her face? My mother had shiny dark brown hair and soft, smooth skin.

Margaret shrugged.

"Why is half the schoolyard divided in two and why aren't there any boys in our class?" I asked Margaret.

The fenced in school yard stretched the width of the building in two halves at the back along St.-Laurent.

She stopped and stared at me as though wondering whether I'd just gotten off the boat. "That's the boys' side of the school. They come out after we go back in 'cos the nuns don't like us talking to each other."

"The school I came from had boys and girls in the same class," I told her. Why would they want to separate boys from girls, I wondered? I had a lot to learn about my new surroundings.

Recess ended in a blink, the return to call signaled by another piercing bell. Once more we lined up in pairs, class by class, for the silent procession back to our desks, just as the boys were let out for recess and began to fill the other half of the yard. Some of them ran to the dividing line to hoot and whistle as we girls made our way back inside. When an older girl from seventh grade turned towards the call, her teacher shouted, "Head forward, Anna!"

The rest of the morning fled, and the piercing ring of the bell announced the lunch break.

Just like my old school, this one had no cafeteria or lunchroom. Everybody went home or, if both parents worked, to a neighbour's house to eat. Maybe the Irish kids' mothers provided hot lunches, but I knew Mamma, like most of the Italian women around us, she would get another job soon and I'd look after myself—which I knew I could since I was nearly ten years old.

I hurried home for lunch; the newness of everything was tiring me out. Mamma stood at the stove stirring something inside a pot, Ricky sat in his highchair eating something I couldn't identify and Teresa had parked herself on the floor in front of the TV mesmerized by the black and white flickering images.

"What's for lunch, Ma?"

"I made you a sandwich."

"And what are you making for supper?"

"Rice and cabbage."

"Ummm," I said, biting into a couple of meatballs squashed between two thick slabs of bread. I did like my food, and rice and cabbage soup, on which Mamma sprinkled lots of Romano cheese, was one of my favourites. Mamma couldn't bear the smell of any hard cheese, but radishes and beets were the only things I turned away.

Mamma never refused to give us something to eat if we said we were hungry, even if it was between meals. In fact, she was always either talking about it in one way or another: how much it costs, what to buy, how to prepare it so as to make everybody happy and finally, how not to waste it.

My father, on the other hand, was stingy with food to the point of hiding the more expensive stuff, like cured meats, to prevent us from helping ourselves without his permission.

I ate my sandwich, sat next to Teresa to watch the show with her before skipping back to school for the afternoon, quite happy to go because I liked Mrs. Keyes very much.

I didn't take much interest in what work my father did to earn a living, but he seemed to change jobs often. My parents argued about it. He had a Grade 5 education, as did Mamma, the highest grade available in Campochiaro. He worked with his hands, that much I figured out, sometimes in factories, more often on construction sites.

He arrived home muddied and exhausted. But our bathroom had no shower and a daily bath was out of the question. We now had a hot water heater, a manual one we lit with a match, and which took half an hour for the water in the tank to get hot, but they said it was too expensive for all of us to take baths every day. We took sponge baths and kept baths to once a week, starting with my father, after which the rest of us took our turns in the same bath water.

When my father arrived home from work, he washed with a washcloth at the bathroom sink, all except for his feet, which needed to be soaked, so Mamma washed his feet. She prepared a basin of warm water where he'd soak his feet for a while, and then she'd get down on her knees to wash and dry them.

It bothered me to see her on her knees tending to him like that, although I couldn't explain why it disturbed me.

"Why do you wash his feet, Ma? Can't he do that himself?"

"He can't reach down to do it properly."

"So, why doesn't he wash your feet?"

"Oh, Elvie. You and your questions."

Once he'd cleaned up, we ate. We took all our meals, sitting around the same turquoise-Arborite topped table we'd used on Saint-Timothee.

Ricky didn't like to sit in his highchair and Mamma often held him on her lap at mealtimes. She put a spoonful in his mouth for every one she took for herself.

"You baby him too much. He's nearly 2. Old enough to feed himself," he said the evening after my first day at school. Mamma didn't replay, she rarely did so as not to start an argument.

"Elvie, go get the fruit," my father commanded after we'd finished our bowls of rice and cabbage.

I pushed back my chair, maneuvered myself out of the cramped space between the table and the wall and went to get the bowl of fruit from the counter. I had just sat down when Mamma piped up, "What about the walnuts?" and suddenly a terrible anger welled up within me and made me hate them both. Get this. Get that. Go to the store and buy me this or that. Look after your brother, take care of your sister, do the dishes, sweep the floor. I didn't want to do any of it.

"I do it," Teresa said. She was the quietest of us, the one who kept her head down all the time, the most easily frightened one of us, and she stuck close to me when Mamma wasn't around, even tried to help me with the chores although she mostly got in my way.

"I finished the dishes. Can I go outside?" I asked, poking my head into the front room where my parents were putting on the last of three coats of paint. I hoped Renee could come out.

"Did you do your homework?" my father asked.

"Yes, I did it before supper." That was a half the truth. I'd done the written stuff but not the reading assignment.

"Fine, but be home by 8:30 o'clock, or else," my father said.

Both Rose Marie and Renee were already outside. I saw the pair of them sitting out on Rose Marie's balcony playing some game. To my delight, Rose-Marie invited me to come up and my jaw dropped when she showed me her bedroom. It was filled with toys. I then joined them on the balcony in a game of jacks.

I lost track of time and when all at once, an ear-splitting whistle cut through the dusk, I knew it was my father calling me home like one of our Saint-Timothee neighbours used to call his dog when it wandered away.

"I have to go." I jumped up and raced home.

My father stood on the sidewalk in front of our house, arms crossed at his chest and looking extremely displeased. He waited until I stood before him then lifted his arm and slapped me hard across the face.

"What was that for?" I asked, humiliated.

"For tardiness."

CHAPTER TWENTY

All in all, I liked our new house and the new school. The only thing that continued to prey on my mind were the rats racing across the ceiling night after night. Despite assurances from my parents, I was convinced those ugly animals would chew their way through the walls, get into the house and crawl into our beds and bite us. The fear made it hard for me to fall asleep and meant Mamma had to drag me out of bed in the morning to get me up in time for school.

We settled into a routine. My father went to work every day at one job or another and in early June Mamma found work at Fashion Fit Lingerie, a few minutes walk away at one of many factories in the tall buildings along Saint-Viateur and Saint-Laurent. I had loved having her at home looking after the house and us, even though it meant putting up with her nagging at me to help around the house.

She worked on an overlock sewing machine so close to home she could have come home for lunch if she'd wanted to. She didn't though because she only had half an hour for the lunch break and preferred to eat her sandwich at her machine while chatting with the other women.

Teresa and Ricky were put in the care of a neighbour six doors from ours, an Italian woman with two daughters of her own, the eldest one Teresa's age. The woman also looked after several other neighbourhood children and later in the evening, her husband came home from work and looked after their kids while she went to work cleaning offices.

My mother wanted me to eat my lunch there during school days, but I only went once, and that was one time too many. I told my parents I didn't want to go there to eat.

"Please don't make me, Papà. I just can't."

"Why not?"

"She's a nice lady but I bet you wouldn't eat there either. It stinks of pee and dirty socks."

"It's the mattresses, Elvie," Mamma explained. "Her girls pee in the bed at night and that's what you smell."

"Next month I'm going to be 10. Can't I come home and have lunch on my own?"

My father reached into his shirt pocket, took out a pack of Player's cigarettes, removed the matchbook tucked inside, and lit a smoke. After a couple of deep pulls, he said, "Okay, fine. But be warned, you're not to bring in any of your friends while you're in the house alone—not during lunchtime and not after school."

It made me feel terrific to have won the argument.

It didn't seem to bother Mamma to have Ricky and Teresa sitting around in the neighbour's dirty household. "She feeds them and keeps an eye on them and doesn't charge too much," she said when I asked her. Mamma liked a clean house—expected my help with that—but she didn't spend all her time cleaning. Getting meals on the table was her top priority.

Lots of children of all ages lived on our half of Saint-Dominique behind that long wall of duplexes. At least two per household. I stuck close to Renee and Rose Marie since they were the only girls my age. Sometimes we played tag or hide-and-seek with the boys, including my former classmate Pasquale, but not often since the boys preferred to stick together, too.

Sundays were the most boring days of the week when the street emptied as families went visiting or received callers and stayed indoors.

One such Sunday, Mamma had a bad headache so she stayed home. After lunch my father sat reading his magazine and Mamma, Ricky and Teri went to take a nap. At loose ends, I parked myself on the front stoop, protected from the rain by the balcony above. I watched how the raindrops collect in puddles.

When I lost interest in puddles, I went and knocked on Renee's door, hoping she might be home. Her mother answered, thank goodness, since her stern, silent father scared me a little. He intimidated me.

"Is Renee home?"

Renee's mother looked much older than mine. Besides, she had an adult son, married, who lived in the flat above them. She wasn't as pretty as Mamma, white streaks in her hair and deep furrows in her face, and a thick swollen lower leg but she was always nice to me. "She went to Rose Marie's a little while ago. Try there."

I hurried to Rose Marie's, only three doors up, but hesitated before pressing the buzzer. *Should I?* Rose Marie might shut the door in my face but I was desperate for something to do so I took a chance and pressed her buzzer.

An answering buzz unlocked the door, and I pushed it open. Rose Marie gazed down at me from the top of the stairs.

"Hi. Renee's mother told me she's here," I said. I had my fingers crossed behind my back hoping she'd ask me in.

"Yeah, she's here. We're playing snakes and ladders."

I looked up at her and waited but no invitation came. I didn't lower myself to ask outright whether I could go up, so I closed the door and went home feeling a new darkness close in around me. Why did Rose Marie treat like that? What had I done to make her dislike me?

I went home, lay down on my bed and had a quiet cry.

When school let out at the end of June, we'd been in the new house for two months, long enough for the newness to wear off and for my parents to start arguing again. My father had been pretty relaxed until

Mamma went back to work and I wondered whether that was why he started picking fights with her again, asking her pointed questions about her colleagues, her bosses, where she spent her lunch break and with whom until she got upset and shouted at him.

As the tension between them mounted, Teresa and Ricky and I left the house when we could and stayed out of their way. Teresa in particular clung to me, stared at me with big eyes as their shouts reached us where we'd taken cover while Ricky ran up and down the sidewalk or the back yard making noise.

I ended Grade 4 with surprisingly good marks, given how little effort I'd put into school work. My father nodded in semi-approval whereas Mamma didn't seem to care. She was too busy looking after Teresa and Ricky to care one way or the other about my marks, I resented her for it.

The summer of 1959, when I turned 10, Mamma named me official babysitter to Teresa and Ricky—4 and 2-years-old—to save money with instructions to call on their former sitter, our neighbour, if I needed help. While she sat at a factory sewing machine sewing panties, slips and negligees, I fed *her* children lunch and snacks, washed her dishes, dusted her furniture, swept and washed her floors—at least, that's how I saw it. For a change of pace, I took a stab at cooking, too, which was fun, sometimes with palatable results. But I hated doing the weekly laundry and there was no way for me to get out of it.

Washing laundry consumed an entire day using the wringer-washer. First, I pushed and pulled the machine with its big round tub from its corner at one end of hallway into the bathroom, angling it just right to get it into the small area and close enough to the sink so the mouth of the machine's detachable hose reached the faucet. While the tub filled, I dropped in dirty clothes, separated into whites and darks, threw in handfuls of soap powder then pushed down the lever on the side of the tub to get the agitator going. After about twenty minutes I took each piece out of the tub and fed them one by one through the machine's encased rollers to squeeze out excess water while the tub of dirty water drained away into the bathtub via another hose.

The white loads went in and out three times: first, with plain soap and water, second with hot water and bleach, and a third time to rinse them. Dark clothes only went in twice. On a typical laundry day, I did three loads of whites and two loads of darks, which meant filling and emptying the washing machine thirteen times. Then I went to the back yard, stood on a chair and hung things on the clothesline to dry.

One day as I complained bitterly to Mamma about all the work, my father overheard and he came roaring into the room.

"If I ever, ever hear you complain again, I swear I'll make you regret the day you were born."

At first, the fury contorting his face made me shrivel inside myself, but a balloon inflated inside and got so big I feared it might explode and turn my insides to pulp. I had had to let out some air. "Nobody I know who's my age has to do all this work," I said. I pressed my lips together to keep myself from saying any more.

"I don't care what you think! I don't care what you want or don't want, what you like or don't like. I'm in charge here. And you'll do as I say. Do you understand me?"

I refused to reply, and I held his gaze. Suddenly he laughed, knowing no matter what I said, he could make me do whatever he wanted. "Do you understand me?"

Still, I said nothing. I thought to myself, *I don't care if he beats me to death because if he killed me everybody would know what a terrible man I've had for a father.*

But instead of raising his hand to force me to his will, he softened. "You see how hard your mother and I work, don't you?"

Here we go, I thought, waiting for a repeat of the old, familiar lecture about how hard their lives were in Canada, about the sacrifices they had to make to get ahead.

"You're 10 years old now, Elvie. There are things you're capable of doing to help—or do you want to be treated like a baby all your life?"

The voice in my head answered, *Yes, treat me like a baby! I'm only 10. I want to be looked after the way Rose Marie's and Renee's parents look after them. I want to spend my time reading and playing and maybe doing a little housework not looking after your house and your children...* But I didn't dare speak those words.

"Besides, the sooner you learn life is hard, the better off you'll be. Mark my word, one day you'll thank me for teaching you this lesson. Yes, we're asking you to do a lot right now but I'm also teaching you to do things for yourself, to be independent. Do you see?"

I stared down at the floor with a sudden understanding I could never make this man understand.

"Do you see, Elvie?"

"Yes, I see," I said. But I only saw two people who were supposed to be looking after me—weren't they? They're making me miserable.

CHAPTER TWENTY-ONE

The summer of 1959 turned the city concrete streets into a broiler. I loathed it as much as I loathed the cold. There was no getting away from it, especially as the morning tipped into afternoon and the sun's touch seared my skin and the heavy air heavy with humidity, made me dopey.

Ricky, Teresa and I spent mornings on the sidewalk playing skipping rope or hide and seek or chasing tiny white or buttery yellow butterflies in the weed-filled empty field across the street that belonged to the Patronage. When it got too hot to bear, we fled indoors where the sun's fingers couldn't reach us, leaving both the front and back doors open, hoping to catch a breeze. We watched TV, the three of us sprawled on the couch on top of each other with glasses of red Kool-Aid clutched in our fists.

In 1959, we had two channels on TV, CBC English and CBC French. We switched back and forth at first although I didn't understand the Parisian accent, I got to love old French police films that aired every afternoon.

Summer evenings didn't always give us respite from the temperature and everyone fled their flats, heat had collected the whole day and now hung like smoke, choking us. People plunked chairs on the sidewalk or on their balconies and talked to each other while a small army ran screeching around them.

My father, who'd acquired Canadian citizenship, liked to talk politics. The other men let him talk but they didn't seem to have much interest in what he said. My father supported the Liberal party both provincially and federally and despised the government arch-conservative Maurice Duplessis and the Union Nationale government.

"Duplessis is corrupt, corrupt I tell you. Him and the Catholic Church! Well, they've got this whole province in a stranglehold."

The people around him would shrug and change the subject.

Sometimes on the weekend we might attend a wedding or a christening—there seemed to be so many of them but what with new clothes and the requisite gifts, my parents only attended when it involved close family. But there were lots of Italian church festivals celebrating various saints and my father sometimes took Teresa and me to give Mamma a break.

I went along with my father whenever he went to his cousin Giulio's Saturday evenings or Sunday afternoons where they played cards, Scopa, Briscola or Tresette. They played long into the night and drank beer, and while some of the men got drunk, my father never did. While the men played, I loved spending time with, Fil, my adopted big sister, whom I worshipped. At fourteen, Fil stood five-feet-five inches, taller than most Italian girls, had glossy auburn hair and large dark brown eyes. I was so happy she let me, a kid of 10, stick around with her and her chic friends. I didn't care for Fil's mother, though. She was a sour woman who barked endless orders at her. Fil was the middle child of three and the only girl.

"Don't you hate how your mother is always after you to do things around the house but not your older brother?" I asked Fil.

"It's just her way. Besides, even if I did mind there's nothing I can do about it."

Her calm acceptance perplexed me. Maybe she couldn't refuse her mother's orders but how did she manage not to resent the woman for such unfairness?

During one visit that summer, Fil made a shocking announcement. "I started bleeding."

"What?"

"Bleeding. You know, from down there."

I'd heard rumours from other kids about this bleeding business but had had my doubts. "So, it's really true! Yuck. Does it hurt?"

"Nah. It's more like a sore stomach for a day or two."

"Once it starts, do you bleed all the time forever?"

"Nah. It comes every month for a few days."

"Are you sure every girl gets it?"

"Yup."

"Why do girls get it?"

"Something to do with babies."

"Well, I hope I don't get it because I don't want babies."

As the days of summer moved closer to fall, my father's mood darkened and he turned more truculent, so much that we all walked on eggshells in an effort to avoid provoking his anger. He quit his job, claiming his boss didn't like Italians and was out to get him. He soon found another job but just one day later he was complaining about his treatment there too. His anger caused by the people he worked with made him impossible at home, and he devoted himself to finding fault with everything we did, particularly Mamma. He didn't hit her, instead, he wore her down with criticism, chipped away at her self-esteem: she was fat, she was ignorant, she was a bad housekeeper and on and on, until one Sunday afternoon during one of his harangues, Mamma threw a plate at his head.

Had it struck where she'd aimed, the plate would have done damage. But he'd ducked and the plate shattered on the kitchen floor. It thrilled me to see Mamma fight back for once and I prayed she'd do it more often in the future, that is, until I saw the murderous expression on his face. Mamma ran out of the house through the back door and stayed out for several hours. When he saw her poke her head gingerly through the door to make sure he'd calmed down, he didn't say anything until she came in. Then he went to her, and he slapped her face.

He quit his job again and I had to endure his presence all day, every day. The days before the new school term began rolled slowly along like tumbleweeds across a vast desert, each one distinguished only by variations in my father's moods. I studied him, learned to read the nuances of expression, subtle shifts in tone of voice, the way he used his hands. The depth of his frown told me the temperature of his rage; in the width of his smile, I divined the degree of benevolence.

When I adjusted my behaviour according to those readings, we got along better. But I resented having to do it, and I turned inward. The son of a neighbour was a great reader and he lent me books in which I lost myself. As I lay on bed one day, belly down, immersed in a Bobbsey Twins story, a sudden cry of pain—no, a wail—burst from my parents' bedroom. I shot to my feet and the awful lament repeated itself. It was a sound so filled with pain, both alien and familiar, it shook me. Heart galloping, I made my way to the bedroom, where I knew my father had been lying.

The door stood open. He lay on his bed, curled up tight, like a baby.

"Papà?" I asked.

What was wrong with him? Was he sick? Would he die? Was it my fault for all the times I'd gotten really mad at him and I wished him dead?

He straightened up a bit and lifted his head. He looked towards me but didn't seem to see me as though he were seeing through me. He blinked a few times, seemed to come to and then called my name.

"Yes, Papà."

"Come here. Come sit next to me," he said sitting up. His voice was hoarse.

I didn't know what to make of him but I reluctantly went to sit at the edge of the bed, perched there prepared to bolt at any moment. With his puffy face and swollen eyes, he barely looked like himself.

He pulled a handkerchief out of his trouser pocket and wiped his nose. "I hope you have a life less miserable than mine, Elvie."

How could he say such a thing, I thought? Not only was he an adult unlike me, a kid everybody ordered around, he was in charge and could do whatever he wanted. Wasn't that what made people happy?

He covered his face with his hands and wept quietly while I sat anxiously beside him not knowing what I should do. The only time I'd seen him cry was the day he'd nearly made Mamma hang herself. Sometimes, I thought about that day and got scared all over again.

He mopped his eyes and nose with the handkerchief. "Everybody hates me, Elvie. Do you hate me, too?"

I shook my head, a silent lie, but I sat within his reach, too close to risk telling the truth.

He sighed. "Your mother hates me. But then she's an ignorant woman and she doesn't think past her creature needs. You think I'm bad and she's good but when you grow up, you'll understand how sneaky your mother is." A faraway look came into his eyes, and he went silent until he pinned me with the glistening beam of his eyes. "You're not like her, are you, Elvie? No, I don't think so. You're not going to grow up to be an ignorant cow like her. "You're a thinker, you are. Just like me."

I fidgeted; I didn't want to be like him at all. Was I really like him?

"You were born into a different world from mine. You will have the chance to free yourself, to make your life whatever you want it to be. With a good education, three languages under your belt and a bit of ambition, you can go far. Don't let anybody pen you in. Don't let them."

I nodded but had no clue what he was talking about.

He took my hand, looked deep into my eyes, as though he wanted to get inside me. "*Nn spreca l'occasion.* Don't waste the opportunity." He dropped my hand and shut his eyes. "Go back to whatever you were doing, Elvie. I need to rest."

I hurried away in confusion, my thoughts whirling round and round, like a pinwheel whirled by a strong wind. What did he mean about Mamma? And was I really like him? He argued with everybody, and people didn't like him while I didn't fight with my friends like he did.

Was I like Mamma? Yes, Mamma had lots of friends, but she only cared about everyday boring things like housework. She rarely talked about anything interesting going on in the world. My father read magazines and watched the news on TV.

So, if I wasn't like either of my parents—and didn't want to be—who was I?

CHAPTER TWENTY-TWO

Each day of July and August of 1959 seemed to pass so slowly but suddenly I was getting ready to start Grade 5 and the struggle to get me up in the morning to get there resumed. When Mamma's voice woke me, it felt as though I was trying to pull myself out of quicksand like I've seen happen in a cowboy movie.

"Get up!" she yelled, exasperated, on the first day of school. "Get up or I'll pull you out by the hair."

I wanted to obey her, but my body weighed too much to move and someone had glued my eyelids together.

"Come on, I've made toast, and there's the marmalade you like," she said, giving my shoulder a little shake.

Eventually, I shuffled into the kitchen. My father was still in bed, thank goodness, because when he came to wake me, I had to get up immediately otherwise he'd lift me out bodily. While I ate my toast, Mamma dressed Ricky and Teresa. Until he got himself a job, my father would have to look after them while Mamma worked.

Mamma poked her nose into their bedroom on her way to the factory. "I'm leaving now. If you decide to go look for a job, Sesta said she can take the kids."

I lingered over my toast as long as I dared, too long, and then had to rush to put on the white cotton blouse I'd washed and ironed myself, the pleated navy-blue tunic over it, beige stockings held up by ordinary elastic which Mamma had made into bands to hold them up around the thighs and ugly black and white Mary Jane shoes.

I was thrilled to get Mrs. Keyes as my teacher once more, although the pupils had been shuffled and there were a lot of new faces from the Grade 4 class. We didn't do much learning that first day, but it came with a stern warning that *everyone* had to attend 9 o'clock Mass every Sunday at the school's parish church, St. Michael the Archangel.

Although my parents had registered as parishioners at the Italian church, Madonna della Difesa, they rarely went to Mass. Mostly, they saw the inside of a church for weddings, baptisms, and funerals. My mother said she had too much to do on Sundays, and my father wasn't a believer, he said the priests only wanted to fleece their flocks. I did go to Mass from time to time, when I felt like it, but not at our parish church, which was on Henri-Julien, a half-hour walk away or take a bus. When I did attend Mass, I went to St. Georges, the French-language parish on Bernard, because it was the closest, but I mostly didn't bother.

My lackadaisical attitude towards attending Mass landed me in trouble.

At the end of class one Monday, the principal ordered the entire student body into the assembly hall, something that hadn't happened in living memory, according to the older girls. The assembly room was too small to comfortably hold us all and we stood pressed against each other murmuring, worried about what bad thing might have happened to bring us all together this way.

The principal, a nun, marched in and went to stand on the small stage. She was a tall woman, and stout, and a sad expression had replaced her usual placid face. Without preamble, she said, "Girls, those of you who attended the 9 o'clock Mass at St. Michael yesterday, raise your hands. Remember, God is watching. You can lie to me, but you can't hide the truth from him."

A bunch of small hands went up, far fewer than a third. I squirmed. I hadn't been to Mass Sunday—not at St. Michael's or anywhere else.

"You've done yourselves credit, children. You may go home." The devout kids quickly filed out.

"Now, who among you attended a service at St. Michael other than 9 o'clock?" More hands went up; that group too was set free. About a third of us remained.

"Who among you attended Mass at some other parish church? Remember, children, God sees all."

I broke out in a sweat. Should I lie? Would God's punishment hit me harder for lying or would the principal's punishment be worse? Sunday was the only day I could sleep in and 9 o'clock Mass was just too early. Of course, I could have gone later but Mass bored me silly.

Standing up, sitting down, kneeling, and all that up and down stuff in a language I didn't even understand, not to mention the sermons when the priests went on endlessly about how evil we all were.

Figuring God had more power and could hand out more dangerous punishments than the school principal, I decided to tell the truth.

Only a handful of kids, the sinners, remained. What lay in store for those who'd committed the mortal sin of missing Mass? I wondered.

One by one, the principal called us up to the stage. When my turn came to explain myself, my insides wobbled like the cherry-flavoured Jell-O I loved. What would she do to me? Kick me out of school? Give me the strap? Did they strap the girls at Luke Callaghan? They hadn't at Edward Murphy.

"I hope you have a good excuse for not going to Mass, young lady." The principal in her black, floor-length robes loomed over me. "You know as well as I do that missing Sunday Mass is a *mortal* sin. If God chose to take you to him before you'd had a chance to repent, you'd end up in the fires of Hell."

"Yes, Sister," I said, unable to meet her gaze.

"So, tell me, why didn't you do your duty as a Catholic?"

How could I tell her, a nun, someone who had a direct link to God, that I didn't attend church because I'd much rather sleep in?

"Look at me, child, and explain yourself."

I looked up but couldn't hold eye contact, my fear of her suddenly much greater than Almighty God who now seemed much less real. To save myself from whatever she had in mind for me, I lied, in a small voice:

"My parents had work to do, and I had to look after my brother and sister."

"I see." She thought about what I'd said, stared again at me, and nodded. I wasn't sure she believed me. "Tell your parents you are expected to go to Mass every Sunday."

All the way home, I expected God to strike me dead or at least warn me in some way. Nothing happened, not that day or the next, which made me wonder whether God really cared if I lied or even went to Mass.

Despite the principal's admonishment to go to Mass every Sunday, I often failed to haul myself out of bed in time, for the early Mass, and found excuses for not attending later in the day. Feelings of guilt faded more and more with each absence. In catechism class, Mrs. Keyes had told us that when a Catholic stops feeling guilty about committing a mortal sin—and missing Sunday Mass was a big one—it meant I'd developed a "black conscience." A very bad thing, I'd probably go to Hell.

In early December, Zia Tresa, the last of Mamma's sisters arrived in Montreal with her husband, two children, and pregnant. They moved in with Zia Carmelina, who'd sponsored their immigration application until they could get on their feet. The seven of them, four adults and three children, shared a five-room upper duplex in a newer section of the city, northeast of our house.

I rejoiced when spring pushed the glacial winter back into its hole, and before I realized it Grade 5 ended, and I was home again for the summer, sitting on the front stoop, sometimes with Renee, sometimes with Rose Marie, when she had nothing better to do, and sometimes all three of us together, singing along to the Hit Parade on the radio, as waves of fierce heat rose from sidewalks like steam.

My father hadn't found a job and that meant I had to watch my step and stay within calling distance. One ordinary July day as we three girls sang along with "Itsy Bitsy Teenie Weenie Yellow Polka dot Bikini" we jumped to our feet when loud banging emerged came from inside our flat.

I raced in to see what had happened and found my father pulling down the kitchen cabinets and covered in plaster dust.

"Papà, what are you doing?"

"I'm going to build a new kitchen." His gloom had lifted.

This he did, taking down all the cabinets, removing the sink, the hot water tank, stripping away the old plaster down to the lath and taking up the old linoleum floor. Then he rebuilt it: replastered the walls, put up new white cabinets and grey Arborite countertop, installed a shiny stainless-steel sink and a white tiled backsplash behind it, replaced the old hot water tank with an automatic one—no more lighting it with a match—and put down pretty linoleum checkerboard flooring using burgundy and grey tiles. He painted the walls lemon yellow.

The project shook him out of his blues, and to everyone's relief, once he finished the project he went out and got himself a job.

CHAPTER TWENTY-THREE

When I started Grade Six in the fall of 1960, to my enormous disappointment my teacher was a nun. However, dislike for the teacher paled in the face of profound upheaval taking place within the province and around the world throughout the 1960s and affected everyone, including children.

In Quebec, Maurice Duplessis, premier since 1944 and known as "Le Chef," died of a stroke in September 1959 and that set the province on a new course. Duplessis and his party, the Union Nationale, had dominated provincial politics since the 1930s with a socially conservative, anti-Communist, anti-union stance and actively supported by the Roman Catholic Church. Duplessis' refusal to secularize institutions, including the education system then controlled by the Catholic Church, delayed the province's development by at least a decade.

Once Duplessis died, voters kicked out the Union Nationale as the default governing party and elected a Liberal government the following June. The new Liberal government set about modernizing the province, including rapid and dramatic development of government institutions and taking a big role in Quebec's economic, social and cultural life. The election of the Liberals launched Quebec's Quiet Revolution.

The new environment gradually brought prosperity to French-speaking Québécois, who now demanded greater control over economic resources. The battle also led to an expansion of nationalist sentiment by some among the French, which led to some two hundred bombings throughout the 1960s by the movement's radicals and culminated in the kidnapping of a British government official and the kidnapping and murder of a Québec cabinet minister in what's now known as the October Crisis of 1970.

Québecers' desire for their own state had deep roots in history. The strip of territory along the St. Lawrence River already had a population of 70,000 Roman-Catholic French settlers when Britain acquired it in a treaty with France in1763. The new British governors tried to assimilate the French population but failed. The tight-knit French-speaking community had developed their own way of life, customs and attitudes and the settlers didn't need to assimilate.

The English changed tactics and formed an alliance with French-speaking elites. In return they agreed to recognize the legitimacy of the French language and the Catholic faith, reinstated the Church's power to enforce collection of tithes, which the Church had been denied to weaken it, and legitimized the French Civil Code alongside English criminal law.

The seeds of Québec nationalism were planted in the turmoil of big economic and social changes at the turn of the 20th century. Until then, most French Canadians had worked on the land or in the timber trade. But farmland became scarce as the French-speaking population swelled, they migrated to the cities, where factories needed labourers. With few exceptions the enterprises were owned and directed by English Canadians or American businesses. The factory job paid little, and the incoming waves of workers led to the proliferation of ugly slums for impoverished workers.

By the 1950s, a French-speaking urban middle class had emerged and continued to make gains despite attempts by the autocratic premier Maurice Duplessis to keep Québec Catholic, agrarian, and conservative. When he died in 1959, the province was more than ready for a new path.

In 1961 Montreal had a population of about two million. More than 100,000 were of Italian origin and competed with the French-speaking majority for low-paying work. The resentment of the French-speaking majority had grown more overt towards immigrants and English-speaking citizens and they pushed to take control of the economy.

This new path included violence by those determined to take control away from the English overlords. In 1963 two Québecers, Raymond Villeneuve and Gabriel Hudon, and a Belgian, Georges Schoeters, a Second World War Resistance fighter, founded the Front de Libération du Québec, the FLQ. Its members included some of the more radical elements of earlier independence groups, such as the *Comité de Libération Nationale,* and they set out to liberate themselves from anglophone domination and capitalism.

The FLQ issued a manifesto, *Message du FLQ à la Nation,* declaring itself ready to undertake a social revolution by any means necessary: "There is only one way to defeat colonialism, and that's to be stronger than it . . . the time of slavery is over. Patriots of Québec to Arms! The hour of national revolution has come! Independence or death!" It also provided instructions on how to make explosives.

Thanks to the FLQ, Quebec's so-called Quiet Revolution, which transformed the province socially and politically, wasn't entirely quiet. Between the founding of the FLQ in 1963 and 1970 when it fell apart after the October Crisis, the Marxist-Leninist group set nearly 200 bombs, most in and around Montreal, including the Stock Exchange, the CN train station, residential mailboxes in the wealthy English-speaking town of Westmount, federal government and military buildings, a shoe and textile factory, the downtown Eaton department store and the home of then mayor, Jean Drapeau. The bombs that detonated killed eight people and injured dozens more.

At the same time, other French-speaking separatists took a political route towards independence with the creation of the Partie Quebecois in 1968. The pro-sovereignty party came to power in 1976 and soon decreed French as the only official language of business and government throughout the province, and the huge migration of anglophones and other ethnic minorities westward got underway.

Meanwhile, the world teetered on the brink of nuclear war thanks to hostilities between the United States and the USSR.

In November 1952, the U.S. had tested the first full-scale thermonuclear device in the Pacific Ocean, which created a fireball five kilometers wide with enough force to wipe out the core of a major city like Moscow, much more potent than the bombs dropped on Hiroshima and Nagasaki during the Second World War. The Soviets, had their own hydrogen bomb program and was developing devices just as deadly, and also began testing them.

The feuding superpowers had a terrifying arsenal at their disposal, and Canada lay directly between them.

When the Soviets detonated four, above-ground nuclear explosions in September 1961, the Canadian government held a full-scale civil defense exercise, a public dress rehearsal for the day the bomb might fall, including a three-minute wail of air-raid sirens, and a public address by the Canadian Prime Minister, John Diefenbaker.

In the early 1960s the Canadian government launched a campaign urging citizens to "be prepared," including a booklet titled *Your Basement Fallout Shelter: Blueprint for Survival No. 1*. It detailed how to build a shelter from scratch capable of sustaining life for several days. Posters appeared everywhere, radio and television programs broadcast urgent discussions as to what to do in the event of nuclear fallout.

But the government-recommended shelters had been designed to protect against radioactive by-products of a modest nuclear detonation like the bombs dropped on Japan during World War II. They would have been against the new thermonuclear warheads.

The U.S. and the U.S.S.R. had been waging a Cold War since the late 1940s, but the most dangerous moment came in October 1962 with the Cuban missile crisis. After America's failed attempt to invade Cuba in 1961, Cubans turned to their Soviet allies for help in deterring future attacks. But when a U.S. spy plane spotted Soviet ballistic missiles on Cuban soil—a mere ninety miles from Florida—it lit a match under the Cold War and a fearful thirteen-day standoff began.

Americans demanded the Soviets remove their missiles; the Soviets refused, not trusting the Americans to cease incursions into Cuba. Day by day the world held its breath, fearful one or the other of the two leaders would press the nuclear button. On October 28, 1962 the Soviets capitulated and agreed to remove the missiles from Cuba in exchange for a promise by the U.S. to stop attempts to invade Cuba.

CHAPTER TWENTY-FOUR

In the winter of 1961, our tenants gave notice and Zia Tresa and her family moved above us in May. I was thrilled to have my cousins, Liliana, 10, and Pasquale, 11 and the baby, living so close. They'd spent 18 months squeezed in with Zia Carmelina's family in a five-room flat. Zia Tresa, a very particular woman, wasn't shy about telling my father she would have preferred a newer flat in a better neighbourhood and my father had agreed to make a few renovations to get her to take the place.

Liliana, the middle child and two years my junior, became my dearest friend. We clung to each other for the warmth and comfort our parents were too busy or too preoccupied to provide, consumed by the demands of getting through each day.

Like me, Liliana had plenty of chores to do, especially after her mother found a job at one of the factories on Saint-Viateur. But unlike me, Liliana liked doing housework; she had a sunny outlook compared to my brooding, and she let injustices roll off her back while I held grudges.

"Doesn't it make you crazy when your mother makes you do the dishes and sweep the floor after supper while your brother plays with his friends?" I asked her.

She shrugged. "I like it when the house is clean and tidy."

I shook my head. "It's not fair that you have to help, and your brother doesn't."

My cousins had their share of violence at home. Their father, Antonio, drank and when he got drunk, Zia Tresa harangued him until he lashed out at her, and she'd run out and stay with us until he cooled off. On the other hand, he didn't brood like my father did, never missed work and gave Zia Tresa his pay envelope every Friday. Few outside our immediate families knew what violence our families endured. They were ashamed, which made us children ashamed so that we never talked about it outside the family. For our mothers, it was about saving face.

My final Grade 6 marks could have been better and reflected my inner turmoil caused by drills preparing us in case a nuclear bomb dropped on us. At school we practiced taking cover under our desks with our arms protecting our heads and, in our neighbourhood, we listened to the screech of air-raid sirens. In case of war, they were a signal for everybody to find somewhere safe to hide. Each time I heard the shrill, sharp sound, even though we knew it was only for practice, it made me fell cold from the inside out. The siren shriek haunted me, and at odd moments, maybe walking to school, and skipping rope, I would hear something reminding me of the sirens and I'd remember that we might all die soon, burned to a crisp.

My father had always watched the news on TV or listened to it on the radio and now I paid attention too.

"Is the bomb going to fall, Papà?"

"I hope not, Elvie. I hope not."

It further terrified me when he decided to build a bomb shelter. He said the best place to put one was in a basement but none of the houses on our block had basements, so he started to dig but gave up after a couple of weeks, saying it was no use.

In July, days after my 12th birthday, I discovered a few light brown streaks on my panties. At first, I thought I hadn't wiped myself properly after using the toilet so I washed and put on a fresh pair of undies and thought no more about it. But the next visit to the toilet showed fresh streaks and it scared me. Had I hurt myself somehow? Was I sick?

I lined my panties with a wad of toilet paper and paced until Mamma got home from work. "Ma, something's wrong with me," I whispered, not wanting my father to hear.

My stricken expression frightened her. "*Che è success?* What's happened?"

I held out the soiled panties. Her face relaxed. Sighing, she said, "*Mo se fatta femina.* Now you've become a woman."

What was she on about? I'd only just turned 12. Then I remembered what Fil had told me about women bleeding down there. But I was no woman. Besides, I didn't want to be a woman; being a girl was hard enough. I couldn't wait to be an adult when I could be my own boss but not an adult woman like Mamma, not an adult *married* woman like all the married women around me who did nothing but work.

Neither had it escaped my notice that Mamma, a woman, had no say at home. She worked during the day in the factory, and she worked when she got home from the factory while my father, whether employed or unemployed, read or watched TV while she cooked and did whatever needed doing that I didn't do. I didn't want that for myself. It seemed to me that if Mamma hadn't had babies, like Zia 'Ndunetta in the Soo, she wouldn't have had to work so hard. Zia 'Ndunetta had wanted to have babies but God hadn't sent her any but almost every married woman I knew had babies. I concluded if I ever married, I'd *have* to have children unless God didn't want to give me any and therefore it would be better for me not to marry.

The idea seemed like a good solution to being female and cheered me up until I realized if I didn't get married and move away with a husband, it meant I'd have to keep living with my parents, which I truly didn't want to do. Nuns weren't married—well, they said they were married to God and he wasn't around, was he? —and they didn't live with their parents. If I became a nun, I could be a teacher, too, one day, and I'd be a nice teacher not a mean one.

As a twelve-year-old, I'd had no idea that the thousands of Catholic women who gave their lives to God, who did backbreaking work as teachers, nurses and missionaries, had as little to say in the running of the Catholic Church as Mamma did in our household.

Mamma handed back my soiled panties, went into her bedroom and returned with a pile of folded cotton cloths and a couple of safety pins. "Here, line your panties with a couple of layers of these. Change them often and wash them in cold water."

I had many questions: Would bleeding make me weak? Did boys bleed too? But she hurried away as though embarrassed and I took it to mean this bleeding business was something unmentionable, dirty.

I phoned Fil, now sixteen, hoping she could answer my questions, and she did the best of answering all my questions. The next time she came to see us on Saint-Dominique, she took me to the pharmacy and bought me a box of sanitary napkins, Kotex brand, and a sanitary pad belt. The box was powder blue emblazoned with a white rose. When I'd used up the pads, however, Mamma balked at giving me money for a fresh supply.

"What's wrong with the reusable cloths? Those store-bought things are expensive."

"The cloths aren't as thick, Ma. Besides they move around and stain my panties. And I hate washing them! They're really icky."

She rolled her eyes but gave in. But now I faced a dilemma. At the time, pharmacies didn't stock feminine products on open shelves. You told the store clerk standing behind the counter what you needed, and that person fetched it from a storeroom. The clerk on Saint-Viateur was a man and I couldn't overcome my shyness to ask him for sanitary pads.

In the end, Rose Marie came to my rescue, in a manner of speaking. She had no shyness about such personal things. We stood in line at the counter and when our turn came, Rose-Marie loudly told the clerk, "She needs a box of Kotex." Everyone behind us heard.

I blushed crimson to the roots of my black hair, as embarrassed as if Rose Marie had stripped me naked in front of all those adults. She saw my reaction and grunted a dismissal: "What's wrong with you? They're just pads."

The start of my menstrual periods, much as I resented it, brought with it an exciting yet confusing time. Without those hormones bouncing around inside my body that summer I wouldn't have noticed the young boy who'd moved into the upper unit three doors away. The moment my eyes clapped on Serge my heart did a jig, as it did every time I caught sight of him from then on.

He was sixteen, stood six feet tall with a lithe, athletic body. His burnished gold hair enraptured me: slicked back on the sides, and a jelly roll on top that ended in a perfect curlicue in the middle of a broad, beautiful forehead.

His arrival drew me out of the pall situation that had settled over our household with the death in Italy of my maternal grandfather. My mother and aunts plunged into mourning their father. They cried; they wore black. TV, radio, or other entertainments were prohibited. Without films to watch, summer afternoons stretched to infinity. Even worse, Mamma told me stories about how strict her father had been, and how he often beat Nonna when he drank. In her place, I thought I wouldn't cry as much.

Serge's arrival gave me somebody other than a dead grandfather to think about. I filled my mind with stories about the budding star of movies now playing in my head. The thought of him excited me in ways I didn't understand and raised unfamiliar stirrings.

Serge had a younger brother, Michel, who was about my age, a cheerful fellow but without his brother's charisma or looks. The two boys lived with their mother and an aunt. I made friends with Michel but when Serge passed by, I looked away, too shy to even say hello. Besides, ever since I'd started bleeding, my father got mad when he saw me talking to neighbourhood boys. I wondered why it suddenly seemed to bother him? What was wrong with him? Why did it bother him all of a sudden?

CHAPTER TWENTY-FIVE

I mooned over Serge the whole of summer 1961 but never once managed to exchange a word with him. I had the means to befriend him through his younger brother but acute shyness wouldn't let me. Besides, at 16, he was practically and adult and what interest would he have in a 12-year-old kid like me and on top of that, if my father ever saw me talking to him, he'd kill me.

With hindsight, I realize I didn't actually want to get to know the beatific Serge, to have as a real-life boyfriend. But he was perfect as an ideal boyfriend on whom I could hang all my longings and so distract myself from the home life I wanted to flee.

Nevertheless, I yearned to see the beautiful young man. Sitting on my stoop, I had a clear view of his balcony and contented myself with waiting to catch a glimpse of him as he walked by or when he sat on his balcony for a smoke on warm summer evenings.

I began Grade 7 that September, my final year of elementary school, a year closer to adulthood and to the freedom I longed for. Unfortunately, my teacher was the same nun I'd had for the sixth grade, a woman who wore a perpetual upside-down smile and who gave off a smell that bothered me when I got near her.

At the time, I didn't recognize the sharp, acrid scent, which I later learned was carbolic soap.

Our father, who was once again out of a job, when Teresa started school that year, had to fight to get her admitted. Her sixth birthday was in October, a month later than the rules allowed.

At the time the schools continued to struggle to accommodate relentless demand as immigrants kept pouring into the city. The shortage of classrooms and teachers was so acute the year Teresa started classes, Luke Callaghan could only offer the Grade 1 pupils half days.

Teresa was assigned to the afternoon group. She quickly learned to read, loved it and galloped through all the assignments but complained about her teacher, a Mrs. Macdonald, who, she insisted, didn't like the Italian girls in the class and was especially mean to them.

As for me, Grade 7 was much like Grade 6 but with the pleasant addition of lessons in sewing and knitting. The time set aside for those classes flew by because they engaged both my hands and my head and, besides, I was good at it and loved having something to show at the end of the term for all the effort I put into the projects: an apron in the sewing class and a potholder in the knitting class.

The days marched on, school, homework, housework, and hanging out with Renee and Rose Marie in my free time. Both Teresa and I were allowed to stay up on Saturday nights and sleep in on the weekends but whereas I had no trouble falling into bed no matter what time I got up in the morning, Teresa couldn't get to sleep if she'd slept in. She'd wait till our parents went to bed Sunday nights then sneak out of our room to sit on the floor up close to the TV with the sound very low and watched old movies on the CBC channel until the station signed off.

In no time, Christmas peeked around the corner, only that year we would be celebrating it with Zia Tresa and our cousins. It had always been just the five of us, thanks to the enmity between my father and Zia Carmelina, and not much fun playing games like Tombola, a type of bingo, with just five people. That year, minus the baby, nine sat around the table playing Tombola, with each of us taking turns calling out the numbers and the jackpots, to my mind, well worth winning.

In the spring of 1962 after a boring winter spent indoors looking after Ricky, my father announced he'd be going into business for himself. He planned to hire himself out as a subcontractor laying ceramic tiles, flooring, and other construction work. He'd gone out and bought a second-hand, cream-coloured, half-ton pickup, for the purpose, and it now sat parked sedately in front of our house,

"*Maledetto*! You accursed man!" Mamma cried out in dismay. "You not only quit your job, you went and used our savings to buy a truck?"

"But I had to have the truck, don't you see? I need it for materials and equipment. Besides, I can use it to haul all kinds of others things. Why, during moving season alone, I can make a mint."

Mamma looked defeated. Besides, the deed was done, and she could only swallow her bile.

He now turned to me to justify himself. "Your mother has no imagination, Elvie. She was born a peasant and she'll die a peasant. One day you'll understand how somebody like that can hold you back, kill your dreams."

"Yeah? I'd like to see how far you'd get with your dreams if I didn't bring in money every week to put food on the table," she said, a look of disgust on her face.

I didn't understand why my father couldn't seem to keep a job. Neither of my uncles seem to have that problem. The more I thought about it the more it perplexed me that he didn't act like any of the other fathers. Apart from not working, he buried his nose in books and magazines rather than playing cards or bocce ball with other men. In fact, he had no friends other than his cousin Guilio.

Nevertheless, he threw himself into his new venture, hustling for business, and getting it. My father had the gift of gab and easy charm and could talk people into things when he wanted to, even if he didn't always tell the truth. He might have made a fortune in a sales job had he been able to overcome the fixation that bosses and co-workers were out to get him.

When Grade 7 ended, and my father was too busy to reprimand for my mediocre marks. I rejoiced to have finished with elementary school and keen to start high school and be one of the big kids. But I didn't relish another summer of housework and babysitting, although being home meant I would have many more opportunities for glimpses of Serge's golden face.

Since Serge had come to Saint-Dominique, thoughts of him had kept me company and comforted me. When rats scratched inside the wall behind my headboard at night, I blocked out the noise by playing a movie, starring the two of us, in my head. When my parents treated me unjustly and I would have given anything to get away from them, his existence gave me hope that better people and a better future lay ahead.

Serge and I had never spoken, never looked into each other's eyes and yet I thought of him as mine. So, when Serge asked my cousin Fil out on a date, it crushed me.

Fil and I sat on the stoop one hot evening while she was staying with us. Fil was a beauty, tall and slender with narrow hips, long shapely legs and a gorgeous smile, not to mention gorgeous auburn hair. To top it off, she had a sweet nature. If she had one physical flaw it was a stubby nose.

Serge stepped out of his house. "That's him!" I whispered to Fil, my insides a-twitter. Fil knew all about my infatuation with Serge; she'd listened to me talk about him endlessly. Serge noticed Fil when she'd stayed with us that summer.

"*Bon soir,*" he said to both of us, as he passed. His smiled dazzled me, the crinkles it caused around his eyes were enchanting.

Fil and I both returned the greeting. It was the first time I'd addressed him in two years.

"Isn't he gorgeous?" I said, when he'd moved out of earshot.

"Yes, he's very handsome," she said.

The next time we ran into him, Serge stopped to chat with Fil. I was too shy even to look at him. Still, to have him so close, to hear the rich timbre of his voice added to my fantasies. When Fil's job ended a few days later, I expected that would end any interaction with Serge. What actually happened was worse.

The blow came a week later. Serge saw me on my stoop with Renee and walked right up to me.

"*Salut*," he said.

"*Bonjour*," I replied, blushing crimson.

"*Est-ce que ta cousine est encore chez vous?* Is your cousin still staying with you?"

"No. She isn't here anymore." I figured Rose Marie, whose mother was distantly related to Serge's mother, must have told him Fil and I were related. How else could he have learned of it?

He looked disappointed. "Would you mind giving me her phone number?"

The request made me reel. Serge *liked*, as in "was interested in" Fil. It took work to keep my heartbreak from showing. "I'll go write it down for you," I said and hurried inside, disappointment rising up like a tide. I handed him a piece of paper with her number.

"*Merci bien*," he said with a little salute before he walked away.

The image of those two lovely creatures together pressed into my brain like a thorn. I didn't call my cousin to tell her. I didn't even want to think about it. It wasn't her fault he liked her, but I couldn't help but resent her for it. Why couldn't I be 17, tall and svelte like Fil? Why didn't I have auburn or blonde hair like fashion models? I had a nicer nose but otherwise I was a 5-foot shrimp who would never have Fil's long legs. My mother even forced me to wear my nice, glossy black hair cut short like a boy's.

Fil phoned me the next day. "Serge called me."

"Yeah. He asked me for your number."

"He asked me to go to a wedding party with him. I told him I couldn't go."

"You did?" I could breathe again.

"Yes, of course, I did. I know how much you like him."

My eyes welled up in gratitude. I knew Serge would never be mine but to lose him to someone close, well, somehow would have been worse.

I spent the rest of that summer pining my lost ideal and waiting for the hit song of the summer, "Johnny Angel," on the radio. Listening to its lyrics gave me comfort.

Johnny Angel, how I love him

He's got something that I can't resist

But he doesn't even know that I-I-I exist

Johnny Angel, how I want him

How I tingle when he passes by

Every time he says "Hello" my heart begins to fly

I get carried away

I dream of him and me and how it's gonna be

Other fellas call me up for a date

But I just sit and wait, I'd rather concentrate

On Johnny Angel

The summer of 1962 was also the summer when I began injuring myself and kept it up for many years—to varying degrees—particularly during stressful times, until I sought help to learn how to deal with my demons tormenting me. It started with me picking at the hard skin on my heels and progressed to the point where I gouged holes in my heels with the points of a pair of scissors so that I could peel away the skin, layer after layer, like an onion. It hurt when I did it and the wound bled.

When I walked on the healing skin it would split open and although it hurt so much the pain made me limp, the sensation, the "hurting" made me *feel* my body, brought me into my body and out of the frightening thoughts roaming around in my head. Pain made me feel whole.

CHAPTER TWENTY-SIX

The high school years began in September 1962. Special uniforms were required so Mamma and I went downtown by bus to Eaton's department store to buy one. Every Catholic high school had its own outfit and Eaton was the only store that stocked Thomas D'Arcy McGee's uniform, where I'd be going. It consisted of a V-neck, navy-blue tunic with an A-line skirt over a long-sleeved white blouse. There were also additional items, such as a pale-blue blouse for winter use only, and a cardigan in the school colours, navy blue with pale blue accents, which was the only cardigan we were allowed to wear in the classroom, neither of which Mamma could afford to buy. Those of us who couldn't buy a cardigan, and that was the majority, shivered throughout the winter.

In addition to class uniform, we had to purchase an outfit for gym class, which included items of clothing I'd never seen before. What was a teddy? What were bloomers? Plus white socks and sneakers.

I don't know how Mamma scraped together the money to buy everything I needed. She left the store, shell-shocked by the bill—this woman who shopped at the nickel-and-dime stores on Park Avenue and only when they had sales, who trolled factories on Saint-Viateur, some of which opened to the public Saturday mornings, to get whatever she could at wholesale prices and bought dry goods such as bed sheets, towels and tablecloths from an itinerant Hassidic Jew who went door to door.

The day before high classes began, my father gave me another lecture about the importance of excelling.

"You're starting high school now, Elvie. This is the time to get serious about schoolwork. If you don't get good marks, and I mean 80-plus average, I'm going to take you out of school and send you to work next year. You'll be fourteen then and legal to work."

Like hell you will, I thought. He could threaten me as much as he liked but I intended to finish high school even if I didn't meet his standards.

Thomas D'Arcy McGee High School stood five storeys above Pine Avenue West between St-Famille and Jeanne Mance, girls on one side and boys on the other. Unlike elementary school where we had the same teacher all day, high school offered the novelty of a specialist teacher for the various subjects. Although the Congregation of Notre Dame—the same nun community I'd had back in Grade 1—ran the school, I had lay teachers that year.

I loved ancient history, English literature and art. Math and science still came hard but home economics in a well-equipped teaching kitchen was fun. The dishes we made struck many of the newest immigrants in our class as strange if not downright disgusting: Potatoes baked with cream? Carrots sprinkled with brown sugar? Cream-of-corn soup? Yuck. Some of the Italian girls, repelled by such strange mixtures of ingredients lost marks because they refused to taste what they'd made.

The situation at home steadied as my father made money with his truck. For a whole month our life sailed on an even keel. Then the Cuban Missile Crises between the U.S. and the Soviet Union erupted in October, nothing seemed as important as the possibility of nuclear war but once that conflict resolved and the rest of 1962 remained, it was quiet at home until winter came and demand for my father's services waned along with his good humour.

By the spring of 1963, his mood was the darkest I'd ever seen it. He spent entire days enclosed in the darkness of their bedroom, brooding. He stopped watching the news or reading magazines and newspapers.

When we addressed him, he answered in monosyllables. The truck sat unused, buried in snow at the back of the house.

When the snow began to melt and the air turned milder, he came out of hibernation, poked his nose outdoors and went back to normal—well, normal for him. We all breathed a deep sigh of relief until he announced with a wide smile and merriment in his eyes that he'd bought a grocery store.

Mamma's eyes went round and fearful, her face paled. "*Dio mio!* A store, are you crazy? What for?"

"To make money," he replied, frowning, dismayed by her disapproval.

Had he really expected her to jump up with excitement, I wondered? Although I didn't know how this latest of scheme of his would affect me, I was sure it would have an impact on my life.

"*Madonna, aiutami tu!* Help me, Holy Mother."

My father told her he'd put all their savings into this new venture. He'd bought Jerry's Italian Provisions, a tiny storefront on Fairmount Street, just west of Saint-Laurent and a 10-minute walk from our house.

"I got such a deal," he enthused. "The owner is sick. Wanted to get rid of it and he sold it for the value of the inventory. "Just think, from now on we'll get our groceries wholesale."

In a voice that blended rage and despair, Mamma said, "I give it six months before you lose interest. I'll tell you one thing, though, don't expect me to help you. I will not work there. I have enough on my shoulders as it is."

He renamed the store Molise Groceries, in honour of our home region, which had recently been split from the Abruzzo and declared a region on its own. The Saturday he opened the store, he invited all of us to go and have a look at it, but Mamma refused. I took a walk there out of curiosity and brought Teresa along.

The store occupied a narrow space between a kosher butcher shop and a laundromat. A bell tinkled when I pushed open the glass door, my sister at my heels. I hadn't expected a supermarket like the Steinberg's on Park Avenue. Nor had I imagined such a pokey little room. The store had a plate glass window facing Fairmount and a glass entry door next to it, yet somehow light failed to penetrate beyond a couple of feet.

A glass case stood in front of the front window, doing double duty as candy display and checkout counter. On either side of the entry, the facing walls had floor-to-ceiling shelves crammed with non-perishables: glass jars filled with jams and pickles, bottles of oil and salad dressing, cans of vegetables, fruit and soup. They held boxes of cake mixes, Jell-O and cereals, cookies and much more. Crouching in the middle of the room was a large, red Coca-Cola cooler. Bottles of soft drinks, juice and milk, were jammed into ice chips inside. Next to the cooler a tall, stainless-steel rack held crusty Italian loaves of bread, rolls, and commercial sliced white bread. At the back of the store, a refrigerated deli counter took the pride of the place. The store did not sell fresh meat, fruit or vegetables.

There were two other small grocery stores like ours on Fairmount. They didn't carry perishable foods since there were also plenty of butcher stores and greengrocers in the neighbourhood. Ever since we'd moved to Saint-Dominique Mamma shopped for groceries at a small store on Clark Street—across from my former elementary school—owned by an Italian family, and bought fruit, vegetables and meat from Jean Talon open market stalls in season.

"What do you think, kids?" he asked.

"Lots of stuff," I said, eyeing the candy counter.

"Yes, lots and lots," Teresa chimed, big brown eyes aimed at the same spot.

It was almost noon, so my father made us lunch. He took three crusty rolls from the bread rack, sliced some mortadella, an Italian bologna, and made sandwiches. There was only one chair in the store, behind the glass case. Teresa and I ate on the store's front step.

The store hadn't impressed me, but my father seemed content. When he was happy, home life was better. I prayed the store would keep him happy for a long, long time.

Throughout the rest of the spring, he opened the store at 8 a.m. pronto, and didn't get home until 6:30 p.m., at the earliest. It was understood we wouldn't start supper until he came home no matter the time, no matter how hungry we were because he insisted that "families must eat together."

By the end of the school year, however, he'd lost his smile, and a darting furtiveness replaced the earlier sparkle in his eyes. He seemed less and less keen to get to the store and opened its doors later and later. Worse, he began to complain about the storekeeper next door, owner of People's Kosher Meat Market.

"He's watching me," my father said, one evening around the supper table.

I shot a quick look at Mamma, who caught her lower lip between her teeth. "What do you mean he's watching you? Why would he watch you?"

She'd known all along this would happen, and it hadn't even taken the six months she'd predicted.

"You don't believe me, do you? He stands outside my window with an axe in his fist and stares at me. I'm not imagining it."

"Maybe he was just standing there waiting for someone."

He slammed his fist hard against the table, rattling the dishes. "Do you think I can't tell when somebody's threatening me?"

Oh-oh, I thought, putting down my spoon. Peace had been nice while it had lasted.

"Don't you understand? He's a Jew. I'm Italian. Jews don't like us setting up businesses next to them. He's doing this so I'll leave."

146

"But Papà, didn't you buy the store from an Italian?" I said, trying to placate him.

"Exactly! Now I see he left in desperation."

For all any of us knew, the previous Italian owner had done business there for decades. But when my father was like that, you couldn't argue with him.

"He's a butcher, after all. He knows how to kill," he said, pressing his point.

"So, you're saying you want to give up the store? Let's see, I gave it six months. I guess I was optimistic. It's only been three."

"Did I say that?" he said, glaring at her. "Why do you always deliberately misunderstand? No, I didn't say I want to give up the store. All I said is I don't trust the Jew next door."

"*Va buon.* Fine. Let's see if you make to six months after all."

He threw the fork he was holding across the room and stalked out.

My father had periods of dark moods since I could remember, teasing and smiling one day, brooding and unapproachable the next, changes coming for no apparent reason. He'd also shown suspicion of people, particularly strangers, people he couldn't control. But that evening was the first time he'd come out and said someone was out to kill him.

I went to bed that night weighed down with worry about this new development, worried not so much for his well-being but how it would affect the rest of us.

His paranoia deepened in the ensuing weeks.

"I overheard the butcher talking to somebody today. He's definitely planning to kill me," he told Mamma. He didn't seem to realize or care that what he said would frighten his children, especially the younger ones.

Fed up, Mamma rolled her eyes. "It's all in your head. Why in God's name would he want to kill you? You're nobody."

"You think I'm nobody, eh, that I'm worthless. I've always known that's what you thought! But in this case, you're wrong. There is reason for me to worry. I've had my eyes open all these months and I know he's selling stolen meat out of there."

"And how do you know it's stolen?"

He waved his hand in dismissal. "You don't believe me anyway. I don't know why I bother telling you anything."

"So, if you've known all this time and haven't done anything about it why is he after you all of sudden?"

"I don't know. But I saw what I saw, and I heard what I heard."

"Well then, report him to the police."

He fixed her with narrowed eyes. "Either you're too stupid to understand or you want me to get killed. Right now, he's only threatening me but if I report him, I'm a dead man for sure." He leaned against the back of his chair and closed his eyes. "*Chi se ne frega si quishte qua me scanna?* Who cares if this guy cuts my throat? I know *you* don't care. What about you, Elvie, do you care what happens to me?"

His question made me jump. Why did he keep dragging me into their arguments? Why did he keep doing things that upset us? How much easier our lives would be if the butcher *did* kill him, I thought, then immediately regretted it. I must be a very bad person to wish my father dead, I thought.

As beautiful April arrived my father stopped talking and started hiding in the darkness of his bedroom whenever he was home. He cut the store's hours, and some days didn't go in at all. Business, never brisk, slowed down further. At some point he landed on a solution to his problem: me. All at once, I found myself with a part-time job I didn't want and for which he didn't pay: grocery clerk.

CHAPTER TWENTY-SEVEN

I worked at the store after school from 4 to 6 p.m. on Monday through Wednesday, until 9 p.m. on Thursdays and Fridays, and the whole day Saturday. Most of the time, as soon as I got there, my father hurried home. When I showed up for my first shift, I found him hiding behind the deli counter at the back of the store.

"Did you see anyone hanging outside the store?"

"No, Papà. There's no one outside."

"You're sure?"

"I'll look again if you want."

"Yes, look again. Look across the street, too."

I went to check it out. A few people walked past, minding their business.

"There's no one there, Papà."

" *Va buon.* Fine."

Only then would he come out from behind the protection of the deli counter and set about showing me how to work the cash register and deli meat slicer, where to find various products on the shelves, and how to lock up.

"Do your homework between customers, okay?" he said, and moved to the door. "If you have any problems phone me at home."

I stood in utter shock. "You're leaving me here alone?" Apart from the fact I wasn't sure I could work the register; it made me nervous to be alone in the store. What if a robber came in and held me up?

"Don't worry. It's not you the butcher wants to kill. You'll be fine."

Lucky for me, few customers came. Those who did bought small things: a loaf of bread, a soft drink, a candy bar. But the store's meagre incandescent lights cast shadows in the corners, seemingly got bigger every passing minute. The sun went down.

That first day and every day thereafter, I comforted myself by gobbling up candy, chocolate bars, jellybeans, ice-cream, potato chips and washed everything down with soft drinks—my favourite was Snow White cream soda. He never reprimanded me for helping myself and I thought maybe it was his way of paying me.

The unfairness of it all stoked my anger. My father had bought the store and now I had to pay for a bad decision he'd made. I also thought he might have made up the story about the butcher wanting to kill him to get out of having to work. The butcher didn't look threatening to me.

As I sat behind the counter between customers, I complained to God about having given me a bad father. Even when he tried to be playful, he hurt me. Sometimes he tickled me until I cried or rubbed his whiskers against my face and scraped my skin. He got special enjoyment out of pulling on my ears despite my pleas to stop. I had developed eczema on my forehead and behind my ears and when he pulled on my ears the sores cracked and blood trickled down my neck.

I worked at the store through the late spring, summer and fall of 1963.

My father's paranoia about his impending assassination by the butcher became so acute and he took to sleeping with an axe beside the bed, which further fed my anxiety over Mamma's safety and wrecked my sleep. I imagined waking up some morning to find her head split open.

"Aren't you afraid to lie next to him?" I asked Mamma.

"If I'm destined to die by his hand, so be it."

Her passivity infuriated me because it jeopardized not only her own well-being but ours. Didn't she care, I kept asking myself? She tried to reassure me by saying he was mentally ill, *afissato*, obsessed, fixated on his delusions.

Now that his fear of assassination had caused him to hole up in the house, Mamma tried hard to get him to see a doctor.

"I'm not crazy. I don't need a doctor. Don't you understand, you stupid woman? Somebody wants to kill me!"

His breaking point came in October. I came home from the store just after 6 to find an empty house when Mamma should have been in the kitchen making dinner, my siblings in front of the TV and my father hiding in his bedroom. I checked the backyard, peered into the shed but they weren't there either. Where could they be? Had he hurt them? The thought acted like a hand squeezing my heart. He couldn't hurt them, not all of them, would he?

I was about to go upstairs to Zia Tresa's to find out if she knew anything when I thought I heard someone call my name. I stopped, listening hard and soon heard it again, a feeble voice coming from my parents' room. The door had been left open and I peeked in. The curtains that separated it from the front parlour were drawn across the archway and with no other source of light, it was so dark I could make out nothing and no one.

"Elvie, is that you?"

I reached for the switch and flicked it on, but the room was empty.

"Elvie!" My father's voice.

"Where are you?"

"Under the bed!"

I knelt at the side of the bed and peered underneath. "What are you doing there, Papà?"

"Help me, Elvie."

"Take my hand. I'll help you out."

"No. I'm not coming out. That Jew came here today. I saw his face looking in through the window."

I bit my quivering lower lip. What should I do? Should I go get my aunt from upstairs? Where was Mamma anyway?

"If he was here, he's gone now, Papà. You can come out, I promise."

I'd decided to ask my aunt for help when Mamma came through the front door. Relief made me lightheaded as I raced to turn the problem over to her. Her face slackened more with each word I spoke.

"Where are the kids?"

"I don't know."

"Check upstairs and let me know. I'll deal with your father."

I found Teresa and Ricky at my aunt's, sitting at the supper table with them. Zia put out another plate and told me to sit down and eat. Not long after, Mamma came up, too.

"He won't come out." She was pale. Pale as the milk I poured over my cereal each morning, and so tired it made me want to cry.

"I'm not surprised," Zia Tresa said. "He's *pazzo,* crazy, like his father was." She filled a plate for Mamma, who swallowed a spoonful or two and pushed the food away. I, on the other hand, was ravenous.

"I don't know what to do," Mamma said, despairingly.

Zio Antonio, who been silent until now, someone who minded his own business, which was why he was one of the relatives still on speaking terms with my father. "Let me go and talk to him. Maybe he'll listen to me."

Zio and Mamma went downstairs with me trailing behind. Zio went into the bedroom by himself while the rest of us sat on the couch in the family room to await the outcome. I heard Zio's voice but what he said was drowned out by Zia's gruff, whispered accusations against my father's trustworthiness.

"Mark my words, he's up to something. He's got a goal in mind, and this is all playacting," she said to Mamma.

Who should I believe: Mamma, who said he was crazy and couldn't help himself or Zia who never believed a word that came out of my father's mouth?

Zio eventually got my father to come out from under the bed, had him lie down and covered him with a blanket. For the next few days, he seemed calmer, although he remained jumpy and fearful.

I overheard Mamma and Zia Tresa arguing though: "Throw him out. If you don't, he'll take that axe to you one of these days." I agreed with Zia.

"Yeah? You're a good one to talk," Mamma shot back. "Yours isn't a prize either, you know? He's liable to kill you during one of his drunk binges so why don't you throw *your* husband out? But you'd rather die than let *paesani* know your family isn't perfect."

"Well, drunk or not. *My* husband has never missed a day's work so, at least, my husband supports his family, and he doesn't interfere in how I run things."

In retrospect, even if Mamma had wanted to free herself from the man who dominated her body and soul, she had few doors open to her. As a Catholic, she'd absorbed the belief a woman was bound to her husband, no matter the circumstances, a notion reinforced by social conventions in Campochiaro where a married woman who left her husband was shunned. Such a woman would have no place to live and no way to make a living in an Italian mountain village. But although Mamma didn't spend much time at church since coming to Canada, its teachings were deeply ingrained and she now had the means to support herself and her children, in 1963 provincial law favoured my father. She couldn't get a bank loan or even signed a rental lease without his signature, and she would have lost everything she'd worked for, including any share of the house and other assets. As the head of the household and administrator of community assets, the husband could dispose of shared property as he saw fit.

My father never returned to the store after his breakdown, and neither did I. He sold the store soon after. Probably at a loss.

CHAPTER TWENTY-EIGHT

In 1963 the Quiet Revolution in Quebec started making noise as the separatist Marxist-Leninist FLQ acted on its earlier promise to use violence to free the French-speaking majority from the oppression by the English. April brought the first of wave of bombings with three Molotov cocktails at several Canadian military regiments in the province. Bombs exploded in Montreal on the CN Railway line and national revenue building, and one-hundred-fifty detonators and some fuses near the official residence of Quebec's lieutenant-governor. The words, *Liberte* and FLQ were painted on the front entrance and columns of the residence.

Police and various levels of government seemed incredulous: Canadian prime minister, John Diefenbaker remarked, "Is this Ireland?" and on April 3 the Montreal Gazette's front-page reportage was full of assurances by the various police forces that all would be well: "Montreal police, Quebec Provincial Police and the RCMP have combined their efforts in an attempt to bring to a quick end to the acts of sabotage, vandalism and bomb scare calls."

No injury or deaths occurred until April 20 when a security guard died in an explosion at Montreal's Canadian Armed Forces recruiting centre on Sherbrooke Street. Quebec officials were reluctant to lay the blame on the FLQ and fearing it might "provoke" them into more acts of aggression, while a leader of the *Rassemblement pour l'Indépendance Nationale*, a political organization working towards Quebec's independence, blamed the "indifference" of the provincial Liberal government to people's malaise for the unrest. A RIN organizer went so far as to accuse the RCMP and provincial police of setting the bombs to "frighten people away from independence."

In May the tone changed. The FLQ had placed fifteen dynamite bombs in residential mailboxes in the town of Westmount, a wealthy English-speaking enclave. A Sergeant Major Walter Lea, a Canadian army veteran and bomb disposal expert, was critically injured while trying to disarm one of the devices. The explosion blew off most of his left arm and crushing his face and chest. He survived but suffered brain damage, lost the ability to speak and was paralysed on his right side. The next day a front-page editorial in the Montreal Gazette remarked: "No longer can there be any hopes—slight as they ever were—that the terrorists, having caused their first death, might abandon their tactics." A few days later the city government offered a $10,000 reward and $50,000 reward from the province for information on the FLQ.

The first wave of violence came to an end in mid June after police arrested eighteen FLQ members in a surprise raid. Four of the men involved in the death of the security guard at the recruitment centre plead guilty to manslaughter and received sentences from six to twelve years in prison.

As a thirteen-year-old, I'd heard about the bombings, but it wasn't on the top of my mind, what with school and the ups and downs at home. I didn't watch the news or read newspapers and our teachers didn't raise the subject in class, at least not in the early 1960s. The threat to me didn't feel imminent, not like shudders that went through me when we faced the threat of nuclear war, and the air raid sirens came on.

I knew even less about the longing for the freedom Quebec nationalists determined to wrest for themselves. I might have taken an interest if I'd realized their aspirations were not too far removed from my desire to free myself from my father's iron grip and that, like me, they wanted to rid themselves of an oppressor.

To my surprise, my father, who had once paid close attention to political development took no interest now. He'd sunk into some kind of nether world that existed only in his own mind and said little. If I asked him questions, he told me not to bother him.

However, the quiet part of the Quiet Revolution hadn't gone away, in spite of the FLQ's attacks, which many Francophones abhorred, and pushed ahead with economic, social and cultural reforms under the Liberal government of Jean Lesage. In the 1960 election, the Liberals had campaigned with the slogan, *"Maîtres chez nous"* (Masters of our own house), and they set about delivering the promise.

The Liberal government's goal was for francophones to take leadership positions in Quebec and to guide the province into the future. In a few years after winning the election, the Liberal government established a public hospital network; created a ministry of cultural affairs; attacked the political patronage system that had kept the Union National party in power since the 1940s; changed the electoral map to give urban areas better representation and lowered the voting age to 18; wrested control of education from the Catholic Church and established a ministry of education; nationalized hydroelectricity and took control of Hydro-Quebec enormous resources, which became an important symbol for the Quiet Revolution; created the Quebec Pension Plan and added its own family allowance program to supplement the amount provided by federal government.

Quebec became a welfare state.

CHAPTER TWENTY-NINE

In June 1963, Grade 8 ended on a high note. Somehow my marks were high enough to land me in the enriched Grade 9 class. Having to work at the store likely accounted for the good result since having nothing better to do while waiting for customers, I did all my homework.

I thought I'd be spending another boring summer doing housework and babysitting while squeezing a bit of fun with Renee and a couple of other friends who lived close. Once again, my parents turned the tables on me: I was to go work at the factory with Mamma. My father wasn't working, and he'd be looking after Teresa, would be 8 in October, and Ricky, who would turn 6 in August.

"It's time for you to learn the value of a dollar, time you contribute something to your upkeep," he told me.

"I'm not allowed to work. I'm too young."

"That's where you're wrong. You can work at 14, and that's only a week away. It's all fixed."

"Why do I have to go to work when you don't?" The words had slipped out before I stopped to think about the consequences. One look at him told me I'd made a very big mistake and I recoiled. He reminded me of a TV program I'd seen on "Wild Kingdom" and the fierceness of the lion as it leapt on its prey.

I saw his hands start to remove his belt and I covered my head with my hands and closed my eyes in anticipation of the blows. But they didn't come.

"Get out of my sight, you ingrate!"

And I did.

Much later I understood he wanted me out of the house that summer not only for the little bit of money I would earn but to curtail my freedom. It seemed to bother him seeing me around the neighbourhood boys as much as he resented Mamma speaking to any man, strangers or family. In fact, I'd noticed him spying on me from the parlour window. Whenever I talked to Tullio or Peter, who lived on each side of us, he'd come out and order me indoors. It embarrassed and humiliated me when he did that, not that he cared.

I went to work with Mamma at Fashion Fit Lingerie, a lingerie factory. I'd promised myself as 6-year-old I'd never work in a factory after my father had first threatened to pull me out of school if my marks didn't improve. Fashion Fit was a small, family business belonging to Mr. and Mrs. Weldon, and it employed a mere handful of machine operators. They made fancy slips, filmy sleepwear, and panties.

Mrs. Weldon gave me a small pair of scissors and put me to work at a long finishing table snipping the long threads that dangled from the ends of seams. Time crawled, it hovered, it stood still but it refused to move ahead at the pace I would have wanted. Its slowness made me want to run screaming round and round that table. Only after the day ended and I got outside did breathing get easier.

Nevertheless, after a week's work, I was thrilled when Mrs. Weldon handed me a pay envelope containing $7.50 in cash—which worked out to about 18 cents an hour. I was so happy I skipped home, letting Mamma trail behind me, thinking about what I should spend the money on. A new book? A game of Pick-Up Sticks? The pair of pearl-encrusted hair barrettes I'd admired at Kresge's?

I found my father sitting on the front stoop, and I wondered why. He didn't like to be seen by the neighbours as a rule. He made room for Mamma to go inside and invited me to sit down next to him, which made me wary.

"So, you got paid today," he said, smiling.

"Yes." I said, hugging my purse inside of which nestled my first pay envelope.

"How much did you earn?"

"$7.50."

"Not bad." He gazed at the empty field across the street, saying nothing more, waiting, waiting.

As the silence stretched, it hit me like a dodge ball to the head what he was waiting for. My insides turned hot and scorched me as it moved outward toward the surface of my skin. He wanted my money and I felt outraged. Why should I have to give him the first few dollars I'd ever earned? The measly $7.50 wouldn't make much difference to him but it seemed a fortune to me especially since the pair of them never provided any of the extras most of my friends got from their parents.

He wanted the money because he believed that he owned us, his family, and everything that belonged to us in fact belonged to him.

I remained quiet for some time, and he let me think it through, knowing he would prevail because I had no way to stop him. No matter what I said or did, he would take my money because he could.

Close to tears, I took the pay envelope out of my purse. "Here," I said, thrusting it at him.

"I'm glad you made the right decision."

"What would have happened if I hadn't?" My question displayed a boldness I expressed more and more often. I had never hated and resented him as much as I did in that moment.

He tilted my chin upward, usually a prelude to a lecture. "Everybody has to contribute, Elvie." He kept his voice soft, his expression benign.

This time when he turned his gaze on me, I didn't look away. Instead, I stared into his eyes, the same shape, the same milk-chocolate colour as mine, and let him see my hatred. "Everybody? No, not everybody.

Especially not children. My friends' fathers haven't sent them to work in a factory. You did, though, and now you're taking my money, too."

"Don't you take my money when I feed you, clothe you and pay for the roof over your head?"

"You're my father! It's your job to take care of me. Besides, you're not working, are you? Mamma pays for everything."

His doughy features hardened and I prepared myself for a slap. But he didn't hit me.

"How much do you want for yourself?" His voice had the sharp edge he used when he spoke to Mamma.

The offer caught me unprepared. I hadn't expected him to let me keep any of it. How much should ask for? If I asked for an amount he considered too high, he'd make me pay for it in some other way; if I asked for too little, I'd be the loser.

"Well?"

"I don't know. You decide."

"Oh, no. I don't want to hear any complaints later that I've been unfair. No, you tell me what you think is the right amount."

I wanted it all. Every penny, but to avoid potential reprisals I erred on the very low side. "50 cents?"

Nodding, he slipped the two quarters out of the envelope and handed them over then took out the bills, put them in his pocket and gave me back the empty envelope to put in the trash.

Later that evening, when he made me walk to the convenience store to buy him a pack of cigarettes, he handed me the fiver he'd taken from me. I fumed all the way to the store and back and for days afterwards I wished him dead. Over and over, I imagined him dying in all sorts of horrific ways and very, very soon. I knew wishing my father dead was a mortal sin, that it put a big stain on my immortal soul, but I didn't mind going to Hell when I died sometime in the future, if only God would take him now while I was alive.

Like Mamma and her responsibility for running the household, the fact I now had a day job didn't wipe away my weekend chores. I bristled to see my unemployed father lounging on the couch while Mamma and I and even Teresa scurried around changing beds, doing laundry, sweeping floors, dusting. Mamma nagged him to do things, to fix this or that because he was handy with his hands, but he rarely did.

At the factory, day after day I watched Mamma as droplets of sweat dripped off her face; I watched her at home as she got on her knees to scrub the floor and asked myself how she could bear to lie next to him at night. As she turned grey with work and worry before my eyes, I vowed I wouldn't submit to any man that way she did. Better to be poor, better to be alone, better to be dead than put up with such indignities.

As Mamma kept telling me when I groused about him, my father was sick in his head. "He doesn't know what he's doing when he's like that."

I accepted my father's odd behaviour like when he hid under the bed or when he'd thought the butcher was coming to kill him. Was due to mentally illness, as Mamma insisted, but sick in the head or not, taking a kid's first pay proved to me he was also a selfish, unkind man.

CHAPTER THIRTY

By the summer of 1963, my father had improved enough to take on a few hauling jobs with his truck. I couldn't decide whether I preferred it when he was withdrawn and left me alone or when he got better and interfered in my life. That summer, without asking me whether I had any interest in it or not he signed me up for piano lessons.

"Imagine yourself on stage, a celebrated musician. Wouldn't you like that?" he said when I expressed doubt.

He begun to express grand ambitions for me, his eldest. Now approaching his 40s and hope fading for achieving fame and fortune in his own life fading, he thought he could still achieve the high life through me.

An able salesman that he was, he worked hard to get me to buy into his own dream of musical acclaim, embellishing and polishing it day and day. I turned 14 the summer of 1963 and still a child and so despite my animosity towards him, what child doesn't want to please her father in the hope that he would love me better and treat me with kindness.

Besides, I had plenty of imagination—if not musical talent—and came round to his way of thinking. I pictured myself lit up on a stage, audiences on their feet celebrating my great talent, as he described. Not to mention all the money I would earn—and which he no doubt planned to enjoy, too.

Without telling Mamma, he bought a second-hand, upright piano, knowing she wouldn't have agreed to the purchase. She came home from work to find it in the front parlour. pushed against the wall.

"Take it back!" she said, red in the face. "I'm working to keep food on the table and you go out to buy a piano!"

"Listen, listen to me," he said, linking his arm into hers and gently drawing her away from the offensive sight. He talked and talked and talked until she so wearied of listening to his arguments she threw in the towel. She never bought into his fantasy life for me because she understood my character better than he did; I didn't have the drive or the discipline for music.

My piano lessons took place on Saturday mornings, and I was supposed to practice a couple of hours every day at home. For someone who didn't always do her homework because I found more interesting things to do, sitting still and practicing endless scales didn't appeal to me so when Renee or Rose Marie knocked on the front parlour window inviting me to join them, I cut my practices short, and later lied to my father about completing my practice.

My father worked hard to keep me interested in his dream for me, refreshing the image of success at regular intervals. "Your teacher says you have talent. You just have to focus, Elvie! And practice, practice some more. If you do that, you'll end up on the Ed Sullivan Show."

I don't know how my parents scraped the money together to pay for the lessons, although Mamma was genius when it came to stretching a dollar. Had I been given a choice I would rather have spent that money on nice clothes.

As Mamma had anticipated, the piano lessons didn't work out. With each passing week I spent less and less time on the piano bench and my father spent more and more time haranguing me about it. The issue came to a head one Saturday morning in mid-November. I was about to head out for the weekly lesson.

He stopped me on the verandah at the back, a shortcut I used to get to the music lesson on Bernard. "Listen, Elvie, I know I push you hard, but you need to learn discipline. You have none, you know."

I yearned to spit back: *I have about as much discipline as you do*, but wisely swallowed the retort. Instead, I said, "I don't think piano is for me, Papà."

He put a hand on my shoulder. "I want what's best for you. I want you to succeed in life." He wore a peculiar expression, I thought, kind of sappy.

"But there's lots of things I can do, Papà. Why does it have to be piano?"

"What would you rather do?" He caressed my cheek with the back of his hand, which made me feel self-conscious, although I couldn't have said why.

"I don't know yet," I said, taking a half-step back.

He dropped his hand. "*Va buon.* Fine," he said after a long pause. "Today will be your last lesson. Does that make you happy?"

My broad smile reflected the relief that washed over me.

"You're a beauty when you smile like that." He drew me closer. "Do you love me, Elvie?"

His words sent a frisson of apprehension up and down my spine. My smile ebbed as his eyes pinned me to the spot, making me blush.

I looked away. "Yes, Papà" I had no talent for lying; it always showed on my face. How I wished I had a father I could love but this man, the one I'd been given, no, I couldn't love him. I feared him, especially his unpredictability.

The unaccustomed softness in his voice remained. "Okay. Go for your last lesson since it's paid for."

As I turned to leave, he touched my arm. "Give me a kiss before you go."

He kissed me on the lips and held the contact a second too long. I pulled away and ran off, feeling confused. The kiss meant my father loved me, didn't it? Then why did I feel as though I'd done something wrong? It was just a kiss, I reasoned, and forced the incident down into deep caverns of my mind where I stored things I didn't ever want to think about again.

When I got home after the lesson, Mamma, who'd been out grocery shopping, was pacing, waiting for me. She ran to my side and threw her arms around me.

"Are you alright? Has that bastard done anything to you?"

"What do you mean?" I knew what she meant. But how did she know?

She gripped my upper arms. "Tell me! Has that bastard ever touched you? Has he hurt you?"

"No!"

She told me Zia Tresa had been sitting out on her verandah, which just above ours, had overheard our conversation and hadn't liked it. It had worried her enough that she decided to tell Mamma.

"No, Ma, he hasn't done anything to me. I promise. He gave me a kiss before I went for my lesson but that's all." I didn't mention how the kiss had felt nor did I say he'd sought my company more than usual lately, wanting to talk, wanting to play cards. He'd even taken me to a movie starring Brigitte Bardot one Sunday, just the two of us.

"You can tell me the truth, Elvie. I swear to God I won't be mad at you."

"No, Ma, he hasn't done anything to me."

"Swear to God."

"I swear to God."

She hugged me tight. "Why did I ever agree to marry that miserable excuse for a human being?"

Unfortunately for him, my father came into the house entered from the backyard just then. The second he stepped into the kitchen she ran and threw herself at him, trying to rake her fingers down his face as he fought to keep her at arm's length.

"Are you nuts? What the fuck are you doing?"

"You—you disgusting excuse for a human being. It's not enough that you cheated on me while we were engaged and God knows how many women you've fucked since. Now you want to corrupt your own daughter?"

"You really are crazy!"

"Crazy, am I? Maria Tresa heard you! Besides, I know you. I know you have no shame, no morals. Hear me now! If you lay a finger on her, I will cut your throat. I may be wishy-washy about lots of things, *farabutto*, you scoundrel, but this promise you can count on."

My mother didn't, or wouldn't, fight for her own well-being but she'd do anything to protect her children—everything except leave him, I thought miserably.

The veranda incident was the first and last time my father made any such approach. That night and the next Mamma slept with my sister and me because she—the long-suffering wife—couldn't bear the sight of him, let alone lie next him for a short time.

I have often wondered whether my father had, in fact, begun a campaign to groom me with sexual intent or whether he hoped to find in me a potential companion to relieve his loneliness and isolation. Whatever his intentions, Mamma's clear reaction helped me sort out my ambivalent feelings: I couldn't trust my father in any way.

CHAPTER THIRTY-ONE

As if things weren't already chaotic enough in our household, the summer of 1963 dropped a new player into our lives that served as a fresh log to the steady burn in our hearth.

My maternal grandmother, 55, Filomena, recently widowed, joined her four daughters in Canada. Before she even got off the ship, my father observed, "It's going to be war," he said. The man had plenty of flaws but like any good manipulator, he had a talent for reading people.

She came to live in Montreal where three of her daughters lived. As she had with Zia Tresa and her family, once again, Zia Carmelina took it upon herself to sponsor Nonna's immigration, and she lived with Zia Carmelina's family for a year after her arrival.

Nonna landed with a steamer trunk filled with gifts for her daughters and eight grandchildren. She handed out gold bracelets and lots of other pretty things, which predisposed me to like her. But before long, Nonna had us at each other's throats: husband against wife, sister against sister, family against family.

After living with Zia Carmelina's family for a year, Mamma and Zia Tresa had to take their turns housing her. She left Zia Carmelina's and moved in with Zia Tresa upstairs, but since our two households lived upstairs/downstairs, In the guise of helping out both her working daughters, she came and went as she pleased, took control of both households and was vocal about how adults and children alike should behave. This infuriated her sons-in-law and caused friction between the spouses.

Nonna Filomena was incapable of minding her own business, in spite of her daughters' pleas. When husband and wife argued, she took sides; she told tales about what happened in one household to the other and she played favourites, awarding top spot to Zia Tresa and her children, which set the three sisters against each other.

"Don't provoke him," Mamma begged Nonna.

"I don't care if he gets mad. I'm not afraid of him."

"But you're not the one that has to pay the price, are you?"

Nonna nagged and bullied me, the eldest of her grandchildren, in part because I didn't fit the mould of how a good Italian girl should behave, whereas my upstairs cousin Liliana, with her dutiful, housewife-in-training ways did.

"Get your nose out of that book and help your mother," was Nonna's constant refrain.

However, Nonna was no slacker when it came to work. By then Zia Tresa had found a job in one of the factories on Saint-Viateur and Nonna cooked and cleaned for both our families as well as minding Zia Tresa's 4-year-old Lucia.

Mamma had been defending Nonna against my father's attacks, and my complaints about her interference and meanness when things took a sudden turn.

The incident took place on a weekday when the adults were at work and we kids were amusing ourselves outdoors. Nonna was alone in our flat when, as happened from time to time as her employer didn't have enough work to keep all the operators busy, Mamma was sent home early and found Nonna going through the big metal trunk where she stored lingerie she'd accumulated from Fashion Fit over the years. Most of the pieces were damaged in some way—a small oil stain from the sewing machine or a nick in the fabric—although Mamma had, in fact, stolen some of the pieces and justified the thefts by saying her employer exploited her and it was her way of getting a fair wage.

Nonna had put aside a pile of nicely folded panties, slips and nightgowns.

Our front door was open and I heard Mamma's shout, "What are you doing?"

Mamma hated confrontations—Teresa had inherited the trait—and avoided them but she did blow a fuse from time to time.

"You don't need all this. I was going to give a few things to Maria Tresa," Nonna replied.

"*Come it permetti*? How dare you?" Mamma said. "Put it all back."

In a huff, my grandmother picked up the pile and threw the items into the open trunk and stalked out of the house and went upstairs, emptyhanded. Mamma went through the trunk and realized this wasn't the first time her mother had picked through the chest and given her things away.

What a relief to get back to school in September and get away from the old witch, as Teresa and I referred to her. World-changing events were on the horizon and on Nov. 22, 1963, while our class was frolicking in the gym, outfitted in ridiculous teddies and bloomer, the principal's sombre voice announced via the public-address system that John F. Kennedy, the young, charismatic 35th president of the United States, had been assassinated, shot dead.

We looked at each other in utter confusion, and I remembered that John F. Kennedy had been the president fighting with the Russians the previous year when we'd all been scared out of our wits about nuclear detonation. Did that mean we'd have to worry bombs dropping on us all over again?

The gym teacher cut short the class and sent us back to the classroom and our home room teacher, Mother St. Bernard. She sounded bleak when she said, "For the rest of your lives, girls, you will remember this day. You'll remember where you were and what you were doing the day President Kennedy died."

And I do.

John F. Kennedy was the first world figure murdered in the television age. I sat on the floor in front of the TV, as did millions the world over, watching Kennedy's fatal car ride in Dallas replayed again and again. His motorcade inching along Dealey Plaza, his waves to a cheering crowd, how he suddenly slumped against the rear seat of his open car.

My father, too, looked stricken. He had admired the way Kennedy had stood up to the Soviets over Cuba. In a TV address, Canadian prime minister Lester Pearson called the loss of Kennedy "One of the great tragedies of history. But for us, now, it is something more – it is a great, heartbreaking, personal tragedy."

Even as a 14-year-old with no understanding of the assassination's political implications of the assassination, I was affected by global reaction on TV as people wept openly in the streets. Kennedy must have been a very great man, I thought, if people who'd never even met him cared that much.

Meanwhile, at home, tensions grew and grew when it came to our turn to have Nonna living with us in the fall. The hatred between her and my father crackled through the air when they found themselves in the same room with Mamma trying to run interference while Teresa and I did our best to ignore the noise as we watched TV or took cover in our shared bedroom and shut the door.

Although Nonna now showed her contempt for my father in every word and gesture, Mamma said she hadn't always felt that way about her son-in-law. In fact, she claimed Nonna had pushed her into marrying him, despite other suitors, because she'd liked his easy charm and was fond of his kind-hearted, widowed mother and three hard-working sisters. Mamma a respectful and obedient daughter, said she did her mother's bidding. Nonna denied her role in the marriage, but I believed

Mamma. I had never warmed to Nonna but I stopped trusting her ever since she'd stolen from us.

The tension burst out of control in December.

CHAPTER THIRTY-TWO

It was about a week before Christmas, and we sat around the supper table eating a meal Nonna had prepared. Whatever her flaws, Nonna was a remarkable cook, although I for one would have her meals much more if she hadn't rattled on and on as we ate, often to chastise us kids.

Unfortunately, that day she aimed her lance at my father. "And when are you going to get a proper job? Don't you feel any shame at all that your wife works like a dog to support you while you sit around reading magazines?"

My father looked up from his plate, his expression ominously blank. "You need to shut up and mind your own business, old woman."

Nonna didn't know him as well as we did or didn't care. "You can threaten me but I'm not afraid of you even if my daughter is."

"Ma, that's enough," Mamma warned.

"Well, somebody has to talk straight to him if you won't. He's no good, like the rest of his clan."

We three kids had stopped eating. Teresa, who sat next to me, put down her fork. I felt her shudder and she looked towards me, her eyes wide with terror. For once, Ricky was quiet, too. I would have given anything for silence, but the arguing continued, their ugly voices burrowed into my ears and into my brain.

My father's stood up, and I noticed his eyes had that dreadful faraway look. Mamma saw it too and jumped to her feet.

"*Basta*! Enough. This is none of your business, Ma, so just keep quiet."

"Well, that's the thanks I get for trying to help you," Nonna replied, wiping her mouth. "Fine, I'll shut up. Be my guest, wallow in your misery."

Mamma sat down again but my father did not. He stood rigid, staring at Nonna with flames of rage making his eyes glitter. "I don't want you in my house. Get out."

I sat mesmerized by the rapid throb of a vein on his neck.

"This is my daughter's house even more than yours since she pays the bills. I'm not going anywhere."

The effort it took to keep himself from striking out showed in the set of his jaw and fists pressed hard against his thighs. Nonna, however, appeared unperturbed while the rest of us held our breaths and waited to find out whether blood would flow.

"You've been warned," he said, and left the kitchen.

The meal ended in silence. I did the dishes, then I escaped upstairs to Zia's and sat around watching TV with Liliana and stayed there as late as they let me. I went home at 10 p.m. after the program ended and was relieved to see my parents sitting quieting in front of the TV. He watched the screen, while Mamma busied herself with a crochet hook and a skein of fine white cotton thread. They'd made peace. Teresa and Ricky had gone to bed.

"You're back late. You're supposed to be in bed by 10 o'clock," my father said.

"I stayed to watch the end of the program."

"Nobody pays any attention to what I say in this fucking household." He spoke not with anger but with bitterness. "Go to bed."

I got into bed with Teresa and Nonna—there was nowhere else for Nonna to sleep when she stayed with us. I didn't like having her living with us any more than my father did and if, like my cousins upstairs, I'd shown her some affection she might have liked me more. But I didn't have it in me to pretend to like her whereas my cousins loved her. She'd raised them in Italy from the time they were born until they came to Canada four years earlier.

I was on the verge of falling sleep when my father started shouting, "I want her out of here."

"She's not going anywhere!"

"If she doesn't leave, I won't be responsible for what happens."

"What? You'll kill us all?"

At the smack of a hand striking skin and the cry that followed, I threw off the covers and rushed towards my parents' room, Nonna at my heels and hysterical, crying, "*O dio, O dio*, he's going to kill her!" as Mamma came running out of their bedroom with my father chasing her.

The moment my father caught sight of Nonna, he went purple and what ensued was a script for a farce.

"I want you out of this house right now!" he yelled at Nonna.

"*Vaffanculo*! Fuck you!" my grandmother shouted back.

In one quick move, he pushed Mamma out of his way, grabbed Nonna's arm and began pulling her down the hall toward the front door. She was a tiny woman, barely five feet tall but stout, and she resisted with all her might, yelling, "*Aiutami!* Help me!"

Paralyzed, I pressed myself against a wall. By then, Teresa had awakened, and she pressed herself against the wall, crying. Ricky, who slept on a cot in the front parlour, stood in next to the inner front door, scared but silent.

To get him to release Nonna, Mamma grabbed hold of his arm. "Leave her alone! Leave her alone!"

My father, now enraged and out of control, released his hold on Nonna, turned and punched Mamma in the face, twice, while Nonna, barefooted ran out of the house in the freezing cold—it was December—and frantically, repeatedly pressed the upstairs buzzer to my aunt's flat.

"Stop it! Stop it! Stop it!" I screamed at my father. My insides jiggled like the strawberry Jell-O I loved.

When my father turned his head to me, Mamma made her escape and ran for the front door. Breathing hard, he didn't try to stop her but took one last dig. "I really should have let you hang yourself when you got up on that chair all those years ago."

Her hand on the doorknob, she stopped dead, turned and gave him a frigid stare. Then she spat at him, "And that's more than you're worth."

"Get out, and take the other two with you," he said to me.

I took Teresa's hand and tugged her away from the wall where she'd sought safety and hurried past our father towards Mamma who stood waiting at the door, which was near the front parlor, and had Ricky holding onto to her. We filed out into a freezing December night. Mamma shut the door behind us, and we trudged up the stairs to Zia Tresa.

Zia Tresa's husband, Zio Antonio, stood waiting at the top of the stairs. "What's happened?"

"He threw us out," Mamma said.

"I'll go talk to him."

"You can try but he's in no mood to talk."

We'd awakened the whole household and they all stood around in the family room, directly above ours, recounting, and with relish, what had just occurred.

Zio Antonio, put on his coat and shoes and went down talk to my father but soon returned. "The door's locked and he's not answering."

"Well, that's that for now," Zia Tresa said and went about organizing sleep arrangements.

Mamma and Nonna slept in the bed Liliana and her little sister used, and Liliana, Teresa and I slept on the floor in the front parlour with layers thick wool blankets under and over us. Ricky got the sofa and my cousin, Pat, slept where he always did, in the tiny area that corresponded to our mudroom, off their front balcony. That room was unbearably cold in winter but Pat hadn't minded.

By the time we settled down, it was midnight, and that's when my father started making a racket downstairs. It sounded as though he was smashing furniture with an axe, and it went on so long we all got up again. Zia Tresa sent Zio down to see if he could get my father to answer the doors but, again, he ignored the knock.

Mamma was frantic, afraid he'd destroy the little we had. The adults put their heads together and after a great deal of discussion—they were worried about saving face for the family—decided to call the police. I was told to make the call.

CHAPTER THIRTY-THREE

My father was still hammering away when two officers in uniform showed up. With me translating, they questioned each of the adults, and then me since I was the eldest and I'd witnessed the melee.

I told them my father hit my mother, pointing to her swelling lip and bruised eye, that he'd threatened my grandmother and then kicked us all out. I told them we thought he was destroying the contents of our home and that we were afraid to return even in the unlikely event he'd let us in.

"We didn't have a chance to take anything with us. We don't have a key."

"Ask your mother if she's willing to press charges, otherwise there isn't a lot we can do since this is a domestic matter between husband and wife," one of the officers explained.

At that time, domestic violence was considered a private matter. In Québec, battered and abused women had to wait until 1986 for a modicum of relief. Only then did the law affirm the *criminal* nature of domestic violence. The new policy also lowered the province's "social tolerance" for such behaviour; police and courts got more discretionary power to arrest and prosecute serious cases even in the face of a victim's unwillingness to testify against her abuser.

"Will he go to jail?" my grandmother wanted to know.

"If *Madame* presses charges," he said, "he will be arrested and charged. If he pleads not guilty, he will go to trial where a judge will listen to the evidence and decide if he's guilty or innocent. A trial means you and your mother and grandmother will have to testify in court."

"Ask them if they would arrest him now if I agree to do whatever he said," Mamma asked.

"Yes, right now," the senior officer responded.

The adults talked among themselves weighing the best course of action. Their biggest worry was how much damage he'd do to the house if they didn't stop him.

"Yes, I want him to go to jail," Mamma said.

The police officers went downstairs. I stood at the bottom of my aunt's stairs with the front door ajar to listen. At first, my father didn't answer but opened up when one officer gave the door a good pounding. I heard the inner door creak. Then, my father opened the main door.

The officers identified themselves. He let them in, the door closed and after that only murmurs were heard. I waited at the foot of the stairs in my cousin's coat to be sure they took him away.

And they did.

I watched from Zia's doorway as police escorted him to the cruiser, praying he'd never come back but knowing he would. We were stuck with him. Mamma had taken a bold step that night by agreeing to press charges, but she'd done it in a fog of anger. I knew her well enough to expect that once rage cooled, he'd come home begging forgiveness, sad and puppy-eyed and she would forgive him. Mamma would never leave him.

I returned upstairs and confirmed they'd taken him away.

"Maybe this'll teach him a lesson," Zia Tresa said.

"That bastard?" my grandmother scoffed. "He was born bad, and he'll die bad."

"If he was so bad, why did you push me to marry him?" Mamma retorted. Her eyes glowed like hot coals.

"Don't put this on me! You agreed to marry him."

"Only after you hounded me."

"*Abashta.* Enough. What's done is done," my aunt said. "It's late. Let's all go to bed. We have work in the morning."

Liliana, Teresa and I returned to our makeshift bed on the floor. It gave me pleasure to think of my father forced to obey the police. I hoped it would give him a taste of what it felt like to be squashed under someone's thumb. I hoped he was frightened, as frightened as he'd made us. That night I asked God to give Mamma the courage to leave him, so we'd never have to obey him again.

Next morning, we missed school because we couldn't get into the house to get our clothes and schoolbags. My mother borrowed ill-fitting clothes from my aunt and went to work. "I can't lose a day's pay, especially now. God only know how this will end," she said.

The relief from my father's arrest didn't last 24 hours. By midday, we heard movement downstairs. "Did you hear that?" my grandmother cried in disbelief. "It can't be him, can it?"

We waited and listened hard, hoping we'd misheard. But, no, somebody was moving around down there.

"Ricky, go peek through the back yard," my grandmother said to my brother.

"What if he sees me and gets mad?"

"It's not you he's mad at," she assured him. "If he sees you, tell him you want to go in 'cause you kids need your school clothes."

My brother reported my father indeed was in the kitchen making something to eat.

When Mamma got home from work and heard he'd been released, she paled. After supper, my uncle volunteered to talk to my father, assess his state of mind and see what could be worked out.

"At least, try to talk him into letting them get some clothes," my aunt said.

This time my father let him in, and he returned with good news. "He'll let the kids go get whatever you need. But he won't let *you* into the house," he told Mamma.

She shrugged. "How did he get out of jail so fast?"

"Guilio bailed him out."

"That bastard, Guilio! I guess crooks look after each other."

My mother gave me a list of things we'd need for the next few days, and I went down with my cousin, Liliana, to get them. We found the front door unlocked and with trepidation went inside. After all the noise he'd made, I expected to find the furniture in pieces but everything looked normal. What had he done to cause that smashing noise? Had it only been to get attention?

My father sat on the couch in the family room staring at the TV screen. His haze had turned inward. He didn't speak, nor did we. We grabbed what we needed and hurried back upstairs.

My mother and Zia Tresa were chatting in the kitchen.

"I shouldn't have called the police," I overheard Mamma say. "Since Guilio got him out of jail, every *paesano* here and in Italy will soon know all about it. How can I show my face?"

Her words immobilized me. I wanted to beat her with a fist as my father had done to her. She cared more for her reputation than for our wellbeing, I thought, with disappointment, resentment, and anger. Did she want to die by his hand? He'd threatened to do that often enough.

"I can only imagine the gossip," my aunt replied. "That husband of yours has ruined our family's reputation."

The ex-pat Campochiaro community in Montreal would indeed talk. For a wife to turn on her husband to the point of having him arrested came close to unforgivable. This prohibition was among many held by our *paesani.* They might have physically relocated to a new country, but they held on dearly to the customs and beliefs of the old country, frozen in the medieval attitudes of their impoverished villages.

Another few days went by. After supper my uncle would go downstairs to ask my father to let us come home. I was resigned to the inevitable. If Mamma hadn't intended to return, she'd already be making other plans.

"I don't want to go back there, Ma," I told Mamma on the fourth evening.

"No? You think getting away from him is as easy as that?"

"Yes."

She sighed. "You see everything in black and white, Elvie. But life is complicated. How would we manage? He's probably already taken money out of our bank account by now. He may be sick in the head but he's not stupid."

"It's not complicated. You're the one who works and you're the one who pays all the bills. We can rent a place. I'll get a part-time job; I'll help. We don't need him, Ma."

"Leaving your husband is a shameful thing."

Frustration made me raise my voice. "He's the one who should be ashamed for what he does to you, to all of us."

She confirmed my fear that she would take us back into that cauldron of tension and abuse, and at his convenience. Couldn't she see he'd let us return because he needed her to support him, not the other way around? He needed her to pay the bills and he needed his children to boss around, which made him feel like the king of his domain. If I had the wit to understand this, why didn't Mamma? Had she no pride? No self-respect?

On the fifth day of our exile, my uncle returned from his latest talk with my father to announce he'd take us back.

"Of course, he is," I said. "He's probably tired of cooking for himself." No one reprimanded me.

"He's in a bad way," my uncle said.

"Good," Nonna piped up. Where my father was concerned, she would have liked to gut him like a fish and smile while doing it.

"He's not making much sense," my uncle said. "That trip to jail scared the shit out of him and now he's going on about somebody he met in jail who threatened him. He's scared the guy is going to find him and kill him."

"That's nothing new," I chimed in. "He's always going on about how somebody's spying on him or out to kill him."

My uncle turned to me. "Listen, he's still your father. He hasn't moved from that couch and hasn't eaten in days."

"I don't believe it," I said. "He just wants us to feel sorry for him."

"I'm just telling you what he said. It's up to your mother to decide with to do."

I almost laughed. I already knew what Mamma would do. Neither Zia Tresa nor Nonna offered a single word to encourage her to save herself.

"Where will you go if you don't go back, a woman alone with three children?" Zia pointed out. "Besides, if you don't go back, he'll sell the house from under you and you'll be left with nothing."

The house meant a lot to Mamma, more than her children's mental health or her own.

"Go back, *figlia mea*, daughter," pronounced Nonna. "At least you'll have a roof over your head. You have too much to lose, otherwise."

CHAPTER THIRTY-FOUR

Mamma took us home; we couldn't impose on Zia Tresa's family much longer.

We found my father slumped on the couch, looking haggard. He didn't utter a word. Nor did we. In fact, a week went by before my parents spoke to each other. But gradually, the old household pattern resumed. Mamma worked, my father contributed nothing but tried to call the shots. The result: constant argument.

Tension seeped back into the house like smoke slipping under a door. Besides, he hadn't forgiven Mamma for having him arrested, even though she'd withdrawn the charges. His resentment showed in every glance, every word he said to her. I noticed with pleasure, however, that Mamma's fuse was much shorter and she snapped at him if she bothered to respond at all. Something had definitely shifted in her attitude, and it gave me hope.

As for me, I rebuffed his every overture at making peace. Whenever he came into the room, the hairs on my arms stood up. The sight of him, let alone the thought of engaging in the friendly conversation he wanted, repulsed me, and I didn't hide it. I stopped addressing him as "Papà." Teresa and I, out of earshot, labelled him "The old man."

Time and again, he wandered into the kitchen where I did my homework. "Elvie, why won't you speak to me? I'm sorry I hit your mother, but she got between me and that witch."

"I have nothing to say," I replied, head down.

"You're not being very respectful. I'm still your father whether you like it or not. Children have a duty to respect their elders."

"Like everybody else, parents have to earn respect."

He didn't give up, and I wouldn't bend. I was only14. Because Mamma was too insecure and too ashamed to leave him, we all had to live under the same roof. But I wouldn't pretend I liked it—or him.

For Christmas Eve Mamma readied a feast of the usual fish dishes, and for Christmas Day, pasta and roasted meats. After dinner, all but my father—Nonna and he couldn't stand to be in the same room together, and he knew he wouldn't be welcome—trooped upstairs to Zia's to play tombola until well past midnight.

When school resumed in January, my father fell deeper and deeper into silence. Sometimes he retreated to bed the whole day. I didn't care. My teenaged passion had veered to outright hatred. If he stayed in bed, I didn't have to look at his face or listen to his voice. By February, he wouldn't leave his bedroom. My mother wanted him to see a doctor, but he refused.

I thought less and less of her for showing concern. "After everything he's done to you, to us, why don't you just let him rot?"

My words saddened her. "He's my husband and he's sick. I know he's done terrible things, but he's a human being. You're young. One day you'll understand that life isn't black and white."

But it was Mamma who didn't understand. She didn't understand my character. I'd wanted my father's love and approval and tried hard to get it despite everything he'd said and done to hurt and disappoint me. The night he'd hit Mamma with his fist, not once but twice, and then thrown us out into the literal cold was the night my father had crossed the last line. That night I finished with him, and that didn't change until the day he died.

At her wit's end and not knowing what else to do, Mamma called on several of his cousins, people he trusted, to talk to him. They came willingly, more than once, sitting beside him, slowly coaxing him out of bed until he joined them at the kitchen table. It must have helped him to know they cared, or maybe talking to them clarified his thoughts about the future. In either case, in the course of a few weeks, he improved.

As spring approached, my parents spent a lot of time talking in whispers. I took no interest. I figured whatever plans they were cooking up they wouldn't take my wishes or needs into account. When they revealed what they'd worked out, the news had me floating off the floor with happiness.

In mid-March, my father announced his plans: "I'm leaving. I'm going home to Italy where I belong. This country—well, I don't fit here."

I stared at him, hoping he meant it. "Please, please let it be true."

"For how long?" my brother asked. He was upset to lose his father.

At 6 years old, my brother had already exhibited behavioural problems. I caught him stealing money from my wallet and from Mamma's purse. When confronted he deployed the same non-answers and change-the-subject techniques my father used when caught red-handed in a lie.

Those thefts were the earliest hint Ricky shared my father's mental-health problems. Did he model himself on my father, growing up in our chaotic, dysfunctional home? Or did he inherit the same bad genes my father had inherited from *his* father—a man whose reputation had been bad? Likely both.

"How long? I don't know, Ricky. Maybe a very long time."

Let it be forever, I prayed. If my father had detected my joy at his imminent departure, he would have pulled off his belt and beaten me to a pulp.

I scoured Mamma's face to assess her state of mine: it drooped with sadness. I couldn't—no I wouldn't—understand her. Shouldn't she feel relief to be free of him?

I didn't understand that her sadness stemmed from a sense of failure, from lost hope. She had left her home for a new country expecting a better life. Instead of opportunities, her relocation had delivered backbreaking work and a broken family. Now she'd have to raise three children with no husband or support from her wide circle of family and friends back in Campochiaro.

Soon after, my father put the word out to *paesani* that our duplex was on the market. Another Italian family bought it, although they weren't Molisani. The sale closed at the end of April.

I never learned whether my father made a profit from the sale or how much money, if any, he gave Mamma. Given future events, it's likely they agreed to put the proceeds in a savings account—less whatever cash he took back to Italy.

Meanwhile, Mamma and I scouted for a flat. We found one in time to meet the traditional May 1st Québec moving date. My father bought a one-way plane ticket and left in April. On May 1st, we moved to a rented apartment a few blocks away. By then we'd lived on Saint-Dominique five years, and leaving it made me sad.

Still, better to move, I thought, than continue living with my father.

On the day of his departure, my father glowed with such happiness it changed his features.

"See this?" he said, showing me a $1,000 bill. "Isn't it a pretty pink colour?"

Fat lot of good it would do us.

We didn't accompany him to the airport; he didn't want us to—not that I would have volunteered. His farewell tears when he hugged us didn't move me one whit. "I'm going to buy accident insurance at the airport. If the plane crashes, you'll all be rich," he sighed.

"Maybe that would be for the best."

I see through you, I thought. He wanted us to believe he cared about our welfare by buying insurance when, in fact, he hadn't contributed a penny towards our upkeep for more than a year.

I endured his hug before he walked away, a stout man on the verge of 40, hair thinning, in his good suit, carrying a suitcase, a man with great expectations. I hoped I'd never set eyes on him again.

CHAPTER THIRTY-FIVE

When my father left us in 1964, the Québec government had finally unshackled married women from their husbands' legal control.

Prior to that time, the Québec Civil Code stipulated that although marriage created a "community of property," legally shared by both spouses, its *administration* rested with the husband. In practice, this meant husbands could dispose of the couple's property however they wished.

In fact, thanks to fierce political and clerical opposition, Québec women had to wait until 1940 to obtain full suffrage. Until 1954, a married Québec woman—along with minors and the insane—was considered legally incompetent to enter into a contract, to sign a will or any other type of binding legal commitment. Until 1964, a married woman had a *legal* obligation to *obey* her husband, until 1977 to gain the same legal authority over her children as her husband had, until 1981 for new family regulations based on gender equality to come into force, and until 1989 until Quebec women achieved *financial* equality when marriage ended. Full equality came only in 1994 when the government enacted a new Québec Civil Code which stated in plain language: "The spouses have the same rights and obligations in marriage," and upon divorce, their assets had to be shared equally.

Bill 16, "An Act respecting the legal capacity of married women," finally gave a married woman the right to borrow money, write cheques, buy property and sign a lease without her husband's consent. The legislator responsible for its passage was Claire Kirkland Casgrain, the first female cabinet minister in Québec's history. Before the bill passed into law, Casgrain noted that even though she'd been elected to the National Assembly, her husband had to sign the lease for her apartment in Québec City because her signature on the lease wasn't legally binding.

For our family, the new law meant that with my father's departure, Mamma could open her own bank account and sign our lease.

In 1964 the Québec government also took control of public education, until then largely managed by the Catholic clergy. It was one more step towards modernizing and secularizing schools in Québec and the reforms took about six years to implement.

Once in charge of education, the government had an important new tool for the emancipation of French Canadians. With an emphasis on free education, including the creation of publicly-funded cegeps: all-in-one, pre-university and technical colleges across Québec, education stopped being a luxury and became a right.

Until these changes were made, female teachers not only were underpaid but forced to abandon careers when they married. Under the new system, teachers' working conditions and pay improved; they unionized and became a major trade-union force.

CHAPTER THIRTY-SIX

While the government made sweeping changes to the education system it didn't have an immediate impact on the English-language Catholic school system. As a Grade 9 student in 1964 school life went along in much the same way, including having nuns as teachers, once we moved to our new flat on Esplanade Street, a few blocks west along Bernard.

I thought Esplanade is a pretty street with huge trees on both sides—unlike Saint-Dominique with its two-storey brick wall of attached flats across a weed-filled field—and whimsical, twisting wrought-iron staircases and balconies.

However, the third-floor flat proved pokey and dark. It had a narrow hallway the length of a bowling alley tucked on the east side of the flat, with a bedroom and a double room on the opposite side. Attached to the top end of the hallway facing the street we had a parlour with access to a balcony, and at the bottom end were the bathroom and a small kitchen. The only things I liked about the flat were the ten-minute walk to get to Zia Tresa's and that my father didn't live there with us.

Teresa and I once again got the only self-contained bedroom, which had no window, and Mamma put her bed in the inner part of the double room at the end of the long hallway. Ricky, now 7, shared her bed.

There were plenty of kids on Esplanade and it didn't take long for us to make friends. Until then our neighbours had been either francophone or immigrants like us, but this neighbourhood had quite a few English-speaking families, and even a few Hassidic Jews, which made me stare what with their big hats and curls dangling on either side of their faces.

But at last, I could stop worrying about finding Mamma dead—we'd kids had started addressing her as Mommy, like the children on American TV shows—when I woke up every morning. It means I slept better, and also did better at school so that I finished Grade 9 with high marks to earn a place in the Grade 10 enriched program the following year.

For the first time in my young life, I experienced inner peace. But life had also taught me it wouldn't last, and it didn't. Just before the end of Grade 9, Mamma announced Nonna would be moving in with us because she'd been at Zia Tresa's a long time now and it was our turn.

Her very presence set me on edge, a woman with the kind of personality that sucked all the air out of the room. Worse still, she wouldn't be coming alone; she'd be babysitting 4-year-old Lucia, Zia Tresa's youngest. I wouldn't have minded but for the fact that the kid stayed with us from Sunday nights, when Zia dropped her off, until the following Friday, when she came to pick her up, the same arrangement my parents had made for when at that age.

Lucia was a hellion, a spoiled, stubborn, destructive child who caused unending chaos in our home and got under my skin. I longed for quiet, for peace. My mother shrugged when I complained, and my grousing put me at loggerheads with my grandmother.

"You're turning out as selfish as your father," my grandmother accused.

I took her words as a slap in the face as she knew I would. More than anything else in life, I didn't want to be like my father. It made me cringe whenever someone at a gathering said I took after my father in looks.

It would have made so much more sense for Nonna to stay at Zia Tresa to care for Lucia, but her husband, Zio Antonio, wouldn't let her stay beyond the time the sisters had agreed to. Besides, no matter where she lived, it cost money to feed Nonna.

My mother tried to calm the waters: "Nonna will only be here until the end of the year. After that she'd go to the Soo, and Zia Tresa will have to find somebody else to look after Lucia."

For Mamma and her sisters, with every expenditure, big or small, they looked for ways to shave costs even if it meant sacrificing ease or comfort. Sisters were expected to help each other so Mamma was expected to help Zia Tresa by having her youngest live with us so she could save the cost of paying for a babysitter.

My father sent no child support. On her meagre salary Mamma somehow fed, housed, and clothed herself, her three children and her mother during the months she was with us. Nonna's diabetes with its strictures only added to food bills. When Zia 'Ndunetta came to visit that summer, she reprimanded Mamma for not giving Nonna steak more often.

"Look around you, 'Ndunetta. Does it look like we live in luxury? Should I buy my mother steak and deprive my children of chicken?"

Zia 'Ndunetta had no money worries. Her husband earned excellent wages at the steel plant, had built their own house, and had no mortgage and she worked part-time work as a custodian at the YMCA, and had no children to raise.

A summer job gave me relief from my grandmother. I had just celebrated my 15th birthday in July when Zia Carmelina said her boss at the factory would take me on as a finisher. The factory wasn't in our neighbourhood but at the northern end of Saint-Laurent Street, where new factory towers were popping up like weeds.

Getting myself to work by 8:00 a.m., however, was a problem. The bus ride was long, and the buses jammed packed. Sometimes three or four buses went by before I could squeeze in. Sometimes I often stayed with Zia Carmelina, who lived closer. But it was a tight squeeze. She lived in her spacious new three-bedroom suburban duplex in Ville Saint-Michel with her husband, their two young children, and her widowed mother-in-law. I shared my cousin's bed, who was Teresa's age.

Zia Carmelina didn't work in one of those big towers but in an older two-storey building above a garage. It was a small operation, children's sportwear, with only six or seven machines, all women, and one cutter, a man.

Her boss and owner, Morris, whom I liked, set me up at a long table with a pair of scissors and a mountain of tied-up bundles of finished garments. I opened a bundle and cut dangling threads from the ends of seams until I'd gone through all the bundles. The bundles kept coming, my task seemingly never-ending. As soon as I finished one bundle, three more came along as the women worked furiously at their machines.

Morris was youngish, good looking with blond hair and blue eyes, a man who treated his employees with fairness and consideration unlike some of the foremen Mamma complained about who pushed and pushed for the women to worked faster and faster. In most factories, finishers like me stood to do their work. Supposedly, it was more efficient to work that way, and it was, but I found it unbearable to stand in place for eight long hours. Whenever I used a stool to rest my legs for short periods, Morris never objected.

I hated the work. Hated it, body and soul, and the workday seemed to stretch to infinity. For one thing, factories had no air conditioning. Machine motors added to the fierce summer heat and raised the temperature to intolerable levels, although the women working the machines didn't complain, which perplexed me. We kept windows open but that did little good, and fans only moved he heat around. By mid-afternoon, I would have given anything to just lie down on the concrete floor for a nap. How could my aunts, Mamma and thousands of other women endure nine-hour days working in ovens then go home to cook, take care of their families then spend weekends sprucing up the houses they were so proud of? I didn't get it.

In no time at all, I developed a crush on him and started building fantasies whereby he fell in love with me. Well, I had to do something to keep from going off the deep end. As a 15-year-old I hadn't learned how to deal with my restless body, desperately wanting to escape confinement, and caused me the same mental anguish. I got through each day at the factory by setting targets for myself. If I met them, I'd give myself a reward like an expensive slice of Boston cream pie for afternoon break.

I pocketed half my paycheque and turned over the rest to Mamma. She could have used it all but was satisfied with half. It felt good to have money in my pocket, and not to be begging for coins for a movie or a chocolate bar. I bought clothes, too, nice ones. My mother had left Fashion Fit Lingerie for a better paying job making women's sportswear. She bought me pretty outfits at wholesale prices. If I got lucky, she'd picked up a "second," slightly damaged merchandise, for even less.

When summer ended and with it my job, I'd put aside a nice little stash of spending money for Grade 10 in September. Nevertheless, I got work in the school cafeteria during the lunch hour, enough to pay for bus fare and french fries from Mr. Red Hot on the way home from school whenever I wanted.

A month before Christmas Mamma approached me with an idea: I should write my father.

"No, I don't want to. Why don't you write to him?"

"Don't you understand? If you write to him, he might send you kids money for Christmas. If I write to him, he'll think I want him to come back."

I wrote the letter and a few weeks later we got a reply. Included with the note was a money order for $5 for all three of his children. Even in 1964, $5 didn't buy much.

CHAPTER THIRTY-SEVEN

I enjoyed Grade 10. In good weather I walked to and from school with my friend, Joanne, who lived on Esplanade. Joanne was a beauty. At 5 ft. 8 in., with long, natural blonde hair, high cheekbones and hazel eyes, she exuded sexual allure. High school boys circled her all the way along the 3-km trek. I envied the attention and admired the easy way she handled it.

Sometimes on the way home from school I stopped at her house, and we'd listen to Beatles music, mooning over their pictures. I claimed the baby-faced Paul McCartney as my favourite, whereas Joanne preferred the complex, poetic John Lennon. When the Fab Four came to Montreal in September 1964, Joanne was among the vast crowd that welcomed them and attended one of the performances. I did neither, of course. Mamma wouldn't allow it. In fact, since my father's departure, she kept an even tighter leash on me than he had for fear I'd get myself a boyfriend, get pregnant and shame her.

We lived in that dreary Esplanade flat only one year before returning to Saint-Dominique. We rented the flat Rose Marie's family lived in after they relocated to the one next door, the one above Pasquale's, the braggart, maybe that one was in better condition.

In May 1965, once again, we packed up, hired a truck, and returned to the old neighbourhood, where our cousins, friends and neighbours welcomed us. My sixteenth birthday peeked around the corner but there would be no Sweet 16 party for me. Instead, as soon as Grade 10 final exams ended, I started looking for work, knocking on doors in the buildings that lined Saint-Viateur. I had two or three factory jobs that summer. They hired students when they were busy but let us go as soon as the rush ended. It was a dreary, boring summer.

When I started Grade 11 in September, the last year of high school, I still had no idea what I wanted to do with my life. I was in the enriched class and many of my classmates planned to go to university, but I wasn't sure I'd be able to pay my way. I thought I might be better off taking the one-year secretarial program and after that at least I could earn some money.

For years my father had encouraged me to take that route. To someone like him, working in an office seemed a big step up from factory floors. He likely saw no value in encouraging a daughter to attend university, a waste when my real future lay in raising children and I had internalized the message.

Besides, my cousin Fil was already working as a secretary at a big engineering firm and loved it. She'd taken an educational shortcut and had opted for a commercial stream her last two years of high school, and work right after graduation. She enjoyed both the work, dressing smart and most of all she loved camaraderie that came with working at a large firm. It didn't sound too bad to me.

Fate intervened when Joanne talked me into applying to Marianopolis College, a degree-granting institution run by nuns, where she'd been offered a full scholarship. My marks were good enough, but I didn't expect to go even if the school accepted me. How could I come up with the money to pay for four years of tuition? My mother sure couldn't help.

Meanwhile, my classmates and I were in a tizzy preparing for our high-school prom. I had no male friends, certainly no boyfriend, and since our school was segregated by gender, I had no hope of a boy inviting me. My father had never even let me go to the school dances. Mamma didn't allow me to date, although she let me go to a couple of the sock hops in my final year but only because I was accompanied by a girlfriend of mine she knew well. Phone calls from boys were forbidden and since I couldn't give out my phone number, nothing ever came of boys I met.

Many of the Italian girls I knew had parents even stricter than mine. Unlike me, they made secret arrangements with boys they liked and lied to their parents about where they went. But I couldn't, wouldn't lie. Besides, the second I opened my mouth to tell a lie, my face went red as chili peppers.

My mother let me attend the high school prom and didn't object to me asking a *paesano*, a kid my age named Silvio, to accompany me. Silvio was game and I had started shopping for a prom dress when my plans came to nothing.

A few weeks before the prom, my father returned unannounced. Worse—much, much worse—Mamma not only allowed him into our home, she seemed pleased to see him.

I despised the two of them and it hurt to look at them, to speak to them as though the words were barbed wire I was pulling out of myself.

Even Zia Tresa, who usually was all about saving face, opined: "Did you see them on the balcony? Arm in arm like newlyweds. After what he's done to her how could she? It's disgusting."

Within days, he retook control of the household. I was bewildered and angry. Had Mamma forgotten everything that had gone on before? Why hadn't she set some terms before letting him back in?

One of his first edicts was to prohibit me from going to the prom, and Mamma made no effort to change his mind. Rage and disappointment tasted bitter in my mouth.

In fact, the honeymoon lasted only a few weeks and soon the old, familiar tensions snuck in under the doors and oozed through the poorly insulated walls and windows like winter cold.

My father helped himself to whatever money my frugal mother had put aside and used it for a down payment on a second-hand car. I didn't hear a murmur of protest out of her.

"Why did you let him take the money?" I asked her, furious.

"Because otherwise he won't give me any peace."

To Mamma's repeated entreaties for him to "Get a job!" he replied, "I *am* looking but it's not as easy as it used to be."

"How can you be looking when you don't leave the house."

"Go to hell."

My father wasn't a lazy man by nature but his paranoia kept him indoors. He was afraid of strangers, potential employers or co-workers included yet bored at home. While Mamma destroyed her spine bent over a sewing machine working sometimes fifty hours a week, he slackened his ennui by starting a daytime affair with our landlady, who lived below us.

Neighbours saw and talked, word reached Zia Tresa, who told Mamma.

"He goes down to her place the back way," Zia reported. "If I were you, I'd gouge his eyes out."

The two sisters were nothing alike, however. Mamma was conciliatory, my aunt implacable; Mamma was slapdash about housekeeping and her own appearance while my aunt was obsessive about cleanliness and how she presented herself; in the face of conflict Mamma would back off, Zia Tresa turned nasty.

Helpless to do anything to improve the home situation, I resolved to put my interests first, as much I had it in my power. I tuned them out, turned inward.

The acceptance letter from Marianopolis College arrived in May 1966, which put me in a quandary. Mamma would have preferred if I'd gone to secretarial school, that I would start to earn money and save for the future. But she didn't put barriers in my way to attending Marianopolis.

"You'd be better off going to secretarial school," my father pronounced when he learned I'd might be going to college. "Secretarial school is just one year. Besides, it's a good job, especially if you work for somebody important."

"Yeah? I suppose you'd want your share of my pay?" I no longer cared what he expected of me.

Anger flashed in his eyes. "Don't be an ass. Four years is a long time. How are you going to pay for it? Surely, you don't expect me to pay for it?"

I snorted. "You? No, I don't expect that."

"Well, at least I hope you'll study something useful. How about pharmacy?"

I said nothing. He didn't know me at all and didn't try to. How could I be a pharmacist when I'd failed trigonometry and dropped physics at the earlier opportunity?

He pushed so hard for me to attend secretarial school that I went to Marianopolis to spite him.

CHAPTER THIRTY-EIGHT

I spent many weekends at Cousin Fil's place the summer of 1966. She was 20 and had fallen in love with a distant American relative. He was in the army, stationed in Korea. Together we penned letters to him and had fun crafting pretty cards. Although he hadn't asked the "big" question yet, she was pretty sure he would. We blue-skyed her wedding plans. Naturally, she'd have a bevy of bridesmaids and I'd be one of them.

I also hit the summer job jackpot and worked at Juniorite, a five-minute walk from our front door on the third floor of a newish, eight-storey building on the southeast corner of Saint-Viateur and Casgrain. My mother worked in another women's wear factory in the same building on the same floor.

Juniorite, which made women's sportswear, didn't operate like any factory I'd ever seen. For one thing, they had no sewing machines. Finished, ready-to-ship garments arrived on racks from elsewhere and it was my job to put them away on serried racks that took up much of the floorspace, and shelved packaged items, like tops and sweaters. The factory wasn't open to the public but whenever the owners' friends stopped by, I served them.

I loved Juniorite; the order pickers, the shipping guys, the cutters; they were all kind to me. And what bliss, to moving from task to task rather than being immobilized like a pinned butterfly!

Two men owned the company with full-time staff of about twenty. Most of them were all in their twenties and not a single one them was

Italian or French-Canadian. There were quite a few Jews, two black women who were sisters, and everyone else was English speaking. Everyone worked hard and yet the atmosphere was upbeat and joyful.

Many of my co-workers socialized away from work but I couldn't join them. My father wouldn't have allowed it if I'd asked permission and I didn't have the guts to sneak around behind his back.

One of the guys on shipping was organizing a party at his house and everybody was talking about it, looking forward to it but he hadn't invited me. I felt left out but I put it behind me since I wouldn't have been able to go in any case. Despite my social status, another student named Howard asked me to go as his date.

"Oh, Howard, I would love to go with you, but I can't. My father is very strict, and he wouldn't let me go in a million years."

"For real?"

"I swear. Believe me, I'd do anything to go with you. I feel like a freak, a prisoner."

Since I couldn't have real-life romances, I experienced them in my head. Serge had long since moved away from Saint-Dominique and out of the starring role in my mental movies. At Juniorite I found a new leading man named Lenny, a junior manager. Around 25, he was handsome, small-boned and slender and not too tall, which I liked because I hadn't grown past 5'2", and he had quiet self-confidence that set me at ease. Lenny was kind to me but had no romantic interest in a sixteen-year-old kid like me. He was somebody safe to dream about because there was no risk of him every wanting to date me.

If I had ever doubted the idea that my father thought he owned his family, he showed it during an incident one night after a handful of shipping guys and I had worked late doing inventory. We finished at around 10 p.m. and we were walked westward along Saint-Viateur, me just minutes away from Saint-Dominique and they towards the buses on Saint-Laurent. I had linked arms with the guys on either side of me and we laughed about nothing. I didn't pay attention to the silhouette coming towards us until we went past a street light that revealed my father.

I quickly unthreaded my arms from the young men's. "It's my father," I said, wished them good night and hurried to his side. But he'd already turned to return home and I found myself trotting behind him. I smelled his rage; it stank like skunk spray.

He reached our place ahead of me, unlocked the door and went in and shut the door in my face. It took me a minute to find the keys at the bottom of my purse and I hurried up the dim staircase to find him waiting in the feeble incandescent light of the hallway. His arms were crossed, and he was breathing fast, like a horse after a long gallop.

"I came to meet you because it was late, and I wanted to make sure you were safe. Instead, I find you carrying on with a bunch of men."

I opened my mouth to explain, but never got a chance to explain—not that it would have made a difference—because he slapped me so hard across the face my ears rang.

"Go to bed."

"Can I at least put in a word for myself?"

"Go to bed!"

He didn't speak to me for two weeks, which I wouldn't have minded except his rage didn't leave him and it stank up the whole house.

At summer's end, Juniorite asked me to stay on part-time during the school year, which delighted me because if I was careful with my earnings, I might be able to swing the tuition fee. In the throes of my excitement to start for college, I had an easier time ignoring my father.

Marianopolis College was a women's college offering bachelor's degrees in arts and science through the Université de Montréal. Founded in 1908 as Notre Dame Ladies' College by the Congregation of Notre Dame, it was the first in Québec to offer higher learning to English-speaking Catholic women.

ELVIE: GIRL UNDER GLASS

The school on the slope of Mount Royal along Peel Street, between Pine Avenue and Sherbrooke St. Classes took place in a boxy, three-storey, mid-20th century building. A similar nearby structure housed the faculty office, student services and a dormitory for live-in students. The library and administration offices occupied a pair of attractive 19th-century stone buildings.

In a twist of irony, Joanne had induced me to apply to Marianopolis and then turned down her own scholarship to go to work. She'd fallen in love and didn't want to spend four years studying when she yearned for marriage and children.

With no firm idea as to what I wanted to do in life, I signed up for liberal arts. In the first semester, I applied myself. I hit every class and did all the homework. I made good friends and enjoyed hours of heated arguments about life and the world while drinking coffee and smoking cigarettes in the common room between classes. The camaraderie warmed me.

In the second semester I starting to wonder why I'd chosen a women-only school, especially one run by nuns, when my marks would have given me entry to McGill or Sir George Williams but consoled myself with the thought that, well, but for Marianopolis I'd be in secretarial school.

My Marianopolis classmates solved the lack-of-men problem by spending most of their free time at the nearby McGill University student center, where males of our species roamed freely and in abundance. I didn't go with them. I'd never learned how to talk to boys with romance in view, and any "I-think-you're-cute" signals a boy might be sending my way were lost on me. The few times I conversed with boys who attracted me, they seemed put off by my seriousness and soon lost interest.

The occasional boy who wasn't scared off by my intensity, I was forced to turn down flat. I didn't have the energy it would have taken to keep relationships secret. Besides, since I had no talent for lying and my father had a bloodhound's nose for sniffing them out, having himself told so many, I was afraid of what he'd do to me. But this inability to have normal boy-girl relationships deeply wounded my self-esteem and made me feel like an outsider.

Meanwhile, my father grew increasingly erratic, sometimes excited and talkative and suddenly turned brooding and silent. In early 1967, he reluctantly accepted a job offer from a relative of his who was a foreman at a shoe factory. He lasted at the job a couple of days.

"Aren't you supposed to be at work?" I asked.

He marched into his bedroom and slammed the door. A few minutes later the relative who'd given him the job phoned.

"Is your father home?" He was annoyed.

"Yes, he's here." I knocked on the bedroom door. "It's Dominic."

"Tell him I'll call him back."

"Sorry, Dom, he won't come to the phone. What happened?"

"Your guess is as good as mine. He was at his machine one minute, and the next he'd disappeared."

My mother wormed the story out of him that evening. He'd bolted when he became convinced the man who worked beside him was involved in the conspiracy to kill him. At supper that evening, a meal I'd made while he hid in his room, his eyes were bloodshot, and he looked haggard. Was he "crazy"? Or was it just an act to get out of working?

CHAPTER THIRTY-NINE

A couple of weeks after fleeing the shoe factory, my father had a psychotic break. I returned from my classes one afternoon to find the door to his room shut, something he didn't usually do. Even when "resting" in bed he kept it open to hear what was going on in the household.

I didn't bother to check on him. Instead, I went to my room, threw myself on the bed— which I still shared with Teresa in the front half of the double parlour—and waded into some reading I had to do for class.

Around 5 o'clock I went into the kitchen to start supper. The bedroom door was still shut, no sound coming from inside. When Mamma got home from work, she saw the shut door and a bolt of fear shot across her face.

"How long has he been in there?"

I shrugged. "He was in there when I got home around two."

As she opened the door my father let out an anguished cry. The haunting sound made my skin retract. I rushed to find out what was going on.

Mamma slowly approached him as he pressed his body against the headboard, his arms covering his head to protect himself and whimpering. "Get away from me!"

"What's wrong?" She asked in a calm voice.

"Who are you? What do you want?"

My mother was close enough to touch him, which seemed to terrify him. "No! No! No!" he cried out, curling into a ball.

I felt no sympathy, no pity. We'd been free of him for a year, underscoring how much better life could be without his suffocating presence. Besides, I still wasn't convinced my father wasn't just putting on a show for his own reasons.

The tears sliding down Mamma's face confirmed she was buying into the histrionics. Even if he wasn't faking, why did she still care about a man who'd filled her life with misery and pain?

These two deserve each other, I thought, as I looked on. How I wished I had the means to walk out on them both.

Moving slowly, Mamma approached him and perched on the edge of the bed, talking softly, trying to reassure and calm him. I left her to it, went back to the kitchen and finished getting supper ready. We ate while he lay in bed asleep, covered with a blanket Mamma had draped over him.

He slept all evening and through the night. But when he got up the next morning, he recognized us but had an old man's shuffle. At the supper table he announced he'd had a visit from the medieval poet Dante, author of the *Divine Comedy*. They'd had an interesting discussion about the nature of good and evil. My mother shut her eyes in despair.

"He's not getting any better," she said after he'd gone to bed. The last two years had chiselled deep worry lines around her mouth and across her forehead, marring a creamy complexion. She was 39.

I groaned. "You still think this is for real? I think *he* believes somebody's trying to kill him—and for that he needs help. But I don't buy this latest song and dance."

My mother looked into my eyes as though seeing me for the first time: "*Dio mio,* you do have a stone in your chest instead of a heart."

"Yeah? And yours is too soft. How could you be taken in by him over and over?"

My mother's face flushed red. Tears brightened her mournful grey eyes, driving a dagger of guilt into my heart. Her reply, however, chased it away: "He's still your father and he's a sick man. Have some compassion."

"He cheated on you; he nearly killed you; he took your earnings and took care of his own needs first. He used you like a servant, like his property and still you feel sorry for him? Where was his compassion for your suffering? For his children's' suffering? Is there a limit to how many times you'll let him beat you over the head with a stick before you make him stop?

"Listen, Ma. He may be sick; he may be acting. I don't know and I don't care. You do what you think you have to do. But if he gets better and starts lording it over us again don't expect support of any kind from me."

"With an attitude like that you'll go through life a very lonely woman."

"I'd rather be lonely than chained up like a dog."

During the next few weeks, my father showed no improvement. He said little and kept to his room writing in a notebook for hours after "chatting" with dead poet Dante. He roamed the house at night, which spooked me. I heard Mamma calling him back to bed, and the answering grunts of refusal. A couple of times, I woke up in the night to find him standing at the foot of the bed I shared with Teresa.

"You need to see a doctor," she begged him time and again.

"What for? I'm not crazy and one day the whole world will know it."

All winter and into the spring of 1967, our family lived with the spectre of a dead poet. It was less tolerable than the old battles between my parents. I spent as many hours away from home as possible. I left in the very early morning for school and didn't return until supper. As final exams neared, I dutifully went to classes and the library. And smoked in the common room.

Except for the obligatory science course—chemistry, which I barely passed—my freshman year ended with above average marks. By summer break, my father's health seemed improved.

I traded my job at Juniorite for the position of "information operator" at Bell Canada. It paid more than double what I'd earned at Juniorite, which itself had seemed a fortune. To me.

Unfortunately, less than a week later, I discovered I'd made a bad mistake accepting the job with Bell because it confined me to a chair in a cubicle for long, painful hours. I wanted to quit soon after I started but I had tuition and textbooks to pay for as well as paying Mamma a bit for room and board to help out.

The three years I spent working for Bell exacerbated my anxieties and contributed to deteriorating mental health. But I stayed. I stayed for the money, which I now know is not a good reason to do anything something hurts you. I could have found other, better ways to pay my bills.

By early May my father's illness, if that's what had caused his breakdown, had stabilized. That allowed his nasty, jealous nature to resurface when an old high school friend asked me to be her bridesmaid. Antoinette was only 17. Everyone, parents included, tried to talk her out of it. But the girl knew what she wanted and wouldn't be dissuaded. Maybe Antoinette sensed her time on Earth would be short. Ten years later, she would die of an aggressive cancer.

Antoinette assigned me her groomsman, a close friend of her fiancé, to be my escort. On the morning of the wedding, he picked me up and walked me to the bride's home. From there, cars would take us to the church for the ceremony, to the photography studio and finally to a banquet hall for the reception.

When my escort buzzed, my father came to the door.

"Hello, sir, I'm here to pick up Elvira," he said. The young man stood on the stoop looking up at my father glaring down. He didn't invite him in. Instead, he stomped to his room and slammed the door hard enough for the flimsy walls to shake, leaving the poor guy wondering what he'd done wrong.

Mamma hurried to the rescue and invited him to come up, and they chatted for a few minutes until I was ready. My escort said nothing about my father's bizarre behaviour as we walked to the bride's home together.

My father didn't speak to me for days, as though I'd betrayed him. His animus poisoned the air, and I could see how the stress aged Mamma, weary of him, weary of life. The more he sulked, the more the rest of us avoided and excluded him, and he reacted.

I had worked the first half of a split shift, 10 a.m. to 2 p.m. and arrived home to find my father gone, vanished. Where had he gone, I wondered? He hadn't left the house in weeks, or even stepped out on the back gallery for a breath of air. Had he packed his bags and gone back to Italy? Oh, how I wished he had but more likely he'd gotten so desperate he made the effort to run his own bloody errand for a change.

Who cares? I put him out of my mind and when Mamma got home from work around 5:30, I was just getting ready for the second part of my shift. She seemed surprised but not worried by his absence. I thought, I hoped maybe she'd finally gotten as fed up with him as I was.

"Set the table," Mamma said to Teresa.

"Aren't we gonna wait for Papà?" she asked.

"No."

"He's gonna be mad."

"*Nem ne frega.* I don't care," Mamma replied.

My shift ended at 9 p.m. and by the time I got home, my father had yet to show up. Ricky and Teresa had gone to bed.

"Where do you think he is?" I asked Mamma as we watched TV. She preferred French programs because she understood much more French than English but there was only one television set in the house and when we kids were around, we watched English shows.

"Maybe he's in Hell," she replied without taking her eyes off the sock she was darning. "Did you notice whether the car's parked on the street?"

I hadn't noticed. The idea of suicide crossed my mind, but I discounted it. A man as self-centred as my father would never kill himself. I was certain whatever trick he'd planned, he was doing it to get attention.

We got our answer around 11 p.m. via a phone call.

CHAPTER FORTY

I answered the phone, unsure about what to expect but certain it had to do with my father. On the end of the line was my father's elder sister, Luisa. "Elvie, let me talk to your mother," she said without preamble.

Zia Luisa and Mamma were not on good terms. Ever since the time Zia had tried to make excuses for her brother's abusive behaviour years earlier, Mamma had cut her out of her life so this phone call suggested something pretty serious must have happened involving my father.

"It's Zia Luisa," I whispered. My mother shook her head.

"She can't come to the phone right now, Zia."

"Look, your father's here at our house. He's sick and we've called a doctor, an Italian, a friend of a friend who's agreed to come and see what he can do. He's in no shape to make any decisions and your mother needs to be here."

I relayed what she'd said. From her chair, mother replied, "Tell her maybe it's time she gets a taste of what it's like to live with her little brother."

Zia heard her. "I don't excuse and never did excuse him. I know how he is, and how hard it must be to live with a sick man."

"But she still expected me to take everything he dished out *and* to cover it up," Mamma shot back.

Zia sighed. "Listen, Elvie. This is no time to be arguing. Ask your mother what she wants me to do."

Mamma shrugged. "We don't know either, Zia," I replied, and that's where the conversation ended.

We heard nothing more for a week, nor did we inquire. We knew he couldn't stay at Zia Luisa's indefinitely so when she called again Mamma took the call, although she listened, mostly. When the conversation ended, Mamma appeared resigned to her fate. "She says he's better. The doctor's there now and wants to talk to me."

I had known this moment would come, that he'd come home again but now that he was about to come home, I felt as though a noose had been dropped around my neck.

Mamma took a long, silent bus ride to Zia Luisa. When Zia Luisa opened the door, she threw her arms around Mamma saying, "I'm sorry if I said or did anything to make you think I blamed you for anything. I don't blame you." Mamma, incapable of holding a grudge, returned the embrace.

Zia invited us in, led us into the kitchen and began preparing a *machinetta* of espresso, a ritual all the *paesani* engaged in when guests came through the door. They all followed a certain protocol with respect to offering refreshment: a host should not *offer* coffee, beer or whatever because a guest would be expected to refuse so as not to put the host to any trouble. The host would have not only to put food and drink out on the table but persist in encouraging the guest to partake.

As a child Mamma had warned me whenever we went to someone's home not to act *scoshtumata,* boorish, by asking for anything. "But why not?"

"Because it's rude. It's one thing if she takes one out of the fridge and puts it in front of you, it's quite another if you ask her for something she might not have or might be saving for her own family."

The custom likely evolved over centuries of poverty in a people too proud to admit it. The hosts, who didn't have much, wanted to look like they had plenty while the guests didn't accept too readily because they didn't want to appear needy.

While Zia made coffee, I chatted with my cousins—two boys around Teresa's age I hadn't seen in years.

"Luisa, don't bother with the coffee. I really don't want any. Where's the doctor? Let's get this over with," Mamma implored.

A moment later, Zia Luisa's husband, a 6-ft. hulk against his wife's 5-ft. frame, came into the room, the doctor behind him. My uncle shook Mamma's hand and introduced us to the doctor after which Mamma and the wizened old doctor and I went into the front room to have a talk.

He spoke Italian, which relieved me of having to do translation duty. "Your husband has had a mental breakdown, *signora*. From what Signora Luisa tells me it's not his first," the doctor said. "Your husband tells me he doesn't fit in this country, believes people here are out to get him and is convinced that if he went home to Italy he would get better. I have no medicine to offer for this malady, unfortunately. In my opinion, I think he should go home."

If the doctor had been a psychiatrist, he might have known about and offered one of the new psychopharmaceutical drugs out on the market. They might have changed my father's life—and ours—but the good doctor made no such offer.

Mamma and I took my father home that night and two weeks later, he was back in Italy. His departure relieved me of such a heavy load I thought I might float away.

He was gone, gone, gone or so I thought.

The summer of 1967 brought the kind of freedom I'd craved. Without my father around to stop me, I took part in activities galore. It was Canada's centennial year. Among many celebrations, the summer highlight was the Universal Exposition of Montreal, better known as Expo 67. The fair brought the city to global attention and its theme, Man and His World, reflected real optimism for the future, especially among young people who believed they *could* make the world a better place.

Expo 67 was held on purpose-built islands in the Saint Lawrence River. Engineers filled in several small islands and shoals to expand Saint Helen's Island. They created the artificial island of Ile Notre Dame, fashioning the Mackay Pier into the Cite du Havre. In less than three years, they erected some 100 structures to accommodate national, provincial and state, privately-sponsored and theme exhibits, as well as 27 bridges, 75 km of roads and sidewalks, 40 km of sewers, 25,000 parking spots, 256 basins, and 6,000-plus new streetlights. Naysayers had predicted it couldn't be done in so short a time.

Between April 28 when it opened and Oct. 27 when it closed, the site racked up more than 50 million paying visitors—far exceeding the expectations—and more than five million performers, media, official visitors, and employees.

The last of Montreal's three underground Metro lines also opened, just in time for Expo. This third line ran under the St. Lawrence River, connecting the island of Montreal with the South Shore suburb of Longueil with a stop at Saint Helen's Island on the Expo grounds. Each and every time the train raced through the underwater tunnel, I pressed myself against the side of the train, trembling, convinced the tunnel wouldn't crack open and drown us all. But I went anyway, and often.

Expo 67 had a magical, vital quality, and revealed a marvellous world to me and my friends. Sixty-two countries participated in the fair, either in individual pavilions or combined with other countries in regional pavilions. We returned time and again to U.S.'s 20-storey transparent geodesic dome; we were among thirteen million visitors drawn to the Soviet Union's soaring structure, and sat amazed as we experienced Czechoslovakia's interactive movie, the world's first. The major countries had restaurants in their pavilions and getting a taste was a highlight of my visits. I got my first taste of cheese and chocolate fondues at the Swiss pavilion, and never looked back.

That summer, as 50 million visitors celebrated the world's future, trouble simmered inside Québec's body politic. The first sign poked its head during the official visit by French president Charles de Gaulle in July. Speaking to a big crowd from a balcony at Montreal City Hall, he cried out, "*Vive le Québec libre!*" Long live a free Québec. While the crowd responded with thunderous applause, Canada's outraged prime minister Lester Pearson, ordered de Gaulle's visit cut short.

Three months later, René Lévesque, the Québec cabinet minister who'd spearheaded nationalization of the power industry, broke away from the Liberal party to create a separatist party, *Mouvement Souveraineté-Association*, later renamed the *Parti Québécois*, to forge independence from Canada.

I knew the political changes were important, but I didn't want to think how they'd affect me because it would have meant making decisions about what to do with my life. I still had no idea what I wanted to be when I grew up. In truth, I didn't want to grow up at all.

As the summer wore on, my exhilaration waned. While I didn't have my father around to infuriate me, and I could come and go as I liked, my job with Bell sucked the joy out of my life. I'd started as a 411 operator in May that year but by July when I turned 17, regular panic attacks assailed me while I worked, a desperation to flee the cubicle confining me. Each shift felt endless and sitting there for hours giving out numbers out of the gigantic book in front of me felt like torture. Some time in August, acute discomfort crossed over into outright panic and suddenly my mind seemed to split from my body and floated up to the ceiling from where I saw myself sitting in the cubicle. I thought I must have died. The experience that day lasted seconds but it wouldn't be the last time it hit me. For the next thirty years the fearful out-of-body experience occurred every time I felt helpless in a stressful situation. To make it stop, I had to come to terms with the demons that lurked in head.

In so many ways, Bell's authoritarian ways replaced my father's. Beyond my claustrophobia, the company treated its then all-female telephone operators in the controlling, bullying ways my father had. Supervisors, also female, routinely listened in on calls without our knowledge to check for accuracy, speed and politeness. Once a month they sat us down one by one and went over our report cards. Each mistake, such as giving a customer an incorrect number, stayed on your record. For full-time staffers, they could affect promotions.

It amazed me how the full-timers, like many women I'd met in the factories where I'd worked, seemed to easily tolerate the mind-numbing work. They didn't seem tormented by the boredom and sense of confinement. Something must be terribly wrong with me, I thought, and I wondered whether my father had also experienced this. Had his breakdowns been real after all? Would my mind shatter one day, too?

CHAPTER FORTY-ONE

I should have quit Bell after that first panic attack but ended up working there three years, full time when school was out and part-time during school terms. I shed weight and Mamma—no slouch herself in the anxiety department—fussed about it constantly, which made me worry about myself. But the food just wouldn't go down. Sleep was something I prayed for when I lay my head on the pillow at night. Panic attacks struck me almost daily and further exhausted me. My mind felt deadened, a rock that somehow broke off from a dead planet floating in space.

Now that my father was out of the picture and I could no longer focus my rage on him, I'd lost the tether that had held me to the world.

I felt no lift in my mood when classes resumed in the fall of 1967, except the small consolation that I now had to work only two shifts a week. I wasted most of my sophomore year playing cards and smoking in the student lounge, rarely bothering to go to lectures. When I did go to classes, I'd soothe myself writing grim poems instead of taking notes. Many of the courses I'd signed up were English and French literature, which I loved so I did the readings, and pulled through the first semester that way.

Thinking back, it might have done better to have chosen something more practical to study than literature. Marianopolis offered a unique program in applied linguistics which might have engaged me. But it didn't. The path I took seemed both too easy and too hard. Literature, philosophy, theology and psychology dealt with the world of ideas and the meaning of life, something I yearned to discover. The courses were easy in that I could bullshit through essays and exams, but a hard range of ideas and arguments challenged and further confused me. I'd grown as someone who saw the world in black or white, nuances overwhelmed me and further darkened my vision.

Instead of attending lectures, in good weather my friends and I wandered through the heart of downtown Montreal. My then-best friend, Linda, and I had shared an obsession with the Montreal-born poet and songwriter, Leonard Cohen. We went out hunting for traces of him. In a CBC documentary, we'd learned Cohen liked to eat at Ben's Delicatessen, which was within walking distance of Marianopolis. We went there regularly, bite down on our four-inch-tall smoked meat sandwiches on rye and scanned the always-busy deli for signs of him. We never found any; we didn't know it, but Cohen had moved to New York.

To perk myself up in the second semester, I joined the school's theatre club. Despite my shyness—so much so I couldn't bring myself to speak up in class—I got a role in a one-act comedy by Thornton Wilder. The play, *Queens of France*, told the story of a lawyer who extorts money from three vulnerable women by convincing each one she's a legitimate descendant of the long-lost Dauphin and therefore the rightful queen of France. Standing in the wings, I thought I'd pass out with fright but once I walked on stage, I exulted, revelled in the power of having an audience in my thrall. The experience gave me a needed boost.

From then on whenever listlessness and boredom overtook me, rather than dig out the root of what ailed me, I simply did something new and a bit scary. Early in February 1968, I made up my mind to change schools and switch to a co-ed university for junior year. I was accepted at Sir George Williams for the fall of 1968.

I hungered for a taste of the real world where I could meet and interact with boys, and experience learning at a secular institution. All my pals had boyfriends. Even my Marianopolis friends had met McGill boys at the student union. Some had gone through several relationships already, while for me a boyfriend existed only in fantasies.

The thought of a starting in a new school cheered me up but the upswing didn't last long.

The blow came in early June, just before I turned 19. I had a day off work mid-week since I'd be working the coming weekend. It was the middle of the afternoon and I was alone in my flat and getting ready to meet one of my Marianopolis friends downtown. I stood at the mirror in my room putting on some makeup, something my father would have prohibited. According to him, only whores used such trickery. Whores or not, all my friends used it and now I lavished on the eye shadow and double layers of mascara on my lashes when I heard a thump on the staircase.

Maybe Mamma was home from work early? I went to the top of the stairs and peered down and stared and stared because my brain absolutely refused to accept what my eyes saw. There stood my father, looking up, warm-eyed and smiling. "Elvie," he said softly.

I had turned into a pillar of salt like the biblical wife of Lot's. If my heart kept beating, I wasn't feeling it.

His smile vanished and his features settled into the old granite-face when I failed to welcome him. Angry, he picked up his suitcase and started up the stairs. When he reached the top, I still hadn't budged. Nor could I. Two pairs of identical brown eyes, his teeming with fury, mine with hatred, bored into each other.

"Get out of my way," he said, and shouldered me out of the way. I would never willingly move out of his way again.

A wanted to let loose a terrible keening, a profound expression of grief as all the old fears and helplessness flooded back and shattered the flimsy dam that had checked them until that day.

I ran back to my room, picked up my purse and jacket and fled, promising myself no matter what Mamma chose to do with him, I promised myself I would never again live under the same room as my father. As I made my way downtown to meet my friend, it suddenly occurred to me that the bastard had the foresight to hold on to the house key. How crazy could he have been when he'd left 10 months earlier, supposedly after a psychotic break, to have planned for a possible return.

I took the bus, paid the correct fare, met my friend downtown as we'd planned but I felt unreal, ghostly, insubstantial and invisible to people around me.

"Oh, my God, what happened to you?" my friend asked.

I should have known better than to count on this friend for solace. She couldn't deal with her own deep wounds let alone mine. She listened, upset, but when I burst into tears, she tried to change the subject. I cut our meeting short and walked away from our friendship. I had no thought for anyone, just my own survival.

I wandered aimlessly for hours trying to figure out what to do. No way would I go home. I'd rather sleep in the street. I wondered at *my mother's* capacity for humiliation. Dare I hope she'd reached her limit and kick him and his suitcase down the stairs? No, probably not.

What could I do? Where could I go? Not to friends. They all lived with their parents, and parents would tell me to go home. That left me with relatives. But who could I trust not to harangue me into acting the dutiful daughter? Tired, confused and discouraged I took the easiest route and went to Zia Tresa's. She lived a few doors away from our flat, in the same flat in the duplex my parents had once owned.

"I thought I might see you tonight. Come up," Zia Tresa said.

Her words extinguished the spark of hope that Mamma might already have thrown him out. "She's letting him stay, isn't she?"

She sighed. "Have you eaten?"

"Yes."

I followed her into the family room where my cousins were watching TV.

Liliana, now 17 had quit school and worked full-time in a factory, like Mamma, like her mother. She jumped up and threw her arms around me. "The bastard! He has no shame. How could he show his face again?" She hated my father almost as much as I did, and she'd never hesitated to speak her mind when he'd offended her.

"How did you find out he was back?" I asked.

"Your mother was here looking for you," Zia Tresa said.

"What did she say?"

"She said she wants to talk to you."

"I have nothing to say to her until she throws him out. Can I stay here for now?"

"Sure, you can stay. Don't worry about that," Zia said.

She called Mamma to let her know I was with her. "She wants to come and talk to you."

"Is he still in the house?"

My aunt held the out the receiver towards me.

"Tell her I want nothing more to do with either of them. Tell her if she comes here, I'll leave, and she'll never see me again."

CHAPTER FORTY-TWO

After my father's sudden reappearance, I had left the house with only the clothes on my back. Liliana, went to get me some of my things and when she returned, she said Mamma was desperate for me to go home.

I slept on an uncomfortable folding cot in Zia's front parlour. Not that I would have gotten much sleep on even the most comfortable bed the way mind ran on a loop of unanswerable questions. How could Mamma choose him over her children's well being? Why, why, why? A man who'd abused us all, who'd demeaned and exploited her and would do it again?

Mamma's continued submissiveness infuriated me, and I lost respect for her, once and for all. Hadn't the last ten months proved to her we could get along very well without him? We didn't need him, quite the opposite; he was the one who couldn't get along without her.

The days after my father's sudden reappearance tumbled into each other, a week, two, then three. In July, Liliana made a little cake for my 19th birthday. I enjoyed my cousins' company but I couldn't stay with them indefinitely. I thought about quitting school, getting a full-time job and finding a place of my own. But the idea scared me; there was no precedent in my life for a girl living all on her own.

Near the end of the third week, I left the building where I worked at the end of my shift to find Mamma standing in the Bell lobby. I nearly turned around and went back inside but thought better of it. Sooner or later, I'd have to face her.

"How did you know what time I'd be out?" I asked.

"I didn't know. I've come here every day after work this week and waited for hours, hoping to see you."

Well, that showed a determination I hadn't seen in her before. But the picture of her standing there for hours after she'd worked eight or nine hours made me twitch with guilt. I told myself, *remember she'd made the choice to let the bastard stay!*

"Okay, you wanted to talk. Here I am."

"Come home. I promise you things will be different this time. I told him that."

I shook my head. "Things can't be different because he will always be the same."

"I know what he is. But he's my problem not yours."

"He'll be my problem, too, if I live in the same house. He'll take over my life like he always does. No, I don't want to be anywhere near him."

"Listen, I've thought this out," she said, turning so we faced each other and gripping my upper arms. "We'll buy a second television. We'll put it in yours and Teresa's bedroom. That way you can have your own space."

"And you think he'll keep away when the rest of us are there? He won't."

"You leave that to me."

"Why don't you just tell him to get out, Ma? Why don't you?"

Her arms dropped to her sides, and she turned away. "You really don't understand, do you? He will never let me go until he's finished with me. I'm *afraid* of what he'll do to me, to you kids. *È pazzo*, he's crazy."

The Bell office was only a couple of blocks from home. As dusk crept over us, we walked, side by side, in silence. I thought about what she'd said, wanting to believe a compromise could work but knowing it wouldn't.

"I'll think about what you said," I told her when we reached Zia Tresa's door.

She threw her arms around me, "Please, come home. Don't add to my worries."

I stiffened. *Her worries?* What about what *I'd* have to endure if I put myself within his reach? She believed she had no choice but to go on with him; but I did have choice. "I'll call you, Ma."

She walked ahead, a short distance to her own door to Hell, her shoulders shaking as she wept. I talked things over with Zia Tresa. She and Liliana thought it best for me to go home rather than quit school and try to live on my own. In truth, I didn't know whether I could face up to living far from Teresa and Ricky and shunned by extended family for leaving home before marriage.

I went home, not understanding my reasons were a mirror of Mamma's for sticking with her husband. I did set conditions, however: I would not turn over my paycheque but pay an agreed amount for room and board; I wanted no interaction with my father, let alone take orders from him. To all of this Mamma agreed. Whether she told my father my terms, I never learned. Not that it would made a difference because he was the sort of man who'd agree anything to get what he wanted but couldn't be counted on to stick to the terms.

Once I returned home, I spent all my time in the room I shared with Teresa except for meals—and they were far from cheerful affairs. As promised, she and I shopped for a second TV so we could watch it in our bedroom.

Trouble started the first night as the family, minus my father, gathered in front of the new TV set. He didn't like being banished and made it known by banging things on the table, slamming doors and stomping around the kitchen.

"Just ignore him," Mamma advised.

But he didn't stop until we shut off the TV and went to bed. Later, raised voices issued from my parents' bedroom. This time Mamma did much of the yelling.

The following evening, he staged a more overt protest by planting himself in the doorway of our bedroom while we watched a program. He stood there in silence, hands in his pockets, eyes trained on the flickering black-and-white screen, angry and defiant.

It was impossible to ignore him. "I thought you'd told him to stay away?" I said to Mamma, loudly enough for him to hear.

"I did." She turned to him. "Why are you here? You promised you'd stay out of her way."

"I don't like being treated like a dog."

"You reap what you sow," she replied, returning her gaze to the program.

He stalked away. But we all knew he hadn't finished his campaign. Ten minutes later the hammering started. We looked at each other.

"What's he doing?" Teresa asked.

"Whatever it is, ignore him. Whatever he's doing, he's doing it to get attention," Mamma said.

The hammering went on and on. Whatever else he had up his sleeve, he'd succeeded in disrupting our evening. Eventually, curiosity prevailed, and I poked my head outside the bedroom into the hallway. From there I could see the family room and into the kitchen. I caught him standing on a chair pounding a nail into the doorframe leading into the kitchen, just as he'd done all those years earlier when he forced Mamma to climb up on a chair and put a noose around her neck. The sharpness of the memory made me break into a sweat. Was the noose for him or for one of us?

"Ma, I think he's going to hang himself." I despised my father, but I didn't want his suicide on my conscience.

"Let him—but he won't kill himself. Believe me. He just wants to get his way."

Teresa and Ricky pressed themselves close to Mamma, young faces troubled. I took Mamma at her word and resumed my place beside them on the bed. She was right, I thought. Men like my father could no more hurt themselves than they could fly.

We went on ignoring him. When his hammering stopped, he was still alive if not happy. Loud sobs ensued. When those, too, went unanswered, he went to bed.

For months the household quivered, the tension created a constant electrical charge in the flat. My father and I sat at the same table but didn't speak. When words became necessary, the others became our intermediaries. I was certain if he sensed the least weakness in me, he'd take over my life again.

My father's sudden reappearance was the first of two blows that summer. My sweet cousin, Fil, got married and moved with her new husband to New York state. Not that I begrudged her the married life she'd long wanted. Preparing for her wedding had been fun as we'd shopped together for her dress and going-away outfit, bridesmaids' dresses—I was one of four—flowers and party favours.

I hadn't cried in years, hadn't been able to, and yet on Fil's wedding day the damn speech I'd so carefully constructed crumbled and hot tears scalded my face as I wept for the loss of a dear, trusted sister. I promised to visit her often, and I did for many years. But in time, distance along with a very different ways of life left us with little in common.

After Fil left Montreal, I slipped into a deep funk, and I escaped into novels. With Teresa right beside on the bed with the door closed, we buried our noses in our novels where we could live in someone else's world and forget the sound of yelling between our parents in the other room.

CHAPTER FORTY-THREE

In the fall, I began junior year at Sir George Williams, a co-education school. At last! The newness of place and routine lifted my spirits. In hindsight, my relentless search for newness was mental laziness, an unwillingness to apply myself to anything I had to work at to master. My father had been right about one thing: I lacked discipline. Expect for reading novels, which I did ten to twelve hours in one sitting, although even my choice of fiction was a random pursuit with no goal except distraction.

Going to a new school did not alleviate my malaise as I'd hoped. I didn't fit in, not with "hippies" and their free love and drugs culture nor with the politically active student groups who fought against injustice.

My new school, like many university campuses, would experience its share of turmoil before long. Meanwhile, I had to adapt to new surroundings. Amid the constant stream of students washing up and down on escalators, along corridors, and crowding into lounges and the cafeteria, I soon figured out my Catholic education hadn't equipped me for university-level courses. The new professors demanded independent thinking, not memorization and regurgitation. For one assignment in European literature the prof advised: "Read the novel and answer my questions without going to any sources. I'll know it if you do because I've studied them all."

But we'd never learned how to analyse, how to critique what we read. We had not been taught to think. Assignments without my customary crutches were tough and I struggled. I didn't give up, though. I attended classes, did endless assignments, and in between I continued part-time with Bell to earn my keep.

In Montreal a palpable restlessness hovered. Since the early '60s, the FLQ had plagued the city with bombings. But now, on the eve of a federal election, a riot broke out during the 1968 annual St. Jean Baptiste Day parade. In the clash between demonstrators and police, 126 people were injured and nearly 300 arrested. The riot became known as *lundi de la matraque*, Truncheon Monday, as police with Billy clubs charged the crowd when protesters burned cars and threw rocks and bottles at the grandstand where then prime minister Pierre Trudeau sat unmoving and defiant.

By winter, my father and I had reached an uneasy truce. We weren't friendly but the overt hostility between us was gone along with the intolerable tension we had lived with for months.

And then a *paesana* whispered in Mamma's ear and told her the real reason my father had skedaddled out of Italy this last time. The story went something like this: returning to Campochiaro after his last breakdown, he had found himself a job in Larino, an ancient town of 7,000, about 50 km away where he bribed his way into a much-sought-after sinecure at the Italian postal service.

You'd think my father would have been in his element what with good pay for doing little work with the added bonus of the status that came with being a government employee. You'd think he would have done nothing to jeopardize the good life he'd finally established but maybe he needed to inject a little risk in his life to make it more interesting. In any case, he started an affair with a married colleague who happened to have a very jealous husband.

The affair went on for months before the husband found out and my father ran out of there as fast as his legs would carry him, got on a plane and came back to Montreal where he knew he could talk his wife who wouldn't shut the door in his face. Coincidentally, when he fled Larino, the woman with whom he'd had the affair was pregnant but we never heard anything more about her or her progeny.

Mamma took the news as double treachery, lies about why he'd come back plus yet another infidelity, and she had no compunction about sharing the details about what he'd done to anyone who'd listen. Besides, since the news came from a *paesana* it would soon be common knowledge in the community. Mamma, it seemed, no long cared about saving face. He'd finally crossed the last line and the trick mirror she'd used to justify staying with him no longer reflected the image she'd wanted to see. Only I didn't understand this until years later.

Among the things he'd brought back from Larino was a sophisticated reel-to-reel recorder on which he'd taped a number of Italian torch songs. He played one instrumental piece, "Maria Elena." He listened to it over and over as he stared into the distance with a dreamy expression when it played.

I assumed, as did Mamma, that was probably his paramour's name, and she ragged him about it without mercy until he stopped playing it. For weeks they snarled and scratched and bared their teeth at each other. And then, to my dismay, gradually went back for what passed as calm. Mamma didn't kick him down the stairs but continued to feed him and to lie next to him at night.

I suppose Mamma concluded, what was one more infidelity among so many? As for me, that was the time I began to despise Mamma.

"Do you think we'll ever get rid of him?" Teresa asked me again and again.

"Probably."

"When?"

"I wish I knew exactly when, but things can't go on like this forever."

"I hate him," she said in a matter-of-fact way.

Teresa turned 13 in the fall of 1968 and had started high school. She was a shy, silent kid who rarely expressed her feelings, at least not at home. She had a lot of friends, though, and she liked school and was a good student. Ricky 11, moved in and out of the house like a hurricane. Unlike Teresa and me at his age, he had no chores do to and ran wild with his buddies along the nearby train tracks or went to the community centre across the street run by the Christian brothers to play games. Girls were not allowed to use the facilities.

I hadn't completely given up hope Mamma would kick the old man out so the news they'd bought a house came as a near-mortal blow. How had they scraped enough money together for the down payment, I asked myself? Had they set aside most of the proceeds from the sale of our duplex the first time he took off to Italy? Had he saved money from his post office job and was using that? Although that seemed unlikely to me. He never used his own private stash when he could find other ways of financing his projects.

And I was one of the ways: he badgered, hounded and begged me to turn over my savings and a student grant I'd received to add to the down payment.

The new house he picked out was in Ville Saint-Laurent, a suburb northwest of Montreal, far away from where Mamma's sisters, and most of our *paesani,* now lived. He'd chosen a resale, a duplex in an established neighbourhood about as far as he could get from the many Italians who'd bought in the new development in the east-side suburbs of Ville Saint-Michel and Saint-Leonard. He wanted to be far from prying eyes of people who knew him, and, at the same time, the distance served to isolate Mamma from the support of family and friends.

When he took us to see the place, I liked the duplex at first sight. The ground floor, which had a spacious living room, dining room, bright kitchen, and three bedrooms with big windows in every room, would be ours. The second storey had two self-contained one-bedroom apartments, which would pay the mortgage. The closing date was May 1969.

To keep me co-operative, Mamma promised to buy Teresa and me a brand-new bedroom set of our choice, with *twin* beds—we'd shared a double bed almost since her birth.

In the meantime, I continued going to classes. Back and forth I trudged among home, school and work—aware of what the social and political changes going on around me but stayed back, a mere observer. I even failed to witness the action—I had no classes that day—when a student protest at my school exploded into violence.

The unrest at Sir George Williams University began on January 29th, 1969 with a peaceful sit-in protest in the hallway of the ninth-floor computer room of Henry F. Hall building to protest supposed racial discrimination against six West-Indian students by a biology professor. The occupation remained peaceful for two weeks with several hundred students taking shifts to keep it going while administrators and activists negotiated.

On February 10th, after negotiations fell apart, more than a hundred students took over the computer data room where they barricaded themselves, and shut down the elevators and telephones. In response, administrators called in the riot squad. When the occupying students got word police had been called in, they pitched an avalanche of computer punch cards and documents out the ninth-floor windows. I saw it on the evening news as millions of punch cards floated down to de Maisonneuve Boulevard and surrounding streets like the ticker take parades I'd seen on newsreels. By the time the cards stopped raining down, the streets were covered with them, like the aftermath of a snowstorm.

Meanwhile, the riot squad knocked down barricades the students had set up to block entry to the computer centre and in the ensuing melee, a fire started. I sat mesmerized in front of my TV as thick black smoke billowed from the building, the same building where my classes took place.

By then a crowd of thousands had gathered on de Maisonneuve and fighting broke out. Counter-protesters were recorded shouting, "Let the niggers burn," referring to West-Indian students and other Black protesters.

No one died that day, but 97 students were arrested, among them 42 were Black.

The following day school administrators reinstated the professor who'd been accused of discrimination and declared him not guilty after an investigation took place.

As to the fire in the computer room that cost the university $2 million in damages, the fire department was unable to pinpoint the cause. Some claimed the occupiers deliberately started it, which they denied, while others maintained the riot police set it off by accident when they stormed the room.

The heat of overt protest settled down at school and life there returned to normal. February inched towards March and then into April. I experienced an insatiable need for sleep and a growing disinterest in social activities I once enjoyed. I felt like a ghost haunting my own life.

In May, three days before we were to move into our new house in Ville Saint-Laurent, another tsunami flattened our life of cards.

CHAPTER FORTY-FOUR

The moving truck had been booked for the early morning of May 1st, 1969. Most of our belongings had been packed for days, and gallons of wall paint sat against a hallway wall to refresh the interior of our new house.

I had come to terms with the relocation, and I looked forward to having a big new bedroom with a big window and my own twin bed and a desk where I could hole up. It almost made up for the long commute I'd have to get to classes all the way downtown.

But it all came to nothing. In mid-April my parents had one last epic fight.

The trigger, I suspected, came when my father realized he'd lost control over us. All of us. Mamma had ignored his edits for quite some time and when he attempted to assert his authority over Teresa and Ricky, they ran to Mamma, who often overruled him. As for me, I challenged him at every opportunity, even when he was right, just because I could.

"When you get a job and help pay the bills you can be the head of the house again," she retorted when he berated her.

At long last, I thought. After twenty-two years of willing submission, Mamma was finding her feet and it delighted me.

The point of no return came just days before the move. As usual, Teresa and I were in our room when we heard fearful screaming and shouting coming from the kitchen. I ran to see what was happening this time, Teresa trailing behind me, to find our parents assaulting each other.

Mamma was trying to claw his eyes out as the bitter venom she'd stored in her heart for two decades came pouring out of her mouth.

"Stop!" he shouted, using his arms to try to fend her off. "Stop it or you'll be really sorry."

"Yeah? I'm sorry already. Sorry for all the wasted years. Now I'm going to murder you with my bare hands."

She had no hope of winning a physical fight against him and yet I understood her rage, a rage so hot she was willing to go down in flames herself to satisfy it.

She kicked him, a hard jab to the shin. He responded with punch to her shoulder and another to her breast but Mamma was beyond feeling pain. Screaming curses, she threw herself on him and tried to sink her teeth into his flesh.

I turned to Teresa, "Go! Go to Zia Tresa's. Tell her what's happening then go and find Ricky. I'm going to call the police."

At the time, 911 emergency didn't exist. As a Bell operator I knew how to find the number in the phone book quickly, but my hands shook so hard it took a while and I feared he'd kill her before the police could get there. When I finally reached the right police division, they could hear my parents still screaming at each other in the background.

I put down the receiver and hurried back into the kitchen to find them circling, hatred in their eyes, the pair of them panting. My father's face bled from where she'd scratched him, and big red marks had begun to bloom on Mamma's arms.

"The bitch is crazy," he said to me. "Get her the fuck out of here before I break her neck."

"This place is mine not yours. I pay the rent, so you get the fuck out!"

Somehow, I managed to pull her away, edging her backwards out of the kitchen into the family room, down the hallway to the top of the stairs, down the staircase and, finally, outside. All the while she kept up a steady stream of curses, every curse she'd heard as a child in Campochiaro and some new ones, condemning him to the worst tortures to body and soul imaginable.

Zia Tresa stood on the sidewalk in front of her flat, waiting for us. "Will this nightmare never end?"

My mother leaned against the brick wall of the house we'd once owned and lived in and sobbed. Her tears didn't provide relief or healing, tears like a summer downpour on parched soil, instead they were like a torrent strong enough to drown a broken woman.

When the police cruiser showed up ten minutes later, she had stopped crying, but her grey eyes had lost their softness.

The police listened to my explanation but, once again, explained there wasn't much they could do. "We'll go up and talk to him. Maybe he'll be reasonable. If you want to take it further, madam, you'll have to file charges."

The same old story. Why had I bothered?

I'd left the door open when I'd gotten Mamma out of there. Now I was with them as one of the cops pressed the bell. My father peered at us then came halfway down the stairs, ashen. Maybe he remembered what it had been like to spend a night in jail, I thought.

The cops gave their names and asked if they could go upstairs for a chat, and he agreed. As they went up, I heard one of the cops say to him, "You look familiar, *monsieur*. I think we've come across you before."

I waited outside on the sidewalk along with Teresa, Ricky, Mamma and Zia Tresa, along with several neighbours who'd been friends with Mamma for many years.

The two officers spent maybe ten minutes with my father but when they came out all they had to say was: "He's been warned. Now it's up to you to press charges, Madame."

"That's it? Can't you make him leave, at least?" I asked.

"Non, *mademoiselle,* we can't. He has a right to be in the house."

"Where are we supposed to go? It's not even safe for us to go in and get our things."

One of them agreed to come up with me so I could get a few necessities, and after that we were on our own.

Once again, we took refuge at Zia Tresa's but we could only stay a few days. They'd also bought house and were about to move. She knew, as we all did, there was no going back with my father. Momma had to decide what to do and fast—but, oh, how it hurt to have to give up the house in Ville Saint-Laurent.

"Can't we keep it, Ma? What with the rent for the two apartments upstairs, your salary and my contribution we could manage it."

She looked at me with pity. "You think he'll just turn over the house to us? No, he'll want me to give back his half of the down payment. I don't have any money left."

The day of their fight, my father controlled all our assets, house included. For once, however, Mamma was in luck with imminent reforms in the Québec Civic Code which were in the works. By the time my parents sold the house, the laws had changed, and he was forced to give Mamma her fair share of community property.

I never learned what precipitated that terrible confrontation between my parents or even who struck the first blow, but Mamma was never the same; bitterness shrivelled her up.

From that day on she said, "I'm the unluckiest woman in the world. No matter what I do, bad things happen to me." This became her life's refrain.

Since we had given notice, our flat had already been rented to someone else and we had to find someplace to live in about week. Not easy during moving season. The job was left up to me. I found a dank basement apartment on Rue de l'Epee in Park Extension, some eight km northwest of Saint-Dominique, with two days to spare.

After a few days, my father had vacated our flat and decamped to Italy, never to return, which allowed us to sleep in our own beds the few days before moving into the basement apartment. As a precaution, we wedged a kitchen chair under the doorknob at the top of the stairs in case he decided to return while we slept.

Eventually, we sold the house to the parents of a school friend of mine. After they moved in, she invited me many a time to visit with her. Sure, it was lovelier than any place we'd ever lived in but given the choice I would choose the basement every time if it meant living without my father.

We settled into the basement, which was clean and freshly painted but damp. It had two bedrooms, a double parlour, a small kitchen, and accesses to a back yard. The three-storey apartment building was owned by a Ukrainian family, kind people, who occupied one of the upstairs apartments.

Ricky, then 12, enrolled at a new elementary school while Teresa remained at the same high school, my alma mater. As for me, I got through junior-year final exams despite steadily crawling deeper into the caverns of my own mind, as far away from people as I could get. Because I told myself, *you can't trust anybody, can you?*

The upheaval had traumatized and changed us all. Mamma became aloof, unreachable. Teresa found solace away from home with her friends and Ricky made new pals at high school—juvenile delinquents, who pulled him into their gang and into trouble. And he started stealing money out of our wallets.

We settled into new routines, only this time, but no longer as a family. In fact, we kids spent as little time at home and with each other as possible. We had our own friends, and Mamma had her sisters.

Soon after junior year finals, I reluctantly went back to work for Bell fulltime for the summer, wishing I had the courage to quit.

CHAPTER FORTY-FIVE

A new friendship was the one good thing that came from my Bell employment that summer. It cheered my up. Like me, Renee—yes, yet another friend named Renee—was also a student, a true-blue Quebecoise, *pure laine,* as separatists called people of French ancestry but didn't subscribe to the radical separatism so many French-speaking university students embraced. She went to a French-language college, spoke English well and hated working at Bell as much as I did.

We spent a lot of time together going to movies, discos, restaurants, theaters, concerts. The pair of us stuck our thumbs out when we felt like going up to the Laurentian mountains to take in a show by one of the *chansonniers,* such as Gilles Vigneault and Pauline Julien, artists who played an important role in the development of Québec's social and political awareness during the Quiet Revolution.

In fact, that year the Québec government moved one step closer to making French the province's only official language when it passed the *Act to Promote the French Language.* The new law gave The Office of the French Language more power and gave employees the right to work in in French.

The law also made changes in education that infuriated the separatists. They considered them too weak to promote their language since it allowed parents, including the ongoing influx of immigrants, to choose to educate their children in English or French. The *Act to Promote the French Language* had sought a balance between the demands of nationalists and the rights of the English-speaking minority but ended up polarizing the population. Five years later, the government replaced it with a law making French the language of civic administration, services and the workplace.

As the world around me gradually shifted to French from English, the growing animosity between the two sides became more obvious, more menacing. If an English-speaking customer asked for something in English, she now had a 50-50 chance of being refused service. On the other hand, away from school I spoke mostly in French since most of my friends were French speaking. I'd grown up among them and had little in common with the kids that came from Irish, English or Jewish households.

In 1969, I celebrated my 20th birthday with Renee by hopping a train to Ottawa for the weekend. Not that the nation's capital had a sizzling nightlife. It did, however, have the advantage of being directly across the Ottawa River from Hull, Que., which had lots of clubs and discos.

We checked into the stately Chateau Laurier near the Parliament buildings and snagged a cheap bottle of wine on the way—Jordan's sweet rosé—to loosen up. Neither of us were drinkers and it didn't take much of that horrid rosé to make us giddy.

Around 10 p.m. we dressed up and cabbed across the river to Hull. At the time, the legal drinking age in Quebec was 21, which made me illegal. No problem. Using the sharp tip of a ballpoint pen, I changed the date on my laminated citizenship card, turned the "9" in 1949 into an "8" and problem solved. In the half-light of club entrances, the ID passed muster. Renee, also 20, had come prepared; she'd borrowed her older sister's ID.

Renee had gone clubbing with a plan in mind. Her sister, Lise, was a man magnet, which mystified us. Although she had a pretty face and strawberry blonde hair with a peachy complexion, the bottom half of her looked like Humpty Dumpty. Looks alone, therefore, didn't explain her charms. We'd done a little prior research by tagging along with Lisa to study her methods. Turned out she enchanted not just men but everyone using smiles and flattery and giving each person she spoke to her full and undivided attention. With men, Lise played the old seduction game of appearing soft, sweet, and malleable, spiced with a little teasing. All the men fell for it, even hard-nosed bouncers at popular nightclubs let her in ahead of those waiting in line without having to fork over a big tip.

That night in Hull I flirted as best I could, given my inexperience. After four hours spent in and out of various establishments, we'd drawn quite a few men to our tables, danced quite a few dances. But to my great surprise, I was bored, bored, bored with those men and the inane conversations. I'd attracted them but that alone wasn't enough and I had more fun wandering around Ottawa the following day.

On the train going home I kept asking myself what sort of boyfriend would satisfy me? Why was it not one of the dozens of guys in my classes or the hundreds I crossed paths within a big university that lived up to the ideal one that lived in my head?

I entered my senior year in the fall of 1969, a little more mangled, a little more aimless and my thoughts a little darker than the previous year before. Mamma and I were at each other as she tried to constrain my comings and goings, wanting me to behave like a good Italian girl living in Campochiaro, while I insisted on the same freedoms others my age enjoyed in Canada. She didn't want me to stay overnight with friends, didn't want me going to discos or take weekend trips away. She'd felt the shame of losing a husband and didn't want the added shame of a daughter getting pregnant, which was her biggest fear.

She pressed me to get *systemata*, to settle down, like my cousin Liliana, 18, who'd been working in factories since 14 and was already engaged to be married.

"I'm never going to get married, Ma," I told her time and time again.

"You will, you'll see. Not all men are like your father."

How could I make her understand it didn't matter if there were good men to be had? My upbringing with the pair of them had scarred me and I didn't want to risk ending up with a marriage like theirs. Besides, I lacked Mamma's flexibility which had allowed her to bend when the storms came.

And yet that year I fell in love, well, I called it love, not knowing how else to identify what I felt. In truth, I slipped into another obsession, another distracting fantasy—as I had with Serge when I was 12—that let me believe I might be able to have a relationship with a boy like everyone else.

I met Chris in an English literature class. He wrote poetry and exuded sadness—which I could relate to. His looks appealed to me: tall, rail-thin and square-jawed, with a head of brown curls. In short, he didn't look like any of my *paesani,* young men who were often short and muscular, bred for mountain toil.

We had two classes together, Romantic and Canadian literature. As fall edged into winter, thoughts of Chris soothed me, filling up the vast space left by my diminished interest in courses and everything else. By the second semester, I rarely went to classes, except for the two I shared with Chris. Mostly, I sat in the cafeteria or hunkered down in my damp basement bedroom with novels while listening to Charles Aznavour songs on my record player when I wasn't working shifts at Bell. I didn't care if I failed my courses; nothing much mattered.

Chris and I sometimes went for coffee and talked or took long walks. One afternoon he handed me a poem he'd written about me. It ended with these words:

A dream glows & Keeps your insides searching.

Some times mad, angry, passion—Reclining to possible indifference

Chris never asked me out on a real date. Why not, I asking myself endlessly? I didn't have the courage to show him how I felt, except for the one time I got up the nerve to invite him along with a few other school friends to a dinner party at the l'Île-Perrot cottage belonging to a family friend of Renee's.

My heart galloped and my mouth was like sandpaper stuffed inside it when I approached him.

His face fell. "Oh, I would have loved to join you. But I'm up in the Laurentians every weekend. I work as a ski instructor."

"Too bad," I heard myself say, quite calmly. But it felt as though he'd pushed me off the edge of a cliff. Whatever his reasons for turning me down, his refusal hurt so much I shut down. What did I have in common with this white bread, upper-middle-class guy anyway—a ski-instructor for God's sake?

Hope doesn't die just because you want it to, however, my brain hung on to the idea of him. He'd represented the possibility of a different future and for months after I lay in bed staring at the ceiling thinking about him. If I'd made some plan for the future, something to work towards and look forward to, darkness might not have overwhelmed me. But until my father left, my life hadn't belonged to me but to him. Now that I could do as I wished, I didn't know which road to take, and it paralyzed me.

During senior year at Sir George, Daniele came into my life, and thank God. She was a tiny, flamboyant young woman with a big voice and a big laugh. She was in the Fine Arts program when I met her, having switched from theatre arts. When I bothered dragging myself downtown to school, we spent hours in the vast, noisy cafeteria, smoking and sharing our life stories. Her family's dysfunction rivalled mine, her father, an unrepentant drunk, as faithless as mine had been, her mother, a kind, vulnerable woman who'd contracted tuberculosis when Daniele was a toddler, placed in a sanitorium for a year, and her four kids farmed out to relatives. She would have died but for experimental surgery that removed one of her lungs. It saved her life but left her with asthma that regularly landed her in hospital. Unlike Mamma, Daniele's mother wasn't well enough to work, and she had to make do with whatever amount her husband gave her to feed and clothe the family.

Daniele, the youngest of two sisters and a brother, and one older sister still lived at home when we met. Daniele seemed so grounded, laughing her big laugh at the hardships, refusing to be cowed by her father, always finding a way to get where she wanted to go. She was fearless in every way but one: she worried about her health and a ganglion cyst on her wrist once sent her into a tailspin. It was an early hint suggesting that under the bravado bubbled a deep pool of anxiety.

I had registered for five courses in my final year but only managed to finish three of them. I didn't even bother taking the exams for the other two and got big, fat Fs on my transcripts for them. It meant I was two courses short and wouldn't graduate in 1970, as I'd hoped.

Now I'd have to get a full-time job and make up the courses in the evening, which I could do since Sir George offered a plethora of courses during evening hours to make it easier for working people to get an education.

Back I went to Bell for the fourth summer. I could have quit and looked for work more congenial to my personality but Mamma, my cousins, and even some of my friends urged me to tough it out. Not only did it pay well, it was a large corporation with great opportunities for someone about to get her degree, and I let myself be convinced.

Meanwhile, my funk lifted after Renee and I decided to move into an apartment together. The big, big problem was how to break the news to my mother.

In the months since my father had run back to Italy, I'd often berated myself for failing to snatch with both hands whatever life had to offer. All around me young women quenched their thirst in every way, breaking all the old rules about how they should behave. They drank openly and frequently; they smoked dope; they changed sex partners as easily as they changed their underwear; they swore; they traveled the world, sometimes alone, seeking adventure. But as for me, I was timid and afraid to take risks, afraid people would get mad at me.

The door to my prison had swung open but I was afraid to step out.

CHAPTER FORTY-SIX

For months, Renee and I had talked about getting our own apartment but when talk became a reality, I wanted to back out. We found a three-month sublet, furnished, in a downtown high-rise in the student ghetto on Prince Arthur East. We took the three-month sublet from a couple of roommates who were heading home for the summer. Three months seemed ideal for a first taste of independence.

I put off telling her until the day before the move, knowing there would be a scene. Teresa knew all about my plan but as promised, she hadn't said a word.

"You what?" Mamma said, bewildered.

"An apartment. Renee and I. It's for three months."

She stared me with a blank expression as she tried to take in what I was saying. When she finally grasped the implications, colour rose from her chest to the throat and flooded her face.

"Oh, my God, what will people say?" she said, pacing the narrow corridor of our basement apartment. "It's not enough that everybody looks down on us already because I have no husband and my children have no father. You're like your father. Think only of yourself. Shame on top of shame."

Her words struck home and the familiar guilt, that I was about to abandon my responsibilities just like my father had, nearly changed my mind.

"Why are you doing this to me?" she asked, as tears coursed down her cheeks.

And that's what did it.

"I'm not doing anything to you! I'm young and I want to live my life for myself, not for you. Look around you, Ma. You left Campochiaro twenty years ago. Haven't you noticed things are different now."

"It's that girl, Renee, isn't it? She talked you into this, didn't she?"

"No, she didn't talk me into anything."

"Well, what do you expect from a French girl? They have loose morals."

Renee later told me her mother, also upset, blamed me for luring her away from home. Her mother had been raised a strict French-Canadian Catholic, and neither one of our mothers had a precedent for unmarried daughters leaving home before marriage.

As arranged, the following morning a car-owning friend of mine came to help me move my things. As I carried out garbage bags of clothes—I had no suitcase—Mamma stood in the hallway near the door repeatedly banging her head against the wall.

A large, choking lump of guilt rose up into my throat but I pushed ahead. If I didn't follow through now, I'd never free myself. I closed the door behind me, shutting off her wails.

The sublet was furnished. All we had to do was put away our clothes and jump into freedom. Not having to answer to anyone felt odd at first, no one telling me to hurry up and finish the dishes or to turn down the music or to ask me where I'd been and with whom.

The apartment was within walking distance of the Bell offices where Renee and I still worked. By now I felt so abhorred about the job I felt nauseated the instant I crossed the threshold. The claustrophobia induced by sitting in the cubicle had never abated and I spent every minute of each shift struggling to stop myself from tearing the headset off my head and hurling it at the wall.

I had come close to quitting at the end of the previous summer but a supervisor had talked me out of it with the promise of a recommendation for management training once I had my degree. I'd stayed, telling myself I shouldn't turn down a good opportunity with an important company. When I'd failed to graduate in 1970 as anticipated, I made another attempt to quit but the same supervisor promised to put my name forward for a head office and again, I stayed.

Meanwhile, our apartment turned into a revolving door as our respective friends came and went, and we loved it. It made my heart soar when my fantasy boyfriend, Chris, gave me a call. I wanted him to come by, but he said was about to leave to backpack across Europe and, once again, I swallowed my bitter disappointment.

It told myself, *Face it, you idiot, Chris has zero romantic interest in me otherwise he would have been in touch long before he was due to leave. Wouldn't he?* No, I didn't want to let go of him, well, the hope of having someone like him in my life.

Renee, meanwhile, got herself a prescription for birth-control pills. She had no boyfriend but intended to get one, and when he came along, she wanted to be ready.

The birth control pill had been available in Canada since 1957 but only for "menstrual irregularities," not contraception. In those early days, advertising or selling contraceptives could bring a fine or jail time, unless it was shown to be in the "public good." Canada legalized the pill for birth control in 1969 when Parliament also legalized "therapeutic" abortions and homosexual acts between consenting adults.

May flew by in a haze of parties, restaurants and discos. Except for having to work my shifts at Bell, I would have called it a perfect life. Teresa, who went to school at Darcy McGee just up the street often stopped by with a friend or two. But by the time I celebrated my 21st birthday in July, the sheen of this new life had worn off. Now when I looked around the apartment, I saw dirty, worn furniture and walls needing a coat of paint. Even worse, nothing in that tawdry one-bedroom apartment belonged to me.

The relationship between Renee and me had soured, too. Her long-time friends and fellow students from the college she attended were separatists and when they stopped in, I was deeply offended by how they disparaged anglophones. I don't suppose they meant to insult me because they didn't consider me, an immigrant, an "Anglo oppressor." At the same time, I would never be one of them because only descendants of the original French settlers—*pure laine*—qualified as real francophones. They tolerated me because of my friendship with Renee and when I rejected their separatist views, they simply ignored me.

Renee didn't share her friends' radical views about how to achieve separatism, but she never spoke up for me, and so began the end of our friendship.

I spent more and more time with Daniele, the friend I'd made at Sir George. Daniele also came from a French-speaking family but as a kid she'd opted to switch to an English school in Grade 5, for the fun of it. She had the typical artistic temperament, with no interest in politics, flamboyant and eccentric. She dyed her long, light brown hair pitch black; she clothed her small frame with Salvation Army purchases, and she took any and all jobs to finance her education. She stayed true to her motto: live and let live.

By the end of July, Renee and I weren't speaking. We'd both made peace with our mothers and now we avoided each other by spending time with our families at the homes we'd fled. When the sublet expired, we went our separate ways for good.

The independence I'd craved for so long hadn't been the magic wand I'd hoped for. It hadn't even ended the panic attacks, hadn't chased away thoughts of death or dispelled the worry I'd never be able to do something significant with my life.

Mamma agreed to let me come home, just as she'd taken my father back so many times. It wouldn't have entered her mind to shut the door

ELVIRA CORDILEONE

in a daughter's face. But she made me pay for the privilege with constant recriminations.

When I returned to Mamma's house, she'd moved out of the dingy basement into the upper floor of a nice duplex in east-end Saint-Michel, a half-block from Zia Carmela. The large, freshly-painted two-bedroom plus double-parlour upper duplex ought to have made me happy. I should have enjoyed sharing the large, bright bedroom with Teresa, furnished with the bedroom suite and twin beds we'd bought for the house we'd never moved into. But I'd fallen into depression, far down inside myself, tormented by sudden bouts of fear that drained my soul.

Meanwhile, Bell gave me a promotion and a transfer. They took me out of the operator's cubicle and gave me at a desk in a room with fifty other women also sitting at desks, all of us doing work as regimented and as deadening as looking up phone numbers had been.

I stumbled deeper and deeper towards the bottom of a big, black pit, tormented by sudden bouts of inexplicable fear that left me limp with exhaustion. I hid in my room, brooding and silent and found comfort in putting thoughts to paper. I wrote:

It is the middle of the night and the wind is strong and beats against my window like the fists of a malevolent ghost. I love it. I love its fury, as though it wants to tear the world apart with bare teeth.

I can't think straight. I pick up the pen, believing I have much to say but when I hold the tip to the notebook all my thoughts seem trivial, even to me.

I'm a corroded pipe about to burst. Can you understand that?

It has started to rain. I hear it banging on the roof, each raindrop as heavy as a hammer blow.

It's 3 o'clock in the morning and I wish I had been born a tree or an insect or a piece of uranium, anything but a human being.

Not long after I wrote those words, I quit Bell. This time no one was able to talk me out of it, not even Mamma, who truly couldn't fathom why I would give up a good-paying job and all the opportunities for advancement. How could I make her see the job was fueling my despair?

CHAPTER FORTY-SEVEN

During my summer of freedom, Montreal seethed with social and political disturbances. Reaction to the findings of a federal royal commission report set up in 1963 to study on bilingualism and biculturalism did not surprise French-speaking communities across Canada: francophones were underrepresented in the nation's political and business communities and data confirmed francophones were among the lowest paid in Canada, twelfth on a list of fourteen ethnic groups, ahead of Italian-Canadians and aboriginal people.

As a new decade approached, Quebec nationalism had acquired broader appeal among ordinary francophones, fed by labour movement demands and student unrest as occupations swept community colleges where the separatist movement was influential.

Between 1966 and 1970 the number of strikes and demonstrations climbed steadily. In 1969 a man died when a protest by taxi drivers against Murray Hill, an English-Canadian car service company with a monopoly at Dorval airport, turned into a riot and overflowed into surrounding neighbourhoods—and it happened while Montreal police were out on strike. In 1968, the same year separatists established their own political party, hundreds of militant nationalists threw stones at Prime Minister Pierre Trudeau during the Saint-Jean-Baptist annual parade as he sat on the reviewing stand.

The radical elements among separatists had been busy organizing for years, and by the end of the decade the various groups had gathered under the umbrella of the Front de libération du Québec. The FLQ operated under a loose structure with individual cells working independently. One such cell, the Québec Liberation Army, raised money and weapons for the cause through armed robbery.

The FLQ were dissatisfied with reforms the government had made to public institutions and to the social and cultural life of the province during the Quiet Revolution. They also rejected the Partie Quebecois's concept of sovereignty-association—an independent and sovereign Quebec but with strong ties to the rest of Canada—as tepid and advocated guerilla tactics instead.

On Oct. 5, 1970, FLQ struck. Two separatists armed with machine guns rushed the Montreal home of British trade commissioner James Cross and took him by force as he left for work. Its ransom demands included release of twenty-three "political" prisoners—FLQ members jailed for various acts of violence—demanded the government widely broadcast its manifesto, $500,000 in gold; and an airplane to take the kidnappers to a safe haven in Cuba or Algeria.

The government refused their demands. But while declaring it, it remained open to negotiations, police raided FLQ strongholds and arrested thirty people. When the terrorists countered with further threats to Cross' life, the authorities allowed the FLQ manifesto to be read on a single radio station, CKAC, and on the French national television outlet, Radio-Canada.

Negotiations continued for several days and on Oct. 10 the government agreed to give the kidnappers safe-conduct out of Canada if they released Cross unharmed but refused to release the so-called political prisoners.

Only hours later, the Chenier cell of the FLQ upped the stakes with the kidnapping of Pierre Laporte, Québec's vice-premier and labour minister, whom the terrorists had labelled "Minister of Unemployment and Assimilation." They grabbed Laporte at gunpoint as he played football with his nephew on his front lawn and issued communiqués threatening to kill him unless their demands were met.

Negotiators for the two sides met for several days but when talks failed Québec's premier, Robert Bourassa, asked Ottawa for "emergency powers." On October 16, Prime Minister Pierre Trudeau proclaimed a state of "apprehended insurrection" under the War Measures Act, declaring the FLQ an unlawful organization, suspended the civil liberties of anyone associated with or supporting it, and gave police wide powers of arrest. Within the next forty-eight hours later, police made 250 arrests, including labour leaders, entertainers, and writers. More than seven thousand Canadian soldiers were deployed to Montreal and Québec City, where they remained well into December.

One day after the suspension of civil liberties, the Chenier cell announced it had executed Laporte. On October 18, his body was found in the trunk of a car on Montreal's south shore. News reports suggested he'd been strangled with the necklace for his religious medallion.

The majority of Québecers reacted to Laporte's murder with revulsion and shock.

James Cross, however, was still missing. In early November, the FLQ released a Polaroid of Cross playing solitaire while sitting on a crate ostensibly full of dynamite as proof of life.

After fifty-nine days in captivity, the authorities traced Cross to a small room on des Récollets Street in Montreal North. Negotiations with the abductors led to his Dec. 3 release in exchange, for safe conduct to Cuba, supposedly exiled for life. But starting in the late 1970s and for the next few years the exiles—some of whom had left Cuba for France—returned to Quebec and served various prison terms for the kidnapping of James Cross.

Details of Laporte's murder were established at trial. Two of the terrorists, Paul Rose and Francis Simard, received life sentences for murder but were released in 1982. A third accomplice, Bernard Lortie, was handed twenty years for kidnapping, and Jacques Rose, a fourth member was convicted as an accessory and sentenced to eight years. They were released on parole in 1977 and 1978.

By the end of 1970, police had carried out 1,500 raids and arrested more than 450 persons, the vast majority released without charges. Of those charged, only two were later convicted, but after the October Crisis, the FLQ fell apart. However, the desire for independence remained alive, and it gained strength with the election of a separatist Parti Québécois, under Rene Levesque, a former Liberal cabinet minister.

The tussle for freedom now moved to the political level.

CHAPTER FORTY-EIGHT

I had quit Bell in early September so that when the October Crisis hit, I had the leisure to watch it happening on TV news, blow by blow when I should have turned my thoughts to finding a job. To get some air, I sometimes took the short walk to Zia Carmelina's place. We lived on different blocks of the same street, separated by John F. Kennedy High School. The first time I saw the school's football field filled with army tanks and jeeps, and soldiers patrolling armed with semi-automatic weapons, it shocked me. In a second, the TV news reports I'd been watching turned from an interesting spectacle into a real situation that could drag me into danger. I hurried past them.

My departure from Bell hurt my finances but not my mental health. It gave me the time I needed rest my body and clear the fuzziness that covered my thinking. I woke up one morning to realize that I'd been acting like my father had, brooding and scared, and unable to stick to a job. It made me ashamed, and I got serious about finding work.

I combed help-wanted ads in the Montreal Star and Montreal Gazette which in pre-internet times was a good way to find a job. I examined the big display ads and the tiny classifieds listings. I made dozens of telephone calls and mailed resumes as directed and waited for call-backs. I went to a few interviews, but nothing came of them until December when I was invited to an interview for a job as a billing clerk for a company that manufactured fine rings.

I groaned when the call came because I'd thought I was finished with factories. Well, at least jewellery had more aesthetic appeal than pajamas. Besides, a clerk worked in an office not on the factory floor.

The interview lasted fifteen minutes, and, bingo, I had a job. It paid $60 a week, which wasn't much, even for the times, and quite a bit less than I'd earned at Bell, which paid a basic wage plus shift differentials and double time for working Sundays. But I'd quit Bell, hadn't I? When the owner of the company told me the salary, it didn't enter my mind to negotiate the salary. Women didn't do that. Like most women, when the terms didn't suit me, I'd simply walk away.

The next day I arrived for work promptly at 8:30 a.m. The owner of Trico Ring, Mr. Simon, sat at his desk, head down, sketching something and didn't notice me standing there, waiting.

"Mr. Simon?" I said, finally.

He looked up, his eyes unfocussed, as though he'd just awakened. "Ah, you're here." He put down the pencil. "Okay. Come with me."

We went to the large open area beyond his office. It had tall, mullioned windows on two sides and if it had not been coated with thick grime, the room would have been a pleasure to work in. The walls needed a lick of fresh paint and the linoleum floors were cracked. Still, I appreciated the sense of openness and space.

The room contained three pairs of facing desks. One was occupied by a grizzled, portly man in his 60s and another by a tall, thin young guy with a thick head of pitch-black hair.

"This is Elvira, our new invoice clerk. Show her the ropes M. Elbaz," Mr. Simon said to the older man.

"*Bonjour, Mademoiselle* Elvira," Mr. Elbaz said. He escorted me to the factory floor, accessible via a steel door from our area and introduced me to the half-dozen men sitting at workbenches, although it had room for many more. The place vibrated with hammering and metal files rubbing and rubbing against precious metal. Bursts of steam used to clean finished rings, punctuated the racket.

Once the tour ended, he showed me to my desk, opposite his own, next to a pair of tall filing cabinets. The young guy with the halo of dark hair—occupied a desk a dozen feet to my left—told me he coordinated production but he didn't volunteer the information; I had to ask him.

It was nearing Christmas; their busiest time of year and I got down to work. I wrote invoices by hand, item by item, store by store, when the orders were ready to ship, using an adding machine and a small black binder that listed style numbers and prices. Like most things in life, the work wasn't as straightforward, and I had expected that, but as I learned about precious stones and how to adjust prices based on their sizes and the amount of gold in a setting, I settled right in.

It gave me so much pleasure to look at and handle such lovely objects, the sparkling fire of diamonds, the warmth of green emeralds, the smooth velvet of blue sapphires, and softer beauty of semi-precious garnets, amethysts, yellow topaz, citrine, fiery opal, and dozens more—all encased in glossy gold. The play of light struck me as magical.

The closer we came to Christmas, the more frantic the calls from clients who hadn't received their orders, or only partial orders. I wasted hours trying to give them satisfaction and fell behind on clearing on sending out those that were ready to ship.

Trico's operations were a mess. But I took it as a challenge and at the end of each day I went home contented, if weary. I hounded Mr. Simon until he hired someone to wash and wax the floors every couple of weeks, cleared the windowsills of two decades of accumulated invoice booklets and covered it with vinyl wallpaper to keep it clean.

The busyness of the job and the problem-solving it demanded suited me, although the griminess of our surroundings bothered me.

Within a year, I was running the administrative side of things, built a good rapport with customers, most of them independent jewellery stores across Canada serviced by Trico's three travelling salesmen, and had good relations with my co-workers.

I also went to evening classes at Sir George to earn the credits I needed for my Bachelor of Arts degree.

At home, however, things weren't looking so good. Ricky, now 13, had Mamma in a tailspin. He was cutting classes and had gotten involved with a group of "thugs," and he simply ignored her constant unending harangues. Teresa, 15, got herself a job as a part-time cashier in a supermarket. Between working, going to school and hanging out with her friends, the only time I saw her was when we were getting ready to go to bed.

In 1971 I bought a car, a brown Ford Pinto, that freed me to venture outside the city—that is, once I learned to drive since I bought it on impulse, before I had a driver's licence. Once I got behind the wheel, it was pure joy to come and go as far as I liked and as I pleased.

For a whole year I thought I'd sorted my head, and the mirage vanished as Trico's 1971 Christmas season neared. I'd asked Mr. Simon to hire temporary help but instead of hiring a junior clerk for a few weeks, he gave me the services of his wife.

I'd met her a few times and she'd seemed nice enough. She had a natural elegance, impeccable grooming, the sort of woman who leaves a whiff of scent when she walks past. On her left ring finger, she wore a perfect five-carat, emerald-cut diamond, a gift from her husband, of course.

The woman meant well but rather than helping, she got in everybody's way, even her husband's. She delayed production in her attempts to complete a missing item from an order; she got frazzled, got distracted and would put down valuable rings, forget where she'd left them and get everybody to stop what they were doing to search for it.

It got very tense between us after she started double-checking every invoice I wrote and accused me of undercharging clients when I hadn't.

The old sensations of being caught in a snare returned. I didn't linger at Trico as I had with Bell. This time I started looking for another job as soon as the Christmas holidays ended.

Was this how my father had felt just before he quit all his jobs? Maybe. I just hoped I wasn't as crazy as he'd been in other ways.

I quit Trico in February 1972 after 14 months. The next job, cost accounting for a small construction company, lasted four months; the one after that as a clerk with a cosmetics company, also a matter of months. I couldn't believe it myself when Mr. Simon called me in November 1972 and begged me to go back at double what they'd paying me when I quit.

Despite Mamma's warnings that going back would be a mistake, I took the offer. I returned to my old job in November 1972 but quit after two months. Mrs. Simon had promised me a free hand on the administrative side, but she became more controlling than ever. I left after we had a loud argument over the ridiculous number of hours I'd worked in December. The second breakup was acrimonious.

CHAPTER FORTY-NINE

By 1972, Ricky, now 15, spiralled out of control. Mamma and I were watching television one evening when we got a call from the local police station. He was in custody for hash possession, but they didn't charge him because he ate the evidence to avoid more serious charges. It was his first offence and they let him go.

I went to get him at the police station. When he got home, he went straight to bed and slept for twenty-four hours.

Mamma, fearing worse to come, put him on a plane for Italy in early December and sent him to stay with our father in Campochiaro. I didn't hold much hope that one selfish bastard could teach another selfish bastard to behave with decency while Mamma took the opposing view. She thought only a bastard would know how to deal with another.

I rang in the New Year unemployed. The thought I'd quit three jobs in 1972 weighed on me. I buried myself in my room, cast down about the future and berating myself for failing at everything I tried. I was 23 and no nearer to figuring out what path to take.

I took pen to notebook to try to understand my behaviour and to keep my head above the dark pool of depression.

January 2, 1973

Dark day when an angel visited me for the first time.

Snow of the grey sort covered the streets, the sidewalks, the little bushes that in summer line the streets and separate the houses so prettily from the sidewalk.

I think about the purple rose I once wrote about. Something about a search for a rare purple rose as part of a sacrificial offering on some stone altar. And madness at the end of the story either because I found the flower or because I didn't. I don't remember which now.

The angel appeared on that bleak, snowy day. I noticed something odd in the corner by the window when my gaze moved towards the sound of branches rattling against the pane. The air seemed thicker there, like a dense fog. The fog began to swirl until it shaped itself into an angel with large blue wings.

The angel floated towards my bed where I lay defenseless. Is that music I hear issue from its mouth, I asked myself? No, not music. But not words either. I could make no sense of it.

As I strained to make sense of it, a sudden bolt of fear struck me from inside. My chest. Had this creature come to comfort me or to draw me into madness?

The milky shape perched on the edge of my bed, sat at my elbow as one would next to someone who is ailing.

My hand reached out to touch the angel. My hand vibrates to thrums it emits. It soothes me.

January 27, 1973

I tell myself I should get married because that would at least help deal with this emptiness, wouldn't it? No job. No boyfriend. Must there be something wrong with me? There is no place in this world for me. If my angel had let me peer into the future, would I have killed myself. I don't know how long I can endure this agony?

February 10, 1973

Will I marry and have children? No, and no. I can't see myself with children, nor with the kind of man that would father them. I don't have the strength to fight a potential second war over control of my life like the one I fought with my father.

My brother has written from Campochiaro to say he wants to come home. He says he and my father are not getting along. Now there's a surprise. I doubt my mother will hold firm and make him stay.

February 12, 1973

I feel distant and especially vulnerable today. What's causing this lump in my throat? This sense of strangeness within my own skin? This pressure against my heart? I almost want to say "I wish I were dead." But I don't want to die. I want this unending, unendurable, inexplicable anguish to stop.

February 13, 1973

Can't sleep. Haven't slept much for weeks. What I've come to call The Thing, this frightening disconnection between my body and my mind torments me, terrifies me, makes me think I'm on the verge of madness like my father. Please, God, make it stop because if you don't, I may do it for you.

My mother is unwell. She's seeing doctors for terrible pain in her lower abdomen. I am a selfish daughter, worrying about a psychic pain when she might end up in the hospital.

Writing helped but I wrote without a goal, merely to vent. Maybe if I'd tried to write stories or a novel, it might have given me a sense of achievement, of satisfaction. Instead, inch by inch, the black pool in which I found myself pulled me lower, closer and closer to drowning me. The few times I ventured out for a meal or a movie with Daniele, the world appeared surreal. Sometimes I saw it in black and white, sometimes in cartoonish colours but either way I felt myself out of place in it.

I spent many weekends at Daniele's place. She was a senior at Sir George Williams and still lived with her parents. Bother her sisters had married and moved near Quebec City. On weekends we'd sometimes jump in my car and stay with one or the other of them. The outings distracted me and helped me forget my dark thoughts.

Daniele understood and accepted my state of mind. She didn't get upset when I had to excuse myself in the middle of a restaurant meal because the ceiling pressed down on me.

"Okay. I'll meet you outside when I'm finished eating," she'd say.

Nightmares routinely destroyed my sleep. In the middle of the night, a terrifying image hurled me awake. The terror so overwhelmed I cried out my sister's name. She came instantly awake, got out of her bed and lay down next to me.

"I'm afraid," I said. I felt cold from the inside out.

She didn't know what to say, how to handle her big sister's breakdown, the one she'd relied on to fix things. But she rubbed my back and stayed next to me the rest of the night.

The nightmare had been so vivid: I had turned into a lamb and lay on a butcher's block watching a big burly man wearing a bloodied apron. I was alive when he raised an axe and began chopping me to pieces.

In-between my struggles, I applied for jobs, applied for many that didn't interest me because unemployment benefits were meager and wouldn't last forever. I went to many interviews but received no offers. Depression clung to my skin like bad perfume; interviewers smelled and didn't like it.

After four long months, in March 1973, I started working at Marian Hall, a job both wonderful and searing.

CHAPTER FIFTY

Marian Hall was a reform school for Catholic, English-speaking teenage girls in custodial care. Its inmates were placed there by the courts for violations under the then Juvenile Delinquency Act and held under lock and key. I'd applied for a job as a childcare worker and now drove the thirty kilometers from Saint-Michel in northeast Montreal to suburban Beaconsfield in the West Island for the interview with trepidation. Could I do the work? I had no experience in the field or any tangential education such as a background in psychology. A three-year college program for custodial childcare workers was in the works but hadn't yet started.

I exited Highway 2-20, crossed a railroad track, followed the road into a circular drive and parked in front of a U-shaped, three-storey building. Six concrete steps led to a glass double-door which opened into a small vestibule. A heavy oak door with an opaque half-window barred entry, and I saw no one at the desk behind the reception's window to my left.

I was tempted to turn tail and run. Instead, I pressed the buzzer, knowing if I acted on my fears, I'd end up hiding under the bed like my father.

A scarecrow of a woman with frizzy hair and deep red lipstick came to the reception area. I told her my name and why I was there. She disappeared and a moment late I saw her silhouette at the door and heard the key as she slid it into the lock to open it from the inside. I entered an unusually long, wide hallway with closed doors on each side, and on either end.

I made an effort to smile as she beaconed me to follow. The scarecrow introduced herself as secretary to Marian Hall's director, Ms. Barnett, the woman who would be interviewing me.

Marian Hall, I later learned, was founded in 1956 and run by the Sisters of the Good Shepherd— I just couldn't seem to get away from nuns!—until 1972 when Québec centralized youth protection services and took it over. The nuns had only recently left when I applied, except for Ms. Barnett, their Mother Superior, who took a leave from her religious community, to stay on. Ms. Barnett needed to hire people to replace the departed nuns.

The scarecrow ushered me into the director's office. Ms. Barnett smiled, offered a limp handshake, and in a cultural voice, but one lacking warmth, she invited me to sit down.

The interview went well enough, although it troubled me that she avoided my eyes. Something about her felt off, but as a supplicant I was the one under the microscope, I told myself. She asked me questions about my background and work history; she told me about the institution goals and what would be required of me.

"You're young, only 23, I see. Do you think you can treat our charges as a good parent would?"

The questions sent a shiver up my spine. How could I act like a good parent when I wasn't doing such a good job taking care of myself? I answered in the affirmative, of course.

A few days later the scarecrow offered me the job. Of course, I accepted, despite my nervousness dealing with potentially violent teenagers.

The second time I stepped into Marian Hall's vestibule the receptionist area was staffed. A phone call from the woman brought the childcare supervisor, Lynn Fischer. She stood more than six feet tall and had the shoulders of a linebacker. I walked next to her as she led me to her office, feeling like a midget.

We sat down. An open family-size bottle of Coca-Cola sat in the middle of her desk. She offered me some, which I refused. She had a soft voice, warm blue eyes, and laughed a lot. I liked her.

She told me Marian Hall housed forty-five girls who ate, slept, went to school and played inside those walls. They were divided into three units, referred to as apartments. Each apartment its own kitchen/dining room and living room on the main floor, and bedrooms on the second-storey. All the girls shared the gym, schoolrooms and outdoor swimming pool.

"Come on, let me show you around while the kids are still in class. After that I'll turn you over to Mrs. Holt. She's the childcare worker on the day shift in your unit today. She's been here a few years and she'll put you on the right track. By the way, you've been assigned to apartment two."

The entrances to apartments one and three lay at either end of the long hallway. My unit was in between them, about twenty feet down from Lynn's office. Lynn inserted one of the keys she kept on a ring attached to her jeans to open the unit's entry door and we stepped into the quiet. A full kitchen and large dining area with six square stables for four to the left, facing a cinderblock wall painted lemon yellow—the same pale yellow my father had chosen for our duplex on Saint-Dominique. Beyond the dining area was a short hallway with a windowed staff office to the left and an activity room to the right, and ended in large living room furnished with battered couches and recliners along with a stereo and a television set. The living room had a locked door leading into a staircase for up into the bedrooms and down into basement rumpus room.

As we walked through the living room, Lynn remarked, "TV is a privilege they have to earn, as are cigarettes." She opened the door to the staircase, and we went up to the bedrooms.

At the top the stairs we came to yet another locked door, which explained why she tethered keys to her belt loop.

"Everything's locked," I said, more to myself.

"Yes, everything. Even the kitchen pantry. But don't worry. You'll only need one key to open all the doors in this apartment."

The bedroom floor was another long corridor with a series of doors on either side, some open some closed. Suddenly, one of the doors opened and a bare-footed teen wearing tatty pajamas stepped out. My heart lurched.

"Hey, Fischer!" the girl called out, smirking. She had the doughy face all plump and of an over-sized baby, and frizzy, unkempt dark blonde hair.

"Ah, shit," Lynn muttered. "It's *Mrs.* Fischer to you, Mary. Why aren't you in school?"

Mary grinned then turned her attention to me. "So, you're the new jailer?"

"I asked you a question." Lynn faced Mary, arms crossed, staring down at the much shorter girl, who happened to be taller than me by a couple of inches.

Mary couldn't hold the stare. "I'm sick. People get sick, you know," she replied, truculent now.

"Uh-huh? Well, you'd better get into bed, and stay there until tomorrow morning. I'm sure Mrs. Holt won't mind bringing you up a supper tray."

"Fucking bitch!" Mary muttered as Lynn pointed her finger at Mary's bed. "I need to go to the bathroom."

"Fine." Lynn escorted her down the hall to the toilet and bathtub area, where she waited until she finished her business then walked back with the girl to her room.

"In you go," Lynn said.

"I'm hungry."

Lynn once again pointed into Mary's room.

"You're a fucking bitch, Fischer, you know that? I think you like making me suffer."

Lynn didn't engage her, merely kept her index finger pointing.

I thought about quitting then, feeling out of my depth and a little afraid for my own safety. If Mary had defied me, would I have been able to bend her to my will?

Mary turned, went inside her room, slammed the door shut and screamed obscenities.

"Cut it out, Mary, or I'll lock you in." Mary responded by kicking the door.

Lynn slid her key into the lock. Mary went wild, screaming and hitting the door with feet and fists. "I'm going to cut myself and it'll be all your fault," she said.

"The last time she got this mad at me she vandalized the rooms of several of her house mates. That's why I locked her in."

"Aren't you worried about her cutting herself?"

"She might make scratches on her arms with a straight-pin as usual but I'm sure she won't do any real damage. She uses the threat to get attention. Still, I'll ask Mrs. Holt to check on her."

Mary had lived at Marian Hall three years, arriving when the Sisters of Good Shepherd still ran the place. A judge had placed her at Marian Hall because Mary's dysfunctional family couldn't handle her and didn't want her. "She's been getting worse and worse since the nuns left last year," Lynn said.

She showed me the bedrooms—singles, doubles and triples—and a tiny staff room at the end of the hall for the overnight workers—who were hired especially for that shift, thank goodness. There were no showers, only bathtubs, and not enough of them, so the kids had scheduled bath times.

Lynn and I went back down the staircase past the main floor and into the basement rumpus room where they kids would soon be let out of class for recess. My heart banged against my ribs.

Before the inmates were let out of school, Lynn showed me some of the other facilities in the basement, doors she unlocked one by one: a teaching kitchen, a hair salon, and four isolation cells with mattresses on the concrete floor. Those small cells spooked me, and I hoped I'd never have to put anyone in there.

CHAPTER FIFTY-ONE

Lynn left me in the rumpus room in the hands of a stocky, grey-haired woman, Mrs. Holt, the worker on the day-shift in my unit. Two much younger women, responsible for the other two units sat together waiting for the girls to come down for recess.

They welcomed me. I hoped that soon I could be as calm, as easygoing, as unafraid as they were locked up with teenagers dangerous enough to be put in prison. As the moment approached to meet the kids, my fear had risen to such a pitch I yearned to get out of there.

Suddenly, violently, the doors burst open at one end of the room. We stood up as forty-five rowdy, chattering, nicotine-deprived teens rushed to the person in charge of the unit they lived in, hands out, wanting their cigarettes.

"Keep your voices down, girls," Mrs. Holt said. She made no move to hand out the smokes until they quieted.

"First, meet your new worker," she said and introduced me to each one, names I forgot as soon as she said them. Next, she handed out the cigarettes, lighting them with a disposable lighter she then slipped back into her old-fashioned smock.

All at once, the room shook with rock and roll music. One of the kids had put a record on the turntable and turned up the volume full blast. Mrs. Holt instantly moved towards the source of the noise, and I noticed that she limped. She said something to the girl, who angrily shut off the noise. As Mrs. Holt walked away, the girl gave her the finger, but she didn't see it.

I told myself the work wasn't for me. I couldn't see myself—almost a contemporary—handle those kids as deftly as Mrs. Holt had.

Recess ended. The girls returned to their classrooms, and Mrs. Holt lurched up the stairs to our unit. We sat in the dining area as she explained the daily drill over a pot of tea. Lynn came in and gave me my own master key. Soon the lunch hour came, and we returned to the rumpus room to collect our charges. They crowded around the locked door at the bottom of the stairs and as soon as she unlocked it, a dozen girls trooped in, jostling each other, legs pumping as they hurried up the stairs.

"No, running!" Mrs. Holt called out.

The ran past the living room, talking and giggling into the kitchen and dining area where tables had been set for lunch by one of the kids. Each girl had an assigned task for the week, which included washing or drying dishes and sweeping up the kitchen and dining area.

"What crap did the cook send for lunch, Molt?" one of them shouted. They had affectionately abbreviated Mrs. Holt's name to Molt.

Mrs. Holt—who would be dishing out the food, stood at the counter waiting for them to line up in an orderly way—turned narrowed eyes on the questioner. "I don't like your language, Georgia, and I don't like the disrespect you show for the effort Mrs. Lariviere makes to give you good wholesome food." A few of them rolled their eyes.

On weekdays, lunch, and dinner for all three apartments came from the professional kitchen in the basement. On weekends, those who'd behaved went home to visit their families. Those staying behind, including kids who had no families, cooked in their own unit while under our supervision.

Mrs. Holt lifted the cover of the large stainless steel chafing dish. "It's shepherd's pie."

"Get the ketchup, quick!" somebody called out.

Mrs. Holt laughed. "There's no satisfying you girls."

Mrs. Holt prepared a plate for Mary, who was locked in her room, and took it up to her. I took my serving of shepherd's pie and found an empty seat at one of the tables for four, praying she wouldn't leave alone with them for long.

I needn't have worried; they weren't aggressive with me, just curious and peppered me with questions about my age, marital status, hobbies and anything else that came to mind.

When everyone had finished eating, the girls assigned to clearing the tables and doing dishes got to work. The others broke up into small groups, some in the living room, some upstairs to their bedrooms. A pair stuck close to Mrs. Holt until class resumed.

Child-care workers had three shifts: 7 a.m. to 3 p.m.; 3 p.m. to 11 p.m., with night shift, 11 p.m. to 7 a.m., worked by people hired for that specific shift. Shortly before my shifted ended at 3 o'clock on my first day, the evening staffer came in. Mrs. Holt had gone to the rumpus room to get the girls and left us to get acquainted.

"I've given my notice," the woman said to me. "I can't wait to get out of this hell hole." We sat in the staff room. From there we could see who passed along the hallway and what went on in the living room. "I've been here a year and during that time the girls have gotten more and more threatening. We've been begging management to work in pairs, especially the afternoon and evening shift when most of the trouble happens. But here I am alone on duty again after you leave at 5 o'clock."

If *she's* scared, I thought, how should I feel? "What do you mean? How are they threatening?"

"Don't get me wrong. Most of them aren't violent. It's the two or three who are desperate to break outta here. They're constantly plotting to grab the *magic* key we carry around. Once they get out of the building it's not a long walk to the highway where they can hitch a ride.

"The most dangerous time is when we're all upstairs getting ready for bed. You know right away they're up to something when a few of them gather in one of the bedrooms and start whispering. A staffer alone up there is a sitting duck. A couple of them can grab you as you're walking along the hall, tie you up and take the key."

"Has it happened?"

"We've foiled a couple of attempts. You have to keep your eyes and ears open."

"But isn't there a night watchman?"

"Yes. His duty is 8 p.m. to 8 a.m. But they could wait until after he's finished one of his rounds to attack."

God in heaven, what had I gotten myself into?

I spent the evening after my first day at Marian Hall vacillating between surrendering to fear and potentially learning to do rewarding work. I called Daniele, who had a knack for getting to the heart of things.

"You've been there one day!" she said.

"Yes, I know. But apart from being scared shitless, I don't know if I can get a dozen teenagers to listen to me."

"Well, then, find out. You can quit anytime."

And so, I worked a second shift, then a third and a fourth, until the shifts added up to exactly two years of my life.

CHAPTER FIFTY-TWO

Once I'd decided to stay at Marion Hall, I promised myself I'd treat the kids with the courtesy and respect their humanity demanded. I established good rapport with most of the girls in my care, and even had a lot of fun. There were a couple I loathed—Mary, the kid Lynn locked in her room my first day—and several others were so ill they should have been in a psychiatric hospital.

I had a simple formula: you treat me fairly, and I'll do the same for you.

I did my best to engage them. In the evenings, we played board games, watched movies together on television. On weekends, we cooked together, used the hair salon to wash and set their hair, showed them had to do a facial. On special occasions, such as a birthday, I asked permission to take them out for a hamburger. Mostly, however, we just talked and talked and talked—so many ached to be heard.

I enjoyed my work although I often felt drained by the girls' demands for love and attention. Some eight months after I started the good rapport, I'd established with my charges, saved me from a catastrophe provoked by the evil, baby-faced Mary.

She had an uncanny ability to sense people's emotions and moods, and enjoyed poking them when they were most vulnerable, and the other girls despised her. That day, Mary was needling Christine, an intense girl in the throes of depression. I was in the dining area when the shouting started and rushed into the living room where Mary and Christine faced off, red-faced and panting.

"Okay, that's enough," I said, coming to stand between them.

Shouting always drew the other kids, and they stopped whatever they'd been doing to gather round.

"One of these days, somebody's going to put you in the hospital," Christine said to Mary, her voice laced with loathing.

Behind me someone shouted, "Don't worry, Chrissie, the bitch will probably do it to herself."

I shot an angry glance over my shoulder to where spectators had gathered, as big-eyed and excited as boxing fans. "Not another word!"

"Mary, Christine, please go to your rooms. You can come back down when you've calmed down."

"Whatever!" She moved towards the door, now wedged open to allow them free access to their bedroom upstairs. But she went throw the doorway, thinking herself safe, Mary threw kerosene on the fire. With a vicious smile splitting her doughy face she said to Christine, "You're a fucking cunt and I hope you die."

In one fluid motion, Christine picked up a ceramic vase from an end table, smashed it against the wall and rushed at Mary holding a shard. Mary tried to bolt up the steps, but her ungainly body made her slow and Christine soon caught up with her, pushed Mary hard against the wall and jammed the sharp edge of broken pottery up against her throat.

"What did you say, you piece of shit?"

Mary pressed herself against the cinder-block wall. Her terror-stricken eyes begged me to save her. Her housemates, who scorned her, were clustered behind and around me on the landing, as frightened as Mary. It was one thing for them to enjoy a good argument amongst themselves but quite another to cut somebody's throat—they all knew Christine was capable of doing it.

I felt their gazes pressing against my back, their breaths held, waiting to see what I'd do. Mary wasn't the only one at risk. If I couldn't bring the situation under control, I'd lose their trust along with my ability to control them.

In moments of danger, I've never been one to panic. An inner calm overtakes me, and I do what I have to do but once the danger passes, I fall apart. And that's what happened that day.

Poised on the landing, I did nothing for about 30 seconds. I let Christine hold the shard to Mary's throat so that she could make her point that Mary was in the wrong. Then I went up the steps towards the two girls. Mary flattened against the wall moved only her eyeballs side to side.

"Chris," I said as softly as I could. "Christine." I put my hand on her shoulder and felt the tension. Her body vibrated with the effort it took her to keep from cutting Mary's throat.

"Chris, Mary shouldn't have spoken to you that way. You're right to be angry. But she didn't touch you. Please let her go."

Christine stiffened. Nobody moved; nobody breathed. Ten seconds, 15 seconds elapsed, each one fraught with a disastrous outcome. And then I felt Christine's muscles slacken.

"Get out of my face, you pathetic excuse for a human being," Christine said. I held out my hand for the weapon as Mary scampered upstairs like a frightened rabbit.

I was proud of the way I'd handled the situation and it cemented my relationships with all the girls in my unit except Mary, who learned nothing from the incident. I had to take a week's vacation because of the stress it caused me.

In 1974, almost a year after I started my new career, I got myself a nice, newly-built apartment in the West Island, not far from work, and moved in. The short commute was a big bonus.

Because this was my second attempt at having a place of my own, I'd imagined Mamma would take the news with equanimity. Wrong. She cut me out of her life, and we didn't exchange a single word for the next year. I'd pick up Teresa whenever she had a few days off and we'd spend them together. She and I never argued. We did things together, movies, shopping and so on and talked about work and school but we never talked about our shared past or heart-to-heart talks about the pain in our hearts and souls.

It took an intervention by a *paesano*'s to convince Mamma to "forgive" me. I would have preferred him to mind his own business. Nevertheless, we reconciled.

At work, however, we were in the middle of upheaval. At the start of my second year of employment, the provincial government set new regulations regarding the management of "reception centres" such as Marian Hall. Lynn was no longer my boss. Ms. Barnett remained as director, but a PhD psychologist was hired to oversee the management of the girls' care. Supervisors with experience and appropriate post-secondary education in psychology were hired for the day-to-day management of each of the three units. Two of the new supervisors were men, and the third was Lynn, who was put in charge of one of the units. The new supervisor of our unit was a man named David, a good guy. It struck me as odd that at the first opportunity management had hired two male supervisors and a male psychologist to run an institution which had been in the hands of women for more than two decades.

When our new supervisor, David, joined our unit, he met privately with each of us. When my turn came, he asked me to speak openly, describe my experiences, and make suggestions.

"I have to say, David, I don't hold out much hope for this place."

"Trust me," he said. "Lean on me. I'm a brick."

I gazed into his eyes, earnest, kind and filled with determination. I wanted to believe he could make things better.

The girls, of course, were in a tizzy of excitement to have male child-care workers, except for those who'd been traumatized by men. Many of those kids had spent their young lives manipulating men as a survival mechanism, trading sex for money and favours. Now, they flirted openly with caregivers, although I never saw any one of the men on staff respond inappropriately.

The sort of children we were getting gradually changed, too, as the kids who'd been there when I'd started, were released into the care of their families. The new arrivals were street wise and hardened. Drugs became a growing problem and several near-tragic incidents occurred in 1974, one of them on my watch.

It happened on a Sunday evening after Susan returned from a visit home. I'd come on duty at 3 o'clock and noticed she seemed unusually subdued. I kept an eye on her, and when she didn't appear for a snack later in the evening, I found her on the living-room couch, half asleep. "Susan, don't you want your snack?"

"Too tired."

She didn't sound right. "Susan, look at me." She had difficulty opening her eyes.

"What did you take, kiddo?"

"Pills," she said, drifting off.

"What pills?"

"Mellaril," she said, slurring.

Susan hadn't been prescribed Mellaril, a psychiatric drug used for mood disorders, but one of the other kids did take it. We kept all the prescription drugs locked up in the pantry.

Luckily, two of us were on duty. I asked my colleague to follow me into the office and told her about Susan.

"Jesus Murphy!" she cried.

We decided she'd herd the kids into the gym for a game of dodge ball while I dealt with Susan.

I called David and while I waited for him to answer, I wondered whether the Mellaril Susan had ingested had been stolen from the locked pantry. Possibly, one of the girls had districted one of us while in the there getting something while someone else slipped the bottle off the shelf. Or maybe the kid who had a prescription had been saving them and sold the pills to Susan. Or maybe Susan found a bottle at home that weekend and took them before she came back to Marian Hall.

David finally answered. "I'll call Barnett, right away. We need her okay to call an ambulance."

"I'd knock on her door myself, but I'd probably get fired. Please, hurry up. Meanwhile, I'll get Susan walking."

Ms. Barnett lived at Marian Hall in a self-contained apartment. I prayed she was at home. With mobile phones in the distant future, we had no other way of reaching her.

I half-dragged, half-walked Susan out of the apartment and into the main hallway where we stumbled back and forth. Twenty minutes went by. Each minute brought her closer to unconsciousness, I had more and more difficulty holding her up.

Half an hour later, my co-worker ran out into hallway. "Ms. Barnett said 'under no circumstances' are we to notify the authorities until she gives us the go-ahead."

I could have screamed for the stupidity of the order. What if Susan died?

Ms. Barnett practised a cover-your-ass style of management. I suspected she wanted to alert her bosses at the Québec ministry and her lawyer before giving the go-ahead. Reform schools similar to Marian Hall had recently made headlines in the Montreal newspapers about girls mutilating themselves, starting fires in their bedrooms, and the availability of drugs.

I continued to haul Susan up and down the hallway while she begged me to let her sleep.

Ms. Barnett kept us waiting more than an hour before she finally gave me the go-ahead. I didn't want to waste more time waiting for an ambulance, so I bundled the near-comatose Susan into my little Pinto with help from a colleague then. With the hazard lights flashing, I ignored more than one red light and to reach the hospital.

I spent half the night at the hospital while doctors pumped Susan's stomach, praying the delay wouldn't be fatal. She survived but only just, and was kept there under observation for nearly a week.

After that incident, relations between Ms. Barnett and her staff crumbled. She'd been a Mother Superior of a group of nuns, then a director of an establishment staffed by women who didn't question her authority to do as she saw fit. But now she'd put men on staff, and they weren't compliant. She'd shown willingness to put a child's life at risk for bureaucratic reasons and that decision destroyed the last vestige of goodwill.

CHAPTER FIFTY-THREE

Our new supervisor, David, who was determined to do right by those kids, inevitably butted heads with Ms. Barnett, an autocrat. He pushed back when he disagreed with her directives; demanded meetings; lobbied for changes and offered alternatives, supported by the other two supervisors. The animosity grew unmanageable in late 1974 to the point staff tension began to affect the girls, many of whom came from dysfunctional families, and they showed it through growing defiance and unruliness.

As for me, after eighteen months at the job, my emotional reserves were exhausted, and with no support or sympathy from senior management, staff turned to each other for comfort. For the first time in my life, I leaned on a man to get through hard days. David and I connected on a deep level. When he'd first come on board he said, "Trust me. Lean on me. I'm a brick." And I had. In so doing we connected profoundly, and I fell in love with him. He was a psychologist by training and not only good at his job, he was also a gentle and caring human being. He even wrote poetry, which further endeared him to me, and we spent many evenings together sharing our work.

Colleagues picked up on the electricity between us and, in fact, he was the perfect man for me, except for the fact David was married. As far as I was concerned, that put him out of bounds. I had no desire to be his mistress, always taking second place, of having to sneak off to be together. As usual, I wanted all or nothing, and as a result I sure did end up with nothing.

Only much later did I find out his marriage was already on the rocks. If I had allowed him speak about what he felt for me, I would have known that. At the time, his marital status was an excuse to avoid commitment.

Nevertheless, at work we were comrades in arms, battling the mismanagement that made doubling the burden of the work we did. David and I weren't the only pair to find comfort in a co-worker. There was a revolving door of childcare workers and at one point we had almost as many men as women on staff, and some of them didn't have the same scruples I did. One couple got the boot for having sex in a bedroom sometimes used by staff if they were on a swing shift.

Meanwhile, hostilities between staff and management grew so bitter the social services ministry got involved. The ministry hired a therapist to try to get the two sides talking. Once a week for several months in early 1975, the entire staff, including Ms. Barnett, gathered for group therapy.

The sessions got ugly, as the more vocal workers heaped scorn on Ms. Barnett's chronic understaffing and failure to allow us to create systematic, comprehensive, treatment plans for each of the kids because Ms. Barnett refused to give us access to the girls' files. Unless the girls told us themselves, we knew nothing about their family histories or what had brought them to Marian Hall. Even then, we couldn't be sure they told us the truth.

Every one of those awful therapy sessions ended with someone in tears but Ms. Barnett wasn't one of them. No matter what we flung at her, she showed no emotion and sat as immovable as Everest.

The attempt to resolve hostilities failed, and staff decided to unionize, leading Ms. Barnett to resign along with several of my wrung-out colleagues. One of them was David. When he took me aside to tell me he'd be leaving, the news came like a knife thrust to the gut. I was unreasonably furious that after all his promises of strength, he had crumbled.

David had lasted a year at Marian Hall but by the time he quit, he was a shadow of the man I'd first met, depleted in every way. Ms. Barnett had worn him down, had made it impossible for him—for all of us—to do his job and his body and soul had run out of gas.

"I'm so sorry but I just can't go on here," he said.

My anger spoke first. Intending to wound him, I said, "The first time we spoke you told me to lean on you. I leaned on you and now you're quitting."

It was a childish thing to say. He had to leave to save himself, nevertheless, I felt betrayed.

"I'm so sorry."

I looked away. I couldn't stand to see the pain and hurt in those warm brown eyes, the pockets under them, his thinness.

"There's no need for us to lose touch, though." He reached out to touch me, but I pulled away.

"Yes, yes, there is. Best to end things here and now."

He looked down at his hands. We were sitting at right angles to each other in the unit's staff room. A nearby lamp cast deep shadows on the sharp planes of his face. "I'm sorry I let you down."

"That's not it."

"Then what?"

I wanted to say, "you're married." But my throat had closed and I couldn't get the words out. But even had I said them, they would have been a lie. David had sometimes hinted things at home weren't all they should be but now that a door had opened, I was too scared to commit.

"Please, just go."

David didn't press me. He didn't ask for an explanation. He left the room with stooped shoulders, and I never saw him again.

With David gone, my mood, which had teetered on the verge of depression, spiralled downward, and my work, including my relationships with the kids, suffered. They sensed my aloofness and disconnectedness.

In January 1975, staff moral, which had fallen to an all-time low, tanked after the Montreal Gazette published a series of articles that took the lid off what was going on in places like Marian Hall. Gillian Cosgrove, a young Gazette reporter, went under cover as a childcare worker at Maison Notre-Dame de Laval, and revealed mistreatment horrors there.

Cosgrove's reportage shocked and outraged the public, especially excessive use of solitary confinement cells there. During the time I'd worked at Marian Hall, solitary confinement wasn't used much, except to stop a kid from hurting herself.

The Québec government reacted quickly to the Gazette stories. It sent investigators to Maison Notre-Dame de Laval, and launched a major inquiry into youth protection and detention services. The committee's eleven-volume report confirmed children were being detained by the *courts* for "unacceptable" reasons. It found the detention system had spawned "aberrant practices" that caused some children irreparable harm, called for reform in the youth-detention system and demanded more be done to protect children's rights. The report led to passage of the Youth Protection Act, which overhauled an antiquated, paternalistic system.

In March 1975, I quit Marian Hall, exactly two years into the job. I felt shredded and took a month off to recuperate. When the lease on my apartment came to an end at the end of April, I sold all my belongings and stayed with my mother for the month of May. Daniele and I had to head west across Canada in June—by train, in bone-shaking coach class.

Once again, I repeated past mistakes and instead of getting help to sort out why I couldn't keep myself on an even keel, I ran away, looking for something new to cheer myself up.

I spent a wretched month at my mother's, who was in the throes of her own depression because of Ricky. He was almost 18, and out of control. He took drugs that made him both unpredictable and dangerous. One night, when she tried to keep him from leaving the house, he came so close to punching her in the face Teresa and I were screaming. Luckily for her, he had enough self-control to pivot and ended up putting a hole in the wall instead. But when a few weeks later he was arrested for trying to rob a bank with a baseball bat, she'd had enough. After appearing before a judge and he received a suspended sentence, she shipped him back to our father in Italy.

Teresa couldn't stand the sight of him, and they couldn't be in the same room without yelling at each other. He'd been stealing from us since he was 15, robbed all three of us of the few pieces of gold jewellery we'd possessed, and we had to keep our wallets hidden when we were at home. Zia Tresa also suspected him of being behind a break in at her house that cleaned out her jewellery box.

I drove Ricky to the airport days before my own departure. Ricky seemed relieved to go as the rest of us were relieved to see the back of him.

As to Marian Hall, its days were numbered. The government had replaced Ms. Barnett with a management team unable to clear its "antiquated and paternalistic" atmosphere. Self-mutilation and vandalism incidents increased so much the government sent in investigators. In 1976, a year after I left, the government abruptly shut it down, citing "its overly jail-like conception" as the reason.

CHAPTER FIFTY-FOUR

Daniele and I took a month getting to Vancouver. Along the way, we stopped in Toronto, Winnipeg, Calgary, Edmonton and Banff, travelling coach by night whenever to save having to pay for hotels. We stayed in each city as long as it held our interest, sleeping in rooming houses or cheap hotels.

Daniele and I had grown up in an exciting, cosmopolitan city. In the '70s places like Calgary and Winnipeg were hardly more than small towns. To my eyes, their residents lacked the *joie de vivre* of Québecers. Even Toronto, our first stop, a large, prosperous city didn't pass muster, as far as beauty went. I was accustomed to the grace of Art Deco and Gothic Revival, and the fancy of swirling wrought iron staircases in dense, lively residential areas. By comparison, Toronto's downtown was filling up with boxy skyscrapers, and the residential areas we saw had miles of boring semi-detached homes with unembellished, roofed porches. To me it all seemed so utterly utilitarian and conservative.

Hearing only the sound of English voices was disorienting. I missed not only the music of French but also the waves of Italian, Greek, Ukrainian, and German drifting along downtown Montreal streets.

All was well again when we got to the Rocky Mountains. Those purplish-grey behemoths made me catch my breath and stirred undefined longings. Mountains had shaped my forbears' bodies and their way of life. Was their experience also embedded in my DNA?

In July 1975, Daniele and I arrived in Vancouver, stiff-necked from sleeping on trains and exhausted by the itinerant lifestyle. A couple of days later, I turned 26.

We stayed with a dear friend, Jane, a Vancouverite I'd met at Marian Hall with whom I'd kept in touch after she and her husband returned home. Jane had worked at Marian Hall only a few months; she'd had too much kindness for such work. But when she showered that kindness on me, a no-strings-attached thoughtfulness no one had ever shown me, it felt like a healing balm on my spirit.

In Vancouver Jane had a small birthday party for me, complete with her signature angel-food cake, iced with frothy whipped cream and covered with fresh, sliced strawberries. I held back tears; nobody had ever made a fuss over my birthday.

Daniele and I stayed 10 days with Jane and Rocky until we rented a room in a large house owned by an odd elderly woman. The room was tiny, a large closet really, with only a single bed. But we could afford its $70 a month for the two of us, and we took turns sleeping on the floor.

The old lady lived alone and didn't appear to be coping well. Apart from her forgetfulness, she couldn't keep up with the housework and big house stank of old grease and ground in grime. From time to time, her son visited but all they did was argue.

From the beginning, Daniele had planned to go back to Montreal in September, but I got myself a full-time job and wasn't sure I wanted to return to Montreal. I was hired as a ward clerk in a psychiatric hospital affiliated with the University of British Columbia. With full-time work, I could get myself a small apartment, two rooms in the upper level of a big family house on Kitsilano only minutes from English Bay. It was clean and furnished with an old-fashioned sofa and a table in one room and a bed and chest of drawers in the other. The bathroom was along a landing outside my two rooms. The kitchen had been fashioned out of a former closet and everything in it was doll size: toy sink, two burners for cooking and a bar fridge.

The big, well-kept house belonged to a young couple with a toddler. I liked the wife, who was easy-going and kind but her husband, a university science lecturer soon butted heads. At first, I turned down the rental because he wouldn't allow Teresa, who'd planned to come for a visit, to stay with me. A few days later, after interviewing other potential tenants, he called to say he'd changed his mind. I should have known better, but I moved in. When I arrived with my suitcase, he presented me with a typewritten list of more than a dozen house rules, a copy of which was taped to the door inside my little apartment. The rules included no cooking after 9 o'clock, no loud music, and absolutely no overnight guests—excepting during Teresa's two-week visit.

A few weeks later, I found him waiting for me on the landing when I came home from work. He was there to advise me I had broken one of his rules: "Your friend spent most of the weekend here. You agreed to the rules."

He was referring to Daniele. Yes, Daniele had spent most of the weekend with me, but she was my Vancouver lifeline. Besides, she'd soon be going home to Montreal.

"My friend did not sleep here," I said, working hard to calm my rage. "What's the problem? Did we make noise? Did we disturb your family in any way?"

"No. That's not the point. You agreed to my rules."

"Fine. Consider this my month's notice."

I moved into a furnished two-bedroom flat on the top floor of a duplex in the same neighbourhood. The new place had roaches and needed a thorough scrubbing but it had its own front door and a landlord who didn't insist on vetting guests.

When Daniele left in late August, however, I lost my moorings. Outside working hours, the work at the hospital wasn't taking, I saw no one. Between Friday afternoons when I left work until Monday mornings when I returned to the hospital, I saw no one and uttered not a word. I made a few casual friends at work but had no interest in or energy for socializing. My friend Jane made time for me as best she could but had her own obligations. She was studying full-time for a master's degree along with a big load of household and extended-family obligations.

I should have recognized the signs, seen that I had skidded in the black hole again, but I didn't have that level of self-awareness at the time. I didn't understand why I kept having these bouts of despair.

My friends lived in the pages of many novels I read; my reality was their fictional worlds. On the worst days when the pressure against my chest felt as though it would crush me, I walked to English Bay to sit on a boulder and watch the water smash against the rocks. Sometimes, on these walks, I wrote in my diary.

October 1, 1975

Darkness hangs over me like a thick mist, like a protection.

I tried to run away from it. To think I traveled thousands of miles only to prove a statement I'd written in this diary years ago: "Change comes from within. Circumstances change but you can't run away from yourself." I've been in Vancouver four months now and I've dug another rut for myself. I want to go home but I have a job here and this makes me hesitate.

This loneliness is a white room with no windows or doors.

By November, the depression had set its claws deep. Everything I did, going to work, making a meal, exhausted me. A dreadful numbness stole over me, made me wonder whether some essential part of me had died. The thought shook me so hard I phoned Daniele in Montreal.

She listened while I unburdened my pain in a flat voice. Then she said what I needed and wanted to hear. "Oh, why are you torturing yourself with all your shoulds and shouldn'ts? If you're miserable and want to come home, just come. You answer only to yourself."

But I was ashamed to quit yet another job. Would I never find my place in the world?

How ironic that I worked in a psychiatric hospital but never thought to seek help for my misery. Maybe I hadn't reached the stage where I could face the reasons for my anxieties.

The day after I spoke to Daniele, I gave my notice at work.

October 19, 1975

The staff reacted with disappointment when I announced my departure. Many told me how sorry they were to see me go. Some even tried to talk me into staying. And I've never had that many invitations to dinner in a single week.

Jane and Rocky were saddened, too. Rocky, always one to get to the point said, "Montreal is very far away." Yes, I guess that sums it up.

The weight of sadness had lifted the instant I'd made the decision to go home. Now I can make a new start, I told myself.

CHAPTER FIFTY-FIVE

When the plane taxied to the terminal at Dorval airport on Nov. 19, 1975, I couldn't wait to breathe Montreal air. Teresa picked me up in the little brown Pinto, I'd given her when I'd left four months earlier. I'd bought it new in 1971 but only four years the little car was badly rusted and not worth much.

Her appearance, however, shocked me: her face was a mass of angry pimples and boils. We'd both inherited Mamma's creamy complexion and neither of us had problems with acne during our teens. But there she stood now, 21, her face swollen and almost unrecognizable.

"What happened?" I asked

She shrugged. "Stress."

Teresa had quit in the second year of the liberal arts, three-year, CEGEP pre-university program and enrolled in a full-time hospitality-management program at a private college, a couple of university management courses in the evening and working to pay for tuition and help Mamma out with a bit for room and board. Ricky had been in Italy since May, thank God, I thought, otherwise he would have made her life even more stressful for her.

I moved back in with Mamma and Teresa, and we got on like good roommates. I applied for unemployment benefits first thing but also started job-hunting but ended up spending the winter cocooned in our comfy, shared bedroom. Daniele and I went to a lot of movies, had meals at each other's homes or we ate out, and we talked and talked about our experiences, about the world. I had other friends in my life, whom I saw from time to time, but Daniele and Teresa were the only two people with whom I felt completely at ease because they knew all about my panic attacks and didn't judge me.

In May 1976 I landed a nothing job in a tiny company that published commercial directories. The man who hired me promised the job would put my bachelor's degree in literature—not to mention my dream of making a living as a writer—to good use. His promise came to nothing. The directories had no editorial content, just company names, addresses and phone numbers, industry by industry, with display ads taking up the rest of the space. Still, it gave me a regular paycheque along with the means to get my own place, which I soon did.

Living with Mamma and Teresa wasn't bad, but I jumped at the chance when Daniele, still living with her parents, told me about a one-bedroom flat available right across the street from her. Mamma's concern about what *paesani* would think of an unmarried girl living on her own meant she wasn't thrilled about my moving out. But she accepted it this time.

In June, I moved from the northeast end of Montreal to Ville Emard in the southwest. My new flat was on the second floor of a four-plex—two up, two down, identical one bedroom apartments—in a red brick building, on a long residential street occupied by similar buildings linked to each other, with a bungalow or a duplex with outside wrought iron staircases now and then adding visual interest. My building had a patch of weedy grass on either side of the front door, which opened into a staircase leading to the four units. I liked the street because it had so many trees.

I settled into my little double parlour—the inside part of the double room was my bedroom—and big eat-in kitchen. Work wasn't so good I loved that Daniele lived so close. I kept myself busy shopping for furniture, crockery and the many other things I needed. Unlike my married female cousins who'd received most of the housewares needed for a new home from showers, engagement and wedding gifts, I had to pay for my own.

That summer, Mamma, who had applied to the courts for a divorce, got the final decree. She had finally rid herself of him, but cutting the final tie failed to rid her of the bitterness in her heart, and corrosive influence remained for the rest of her life.

My job failed to give me the smallest spark of satisfaction. Bored and listless, I tormented myself for landing another big, fat failure. But by July the old malaise was creeping over me. I recognized the signs but didn't know how to turn things around other than to quit and try something else. I turned to my therapy: words on paper.

July 8, 1976

I don't know what I'm tense about now. Work is okay. Money is okay. Social life is okay. I'm so sick of myself. Why can't I just take things as they come and be content? Why do I have to analyze and agonize over every little thing?

I suffer aching loneliness and blame myself for the lack of a man in my life. And yet the thought of submitting myself to the demands of a boyfriend, as many of my friends have, leaves me cold. I see how my once carefree friends change when they tie themselves to men. They become "a couple." The men take priority even over my friends' own needs and wishes. Still, now and then, I go to discos with single friends, to plays and to movies but hard as I try none of the men who approach me stir my interest.

In truth, I didn't want a relationship even though I wouldn't have admitted it. The idea of being under a man's control as Mamma had been, terrified me. I rarely thought of my father now, believing I'd finished with him for good. How naïve. Although I'd had no contact with him for seven years, his influence had chiselled grooves in my brain which affected my thoughts and comportment as much as his chromosomes were part of my DNA.

I didn't know it then but I'd grown up to be a very angry young woman. Feeling helpless in the face of such a powerful negative force, my bouts of despair were signs of that rage turned against myself.

My father fueled the rage when after years of silence, he wrote to me. The letter reminded me that he was a man who had no shame when it came to meeting his own needs.

Campochiaro, September 23, 1976

Dearest Elvira: I turn to you for help. I don't know who else to ask regarding the procedure to obtain a Canadian disability pension as described in the attached letter I received from the Canadian embassy. The letter gives the phone number where you could inquire on my behalf.

I don't think you'll refuse me this kindness. However, although it's your decision, I do hope to get news from you. I know you have a big heart.

I know you're smart so don't let me lose this opportunity. Know that I am nearly blind, and you can't just abandon me in this hour of need. Read the embassy's letter carefully and apply for the pension on my behalf—in spite of your life being what it has been. What happened, and there's nothing that can be done about what occurred in the past.

I ask this favour of you! I am certain you will do it. Do as I ask and give me the assurance you will not abandon me.

I send you and Teresa a paternal embrace and greetings to your mother.

Your father,

Erminio Cordileone

I await news as soon as possible!

P.S. Your brother is well. He's grown so much and has filled out. He says you will not help me, but I don't believe him. I have faith in you, dear Elvira.

A hurricane ripped through my mind. How dare he! Not only had he abused and abandoned us, the bastard wanted me to help him! "You have a big heart," my ass! He'd written, to manipulate me into doing something he knew I didn't want to do. It took me days to calm down before I sat down to reply:

Montreal, October 1, 1976

Father: Imagine my surprise when I received your letter! I'm sure you would have been surprised to receive such a thing after being ignored for seven years. Now you want a "favour?" That's human nature, I guess.

I owe you nothing. God knows I don't. Why didn't you ask Teresa to do it? She's the one you cared so much about you sent her a token of your esteem a couple of years ago, a gold bracelet—the same bracelet your son later stole. For that matter, why don't you ask the son living with you to make inquires by mail? No? Why me? Ah, because you know I can do it. And you want results, don't you? Good, old Elvira to the rescue, the same Elvira who didn't merit a token as Teresa did.

Let me be frank, "Father": to you the past may be forgotten but as for me the past affects every single day of my life, every single action.

I could accept your despair, your unhappiness and feel pity and compassion. But you're trying to trick me into an obligation I don't owe you. You gave nothing to anyone your entire life. You took and took. You only ever wanted something from us. You still want something from me.

Your son was right. I'm not interested in your predicament, but I will make inquiries because I wouldn't refuse anyone such a request. I don't care enough to want to seek vengeance but I did want you to know where I stand.

I am typing this letter so there will be no difficulty deciphering my handwriting. I hope your son is literate enough to read it to you.

I'll send you information about your "pension" as soon as it is available to me.

My father always wanted the last word, so he wrote back:

Campochiaro, October 25, 1976

My dear daughter, Elvira: This is the first dialogue between two human beings. One is a writer with a degree, the second has only an elementary school education. Between the lines you wrote there is only the anger of a dissatisfied girl and full of sadness who wants to take it out on her father—deceived and more mangled than you, betrayed, and full of disappointments.

I cannot accept your cacophony. I feel in you the bitterness of a disappointed girl. I do not want any mercy from you or compassion. It is I who feel for you so much tenderness and pain. Who do we blame? You, yes, you blame it on your father because you never imagined me as a man who loves his wife and children. And then he sees himself deceived and whipped and alone. And with the passage of time, he kills himself with the pain of knowing that he does not have the joy of seeing those dear creatures whom he raised as infants, a father who loves them so much even without ever saying a word.

Teresa received my gift, as you would have received it! But I did not send you one because I knew it would not be well received.

Riccardo needed me! He came and I made him into a man!!! This would also have applied to you had you needed me. I am the father with open arms for those who return to me even only for a single day.

Now don't think I want to move you with my talking. You just have to know this, that I'm proud of you. But do not think that I am one of those people you can swirl around your little finger.

Come for Christmas. Your home is here!

I send you my thanks. I embrace you.

My father's self-pity, the lie that had I *asked* him for help he would have given it, infuriated me. The one time Mamma had forced me to write him a letter that one Christmas, hoping he'd send us money, he'd sent us a money order for $5 for all three of us.

His second letter, his refusal to admit he'd had a duty to us, his children, which he'd completely neglected, came as the last straw. I would not now or ever beg him for help but neither would I lift a finger to help him. He could make his own bloody inquiries.

CHAPTER FIFTY-SIX

I stayed at the publishing company for a little over a year but without a smile on my face. To cheer myself up, in the summer of 1977, Teresa, Daniele and I took five weeks off and high-tailed it to Europe. As we planned our itinerary to France, Italy and Spain, Teresa and I debated whether we should make a stop in Campochiaro. If we went, we'd inevitably cross paths with the old man, and neither of us wanted that but at the same time we both longed to see the place of our ancestry. In the end, we decided we wouldn't give him the power to keep us away.

Teresa and I spent an enchanting week in Paris after which we got on a train to Italy, headed to Campochiaro for another week. While we were in Paris and Campochiaro, Daniele was in Istanbul, and we'd planned to meet in Naples.

Teresa and I took an overnight train from Paris to Rome, a one-thousand-km slog in coach when high-speed trains didn't exist. In Rome, we switched to a local train—the milk run—to Boiano, the station closest to Campochiaro. It was July and our enclosed compartment was baking hot. We arrived at Boiano's tiny train station after dark. We got off, dragging our suitcases, along with a few other passengers, who slid into waiting cars and disappeared into the dark. We were alone and headed towards the small station, hoping someone could direct us but saw no one. What to do? There was a pay phone but how where should I call for a taxi?

Suddenly, the station master appeared. A little man with a mustache dressed in a dark uniform. "*Chiudo*! Closed!" He pointed at the door and showed us his key.

In my best imperfect Italian, I asked, "How do we get to Campochiaro? Can we get a taxi?"

"No, no taxis."

He edged us out the door, locked the station and vanished. From Rome I'd called ahead to my maternal great aunt, with whom we were to stay while in Campochiaro, to let her know when we'd be arriving. She was expecting us, and I thought she might worry if we didn't show up but there was no pay phone outside the shuttered station house.

Suitcases didn't have wheels on them in those days and we half carried, half dragged our suitcases to the other side of the building, hoping a taxi might be idling somewhere, but found only a well-dressed man, leaning against a black sedan as though waiting for someone.

"Do you know how we can get a taxi?"

"Where are you going?"

"Campochiaro."

"I can take you."

Teresa and I looked at each other, both of us wondering whether he'd take us into the mountains and rob us.

She shrugged. "We don't have a lot of choice." Ricky later explained that a lot of men with cars made a little extra offering rides as our driver had.

He delivered us safely to Campochiaro, drove right up into piazza at the end of a long road lined with poplars. It was past 11 o'clock and the piazza teemed with the village residents. Young women, arm-in-arm, strolled up and down under the watchful eyes of young men lined up around the perimeter. Everyone stopped and stared as we exited the car. Ricky, who was among the crowd, came to greet us. We hugged.

I turned to driver. "*Quanto?* How much?" He named a sum but when I reached for my purse Ricky stepped in.

"Are you joking?" he said to the driver. "Come on, it's a 20-km ride." The two of them went back on the fare and finally agreed on an amount. Bargaining, it seemed, was an expected part of just about every transaction in this part of Italy.

"Is Zia Maria here? We're supposed to be staying with her," I said to Ricky.

One of the reasons our suitcases had been so heavy was that Mamma had loaded us down with gifts for Zia Maria, a widow in her late 60s, her two married children, a teenaged daughter still at home, and her grandchildren. She'd saddled us with packets of espresso coffee, cacao, and chocolate bars, as though Italy was still experiencing wartime shortages. Mamma had also made it clear she expected us to give Zia Maria a substantial gift of money for her hospitality—"and don't embarrass me!"

"Zia's an old lady. She's probably already in bed," Ricky said. "I wouldn't be surprised if the old biddy forgot you were coming."

"So, what should we do?"

"Well, you can stay at the old man's house for tonight. I'm sure he won't mind."

"No, I don't think so," I said.

"Oh, don't worry, he won't be there with you. It's only a kitchen and a small bedroom. He can sleep at his mother-in-law's. That's where I've been living since he got married."

Yes, my father had remarried that winter. He'd gotten his girlfriend, a young woman a couple of years older than I, pregnant. In a village of a few hundred people, he couldn't continue living in Campochiaro if he didn't do right by her. In fact, as Teresa, Ricky and I stood talking in the piazza, his new wife was in hospital having just delivered a daughter.

We followed Ricky to our father's house to avoid disturbing Zia Maria at that late hour. If there had been a hotel, I wouldn't have accepted my father's hospitality; it made me feel like a hypocrite until I reminded myself, he'd done so little for us, one night's lodging was a lot to ask.

We climb a steep cobbled slope to his minuscule house and entered the kitchen, where my father sat at a table reading. He looked up, smiled and got to his feet but neither Teresa nor I moved towards him.

We hadn't seen our father in eight years. He was 52 but looked a decade older. He was much thinner and seemed shorter than I remembered. Maybe that was because he had to work to make a living now that he didn't have Mamma to bring home a pay cheque. A black patch covered his right eye, in which he'd lost his sight. We'd heard all about it in Montreal from *paesani*. He supposedly claimed he'd shot himself in an act of suicide, but others believed he'd crossed someone— a cuckolded husband or maybe the Mafia—and was rewarded with a bullet. We never did learn the truth.

He didn't look like the image of the father I'd held in my mind's eye, and I felt no stirring of emotion, not even a flicker of the anger I'd stoked for years.

"I'm glad to see you. You both look well." He fidgeted and his gaze didn't hold ours.

He prepared a *machinetta* of espresso as Ricky explained the situation with Zia Maria and he immediately offered us his house. In truth, I was suspicious of both my father and Ricky. The possibility that the pair of them had set things up so that we'd have to appear on friendly terms with our father so that he could save face.

"I'll sleep at my mother-in-law's tonight," he said. "I'm building a proper house on the other side of the piazza."

A new house? How nice for him.

He gave us fresh sheets and towels and told us to feel free to take baths as he had plenty of hot water, a rarity in Campochiaro. After that he skedaddled as though he couldn't get away fast enough. Ricky stayed for a while; he missed speaking English, then went back to the piazza.

"How does he earn a living?" I asked.

"He hauls things around in his truck for people. He and Amalia raise and slaughter a pig every year, they have chickens and eggs, and they grow vegetables."

"Yeah? Doesn't he also make money by cutting down trees on property belonging to Mum's family that he sells for firewood?"

My mother and aunts in Montreal sent regular, furious letters across the Atlantic to the cousin to whom they'd given power of attorney over their land holdings, demanding he take action. The cousin, who himself had also been chopping down trees for firewood and also not wanting to antagonize my father, did nothing.

Teri and I enjoyed luxurious baths that night and slept like the dead until Ricky woke us up with a loud knock on the door to show us the way to Zia Maria's house, the same house where Mamma and her sisters had grown up.

Zia Maria's house lay at the end of a narrow street off the piazza. In the distance I caught sight of a woman dressed in black sitting on a chair against the stone wall of a house. She jumped to her feet when she caught sight of us, and when we got to within ten feet of her, she began to shout and gesticulate, which brought out curious neighbours.

Teresa and I stopped dead, struck dumb by such behaviour.

"That's Zia Maria," my brother said, grinning.

"How could you?" Zia Maria screamed at Teresa and me, her face twisted with rage. "How could you step one foot in *his* house after what he's done to your mother? It'll break her heart when she hears about it.

"No one in *our* family has anything to do with that *animale*. How could you shame your mother this way?"

I turned Teresa. "Should we just get the hell out of here?"

"It'll make things worse, what with all the gossip that gets back to Montreal. We're here now. Let's tough it out. Besides, it's only for a week and it's so pretty."

Ricky interceded. "It's not their fault, Zia. I took them there because they got here really late, and we didn't want to wake you."

I wanted to add but bit my tongue: "And it's not as if you waited up or showed any concern for us, old fart."

The storm of words ended, and we followed her into the house where Mamma had spent her girlhood.

Zia Maria didn't improve with familiarity. Her children and the many other distant relatives, however, were warm and generous. We explored the village and environs with Ricky as our guide. It had a simple, unvarnished beauty with its tired, sun-burned structures, its all-but-one abandoned churches, and fresh, so fresh, locally grown food.

I had so looked forward to going back to Campochiaro, anticipating a visceral connection to my birthplace, but it never came. Maybe, my father's presence got in the way even though we didn't see again but once, and that was in passing one afternoon in the piazza a few days before our departure. How like him to invite us for a meal that evening, knowing Mamma's girlhood friends were lionizing us, we would already have made plans. No, I thought, he hasn't changed his spots.

We took Ricky with us for the remainder of the Italian part of our trip—good riddance to Zia Maria, the witch, and my father's ghost—after he returned to Campochiaro and we went on to Spain.

CHAPTER FIFTY-SEVEN

We flew to Montreal at the end of July 1977. I returned to my nothing job but immediately started looking for something else.

The separatist Partie Quebecois had been elected the previous year, and in short order I saw its impact on my ability to find work as a non-francophone as its more stringent laws to make French the only official language in the province took effect. I spoke French well, but my written skills remained imperfect.

In August 1977 the Partie Québecois government passed Bill 101, a move that enraged the English-speaking community.

Known as *La charte de la langue française*, the Charter of the French Language, the law sought "to make French the language of government and the law, as well as the normal and everyday language of work, instruction, communication, commerce and business." Only French versions of legal documents would be deemed official, and bilingual signs in public were outlawed. It offered businesses incentives to convert operations to French but would be punished if they didn't.

The Charter also revamped laws controlling the language of education and henceforth, only students whose parents or siblings were educated in English could attend English schools while immigrants were forced to send their children to French schools. This provision, coupled with the long-standing outflow of English speakers to other provinces, shrank the English school system to fewer than 100,000 students in 2018 from 250,000 half a century earlier.

The new law also established the *Office Québécois de la langue française*, commonly referred to as "the language police," with authority to investigate and rectify infractions, and fine offenders. Many English-speaking Québecers grew to despise the agency that often punished businesses for violation they considered trivial.

I understood why the PQ passed those laws. The government and its millions of supporters believed, with reason, the French culture would be doomed without protection and promotion. By making French the common language in Québec, it sought to create job opportunities for francophones in senior management at medium and large businesses that had favoured anglophones. But its goal impinged on the freedom of the English-speaking population and those who identified with them, including me.

In years to come, the language Charter did vastly improve the socioeconomic status of francophones, but the road took a bumpy, twisting course. After the passage of Bill 101, Québec's economy took a dive. Between 1976 and 1986, seven hundred companies left for other provinces, taking jobs with them. As the year 2000 approached, unemployment hovered around 10 per cent, compared to 8.7 in 1976. The new language laws also accelerated the out-migration of anglophones and immigrants who spoke languages other than French, exacerbating the downturn. By 2001 one-half of those whose mother tongue was English had quit Québec. Faced with linguistic discrimination and the jobs shortage, young anglophones and even bilingual Quebecers packed up and left.

As nationalists struggled for French dominance and francophones and anglophones traded insults, I went to the office every morning to do a job not worth doing. Worse, the way my employer solicited ads verged on fraud by mailing solicitations that looked like invoices to renew their display ads in Bell telephone's Yellow Pages. Many sent cheques wrongly assuming they were renewing their Yellow Pages ad. As people caught on, however, the cheques got fewer and fewer so that in October 1977, after almost a year and a half, the company let me go and soon after declared bankruptcy.

And what a relief. A double relief because it meant I could claim unemployment insurance without paying the weeks-long penalty if I'd quit.

The panic attacks continued, and they terrified me. In desperation, I signed up for a yoga program, hoping I could learn techniques to calm my agitation. Those first classes challenged my mind rather than my body. I delighted in the physical part of yoga—the grace of moving between postures as the pulse of energy moved through my body. This sense of aliveness felt like a miracle to me, accustomed as I was to the numbness of low-grade depression.

The mental part, however, cast me into a vortex fear when, at the end of class, we lay on our backs for *shavasana,* the corpse pose, the lights dimmed, for the relaxation phase. I couldn't do it, not for months. I couldn't relax, not on my back. As soon as I lay down, my head would start to spin, and I felt as though I had fallen through the floor into a big, black hole.

It took many months to learn how to use my breath to calm the anxious thoughts that fed my fears. Yoga lured me out of my thoughts and back into my body, taught me to feel and enjoy it: the twitch and pull of muscle and tendon, the stretch of skin while warm breath moved into and out of my lungs. It helped me reconnect mind and body so that I could perceive the world around me not through thoughts alone but also through my eyes, my nose, my ears and my skin.

On the home front, only three months after Teresa and I'd seen Ricky in Campochiaro, he came home to Montreal to plague Mamma. My father's boast in his earlier letter to me that he'd made a man of his errant son now proved false. He'd chafed under our father's control for a year and a half, and then he ran away and two weeks later we got a phone call from a Canadian consulate somewhere in Germany, high on drugs, broke and asking for help to come home.

"Send him home," Mamma said, in despair. She couldn't, wouldn't turn away her son.

CHAPTER FIFTY-EIGHT

I remained unemployed four very long months. I counted every penny of my meagre unemployment benefits to make ends meet. Jobs were scarce in the fall and winter of 1977 as employers converted operations to French-only and gave priority to fully-bilingual applicants, preferably those whose first language was French.

I mailed dozens of job applications and made as many phone calls. All the rejections demoralized me. Twenty-eight and still looking for the right road to take. Pathetic, I told myself. But in December 1977, I was hired by a national magazine publishing company as a production supervisor for three of their trade publications. I lasted nine months before they fired me. I wrote in my diary:

March 1978

On December 1 last year, Maclean-Hunter's Montreal office hired me to produce three French-language trade magazines. What a laugh! They give you a title but they treat you and refer to you as a secretary. I'll be damned if I'll let them get away with it, which means, of course, a long uphill battle. I hope I can tough it out.

I liked the work very much, which was like working on a puzzle as I lay out the ads in ways that minimized printing costs. Had it not been for misogyny, and had I had more tolerance and less pride, I would have done well there. The misogynist, Gilles, was my immediate boss, a sycophant, a man promoted from advertising sales to publisher over other francophones in the company because he had refined schmoozing to an art.

Gilles' boss, general manager of the Montreal operation, had hired me since Gilles had just been named to the post and hadn't started his new job. He and I started our respective new jobs the same day.

Ours was a collaboration destined to fail. Gilles' self-esteem deficit led him to needlessly exert his authority over me and I had no tolerance for his bullying and no sympathy for his need to have someone stroke his ego.

My desk sat in a cubicle outside Gilles' office. He took this proximity to mean I was his secretary as well as production coordinator for his periodicals. He made this clear early on when he poked his head out of his office and invited me in for a "chat."

"Sit down." He lowered himself into a big leather chair and crossed his arms.

Oh-oh, not good, I thought.

"I have a problem with your general attitude."

"My attitude?" Now that was perplexing. I always made a point of being polite and respectful to everyone, including him.

"When I passed by your desk this morning you didn't even look up?"

"I didn't look up?"

"That's right. If you'd looked up, you would have seen what a bad morning I've had. You might have smiled and cheered me up. It would have made my day. That's what a good secretary does. In the future, I expect you to greet me with a smile."

My peripheral vision narrowed as though I'd fallen backwards into a tunnel, and it took me a few seconds to force air back into my lungs.

"First, I'm not your secretary. But even if I were, it's not a secretary's job to coax her boss into good humour. If you have complaints about my work — you know, my actual job, producing the magazines—just say so."

He glowered. "This isn't about your work. Your work is fine. It's about your character. You never smile. What's wrong with you?"

Aghast, I stood up. "Is there anything else?"

"No, that's it. But I mean what I say about improving your attitude. Also, you never talk about yourself. I don't know anything about you. This isn't normal for people who work together. For example, I don't know what your interests are or even whether you have a boyfriend."

I replied with a hard stare. When he dismissed me, I went straight to the bathroom and had a good cry. The chat didn't bode well for my future at Maclean-Hunter.

Spring 1978 burst through the sweet damp earth but no rebirth materialized in my relationship with Gilles. By July I was spending more and more time crying in the bathroom than at my desk. Colleagues, several whom I counted as friends, knew what I was enduring but could do nothing other than try to console me. After months of humiliation, the final straw came in late August.

It was near quitting time on a Friday. Teresa had come to the office to meet me since we were going to have dinner together downtown. She stood by as I tidied my desk and we were on our way out when Gilles, who had advertisers in his office, saw me pass his door and asked me to come in.

I poked my head in. "Yes, Gilles?"

"When I come in on Monday morning, please make sure my pencils are sharpened," he said.

"Pardon?"

The two men seated opposite him looked embarrassed when he pointed to a pencil holder filled with half a dozen blunted pencils. "The pencils," he said. "I want you to sharpen them."

I smiled. "Have a good weekend."

"He's serious, you know," Teresa said as we stood waiting for the elevator.

"Oh, for God's sake, he can't be. He was joking. Sharpen his pencils? No, I don't think so."

On Monday morning I didn't sharpen his pencils. When Gilles came in to find the pencils as unsharpened as they'd been Friday afternoon, he called me into his office and let me have it.

"I will not sharpen your pencils, Gilles." Everything in me trembled: my voice, my body, my angry soul.

He would have fired me on the spot but he needed me to finish the production schedule and a new hire would take months to learn the job.

In that moment I was angrier at myself than at Gilles. Why couldn't I just play along like some of my female colleagues? Gilles was the kind of man susceptible to flattery and would have been easy to manipulate. I could have gotten anything and everything I wanted out of him before he knew what I'd done. He wasn't an intelligent man; he'd made his way in the world with good looks and smooth talking.

But I couldn't and wouldn't live by subterfuge; it would make me hate myself.

I wrote a letter of resignation but only to vent. I didn't hand it in because too many times I'd taken that easy way out and quit. I was determined to keep trying, maybe stay at Maclean-Hunter long enough to get a transfer to different section.

In the end, I'd bruised Gilles' ego too badly and he couldn't stand the sight of me. He wanted me out and I agreed to leave in exchange for a letter of reference, and a letter of good conduct so I wouldn't be penalized when I applied for unemployment benefits.

His letter read: "Due to the issues discussed and on which no solution is possible, I am obliged to thank you for your services as of August 25th."

On my last day, I wrote up a two-page list of complaints against Gilles, made two copies and put them in inter-office envelopes along with the letter of resignation I'd written but never submitted. One envelope went to human resources in Toronto and the second I dropped off to the general manager who'd hired me. I was emptying my desk when his secretary called to say he wanted to see me.

He asked me to sit down, which I did. He asked me whether anything could be done to improve the situation. As I spoke, he had his profile to me, staring out the window rather than at me. When finished, he said, "I just hired Gilles. I have to give him a chance to find his feet."

I was expendable. If he fired Gilles, he'd look bad.

Ahead lay another bleak winter.

CHAPTER FIFTY-NINE

I hid in my little apartment reading want ads, filled up notebooks with my thoughts and smoked a pack and a half of Rothmans cigarettes a day, while I waited for somebody to hire me. Smoking was a solace I no longer could afford, but I would rather have gone without food. I lit up a smoke, the first thing in the morning, and the last thing before going to sleep.

September, October and November crawled by me. Writing saved me from despair, a vent for the hot steam of fury and sadness as I let myself dive into an ocean of words, distracting words as I wrote and rewrote, read and re-read, trying to understand my myself and my behaviour. I let the words gush wantonly through the channels of my fingers, without order or goal. Words were warm and soothing water, smoothing the jagged rocks of my mind. They didn't completely repair deep ruts I'd carved into my mind, but they kept me alive.

This last bout of darkness bit deeper than ever. When my brain boiled with the terror of impending madness, I lay down, turned down the lights and played my yoga teacher's relaxation tape. It kept me from running screaming out into the street.

October, 1978

I have taught myself not to care. Not to live. Not to die. To love or not love. Not to work. To write or not write. Pain bounces off me like a ball bounces off a wall. There is no pain. No anguish. It does not matter.

*There have been times when it did matter. All the "No thank-yous"
when I applied for jobs. We don't want you. We don't need your brain
or your time. It hurt.*

*I have been wandering in this desert for years, looking for a place to
build my house. Maybe it's time to stop searching. I am the woman
waiting for an answer to a letter I never mailed.*

Every Sunday I made the long rid—two subway lines and two bus
changes—to my mother's house in Saint-Michel. I did it out of a sense of
duty. Every word Mamma uttered irritated me. She responded to my
obvious anxiety but adding her own: had I found a job yet? I was too
thin. Was I eating properly? But it didn't prevent me from staying over
some weekends to water down my loneliness—I missed Teresa, although
she came to stay at my place quite often to get away from Ricky.

My sadness deepened with the loss of Daniele's friendship that year.
She'd met a man she like a great deal, and as the months went by, she
grew more distant and uncommunicative whenever we were together.
But by then I'd sunk so deep into my own darkness my only thoughts
revolved around how to put an end to my agony. Instead of encouraging
her to talk, instead of trying to find out what troubled her, I shut her out
of my life. Mental illness had made me completely selfish, and my sole
objective focussed and trying to stay alive.

In hindsight, Daniele was likely pondering whether to build a future
with this man, maybe worried about how it would change the rhythm of
her life and the compromises any long-term romantic relationship
demands.

There was no fight, no disagreement. I had promised to call her to
set up a time to see a film but didn't. Neither did she phone me. And
that was that.

December 1978, with Christmas peeking around the corner, it
seemed an unlikely time to find work. After dozens of rejections, I got

excited when I saw a big display ad in the Montreal Gazette seeking an administrative assistant for an unnamed national association. On paper, I met every qualification, including excellent English language and communication skills. My heart skipping, I mailed my application. Four days later I floated off the floor with relief when the call came inviting me to an interview.

The association was the Canadian Chamber of Commerce, and the job was in its public affairs department. The departmental manager, Roger, interviewed me, and I liked the look of him, a tall, pleasant-looking man in his 30s, clean-cut and soft-spoken. We talked for almost an hour; told me he had more candidates to interview but promised to call if I made the short list.

I made it past the first post to a second interview. This time, Roger and two other men were in the room because if I got the job, I'd be "assisting" all three—the media relations manger, the publications manager and Roger, public affairs general manager.

The interview went well. I went home and stayed close to the phone for several days. Unlike my previous jobs, I really wanted this one. I'd liked all three men, how they'd talked to me without condescension. It also delighted me that the Chamber was a workplace of ideas, not products.

When my phone jangled on day four, I picked up the receiver with my heart jumping around in my rib cage.

It was Roger. "When can you start?"

"Today?" I said, laughing. I felt suddenly limp as tension drained out of my body. I thought I might cry with happiness or maybe sing joy or run outside in the snow without a coat.

I started work at the Chamber on Jan. 3, 1979 at their downtown Montreal headquarters on Beaver Hall Hill, in a less-fashionable part of downtown south of Sainte-Catherine Street.

The office manager, a friendly, chatty woman, showed me around and introduced me to people whose names I promptly forgot. The Chamber had a staff of about thirty people, mostly in their 20s and early 30s. Managers sat in offices with glass doors around the perimeter walls while administrative assistants like me, sat out in the open, our floor spaces divided by filing cabinets.

When the tour ended, she delivered me to Roger, and he welcomed me with a wide smile on his face, he came out from behind his desk and shook my hand. He invited me to sit down and for the next hour he gave me background information about the organization and answered all my questions fully. We both smoked as we talked—people smoked everywhere then—taking turns offering each other cigarettes.

My three new bosses took me out to lunch that day, and it touched me. No boss of mine had ever treated me with such consideration.

As the weeks rapidly rolled along, each one faster than the other, I felt near to bursting with happiness, like an impoverished child who suddenly finds herself amid plenty. I couldn't help but ask myself whether it would all be snatched away?

Nobody snatched anything away and things only got better. I worked hard at a job both busy and demanding. I learned how the federal government worked, about impending legislation and its potential effect on businesses, and how my employer lobbied the government on behalf of its members. I met remarkable people, including many of Canada's business leaders and best of all, the work I did fitted the contours of my talents and personality.

In no time, our little department of four became close. We liked each other, spoke the same language even if our politics diverged. The four of us debated social and economic policies, and the role government should and shouldn't play in society. I believed businesses had to be regulated because they couldn't be trusted to play fair with consumers.

My bosses, and the Chamber's policies advocated hands-off capitalism. I enjoyed the sparring.

A year vanished. Roger and I worked as one person. He challenged me with his lightning-quick mind and razor's edge wit. During quiet periods I spent a lot of time in his office learning from him, and smoking.

Roger also intrigued me as a character. I never once saw him lose his cool no matter the crisis. His held his emotions under tight control, so much so it made me wonder whether he had any emotions at all behind that suave exterior.

The comfortable rapport continued for about a year and a half before gradually, oh, so gradually, my feelings of admiration and respect led to something more. But Roger was married, happily married to all appearances. I'd met his wife a number of times, and I'd liked her.

For a second time, I found myself drawn to a married man at my workplace, someone who was also my immediate boss. I did ask myself whether these men attracted me *because* they were out of bounds but had no real answer. Apart from any romantic attraction, I had *liked* David as a friend, and I *liked* Roger. I hadn't felt that way about any of the single men I'd come across over the years. But an affair with my married boss was out of the question, not for moral reasons but for practical reasons. If I were to jump in and things soured between us—as such office romances often do—I, the subordinate female, would be the one who'd have to leave.

That didn't stop me from dreaming, though. Now, at the age of 30, I created a new romantic fantasy just as I'd done the age of 7 when was in Grade 2.

CHAPTER SIXTY

I loved working with Roger, relished his ever-courteous manner and calm demeanour. But after two years of close day-to-day contact, I concluded he used these techniques to keep people at arm's length. Like me, Roger lived in his head, a cerebral man who took great pride in self-control. He was articulate, had deep knowledge of a great many subjects, including fine wines and popular music—he'd once had a radio show—making him a formidable debating opponent.

Roger made the perfect candidate for my romantic fantasy. His married state and his emotional aloofness meant I could dream about him without the risk of entanglement. Or so I imagined. Bit by bit my infatuation with Roger grew unmanageable, a balloon so full of longing it seemed about to pop. Thoughts of him crammed my head every waking moment and he stalked me in my dreams.

Roger continued to behave with circumspection, but my animal instinct picked up his sexual interest. I saw it in the way his eyes softened when we spoke, in the way he sought me out. Had I given the signal, he would have responded. I had opportunities, especially when occasional meetings took place out of town because I believed, ultimately, it would be to my detriment.

When my longing for him hurt so much, I wanted to scream, I wrote him letters, which I never sent.

July, 1980

I try hard to hide what I feel for you, hide it behind a neutral facade. I know there were times when I gave myself away. Remember the slow dance we had during the company's golf day? I think you might have felt the wild throb of my heartbeat because you squeezed my hand and drew me closer.

You, the man I admire, respect and love, if what I feel really is love, have burrowed deep into my heart and mind. We are merely friends and colleagues, but I can't imagine my life without you in it.

Sometimes when we sit and talk, I tuck my hand under me to keep from reaching out to touch your face. When your gaze washes over me, my skin tingles, like silk rubbing against silk. But you are an ethical man— a married man—and also my superior, and you would never take the first step, would you? It would be up to me.

After two years as his administrative assistant, Roger promoted me to publications manager. In my new job I wrote the association's newsletters and other publications. Finally, my dream of writing for a living had come true even though it was only business propaganda. Roger remained my boss but we no longer had close daily contact and our relationship slowly changed. In my place, he hired someone I recommended, Helen, a friend I'd made when I'd worked at Maclean-Hunter.

Helen, tall and blonde with Slavic cheekbones and a kittenish manner, drew men to her the way the Pied Piper drew children, and she was a sexual free spirit, a woman who accepted or rejected depending on her desires in the moment. I wished I could do the same. My Catholic upbringing that sex was bad, dirty outside the bonds of matrimony, and even then, it was something couples did in secret. My parents reinforced the lesson when I hit my teens by prohibiting me from speaking to boys let alone to date as I got older. Add to that my mother's furious reaction when she feared my father may have tried to molest me and I grew up to be a woman with an inability to trust men in any way, not as friends or as lovers.

Helen had no such scruples. "I need men around me," she once told me. "I need the company of men, and the game men and women play makes me feel alive."

I saw her in action many times, observed the leisurely way she stroked her subjects' egos, caressed their bodies with her blue, blue eyes or, sometimes, with the fleeting touch of her hand. Her body's cat-like movements promised delights, which she sometimes provided but not always.

And yet I felt contempt for Helen and for the men she preyed on even while I envied her sexual allure.

"I want to create desire, not necessarily fulfill it," Helen said. "That's what I call fun, the feeling I get when I'm desired. I want an innocent, child-like fun, to laugh, to touch innocently for fun, for warmth. Fucking is a different matter. When I want sex, I take it, and *I* decide with who and when."

In my new better-paying position, I missed talking to Roger and I made up for it by writing to him in my diary.

July 1981

Only two days into my new job and I miss you. You sit two doors away from my office, but I can't see you, don't talk to you. I feel an aching absence; I miss your attention.

I knew there would be a period of adjustment, but I never imagined it would be this painful. When you walk past my office without turning your head to acknowledge my existence, something shrinks within me.

Roger found the new relationship as hard as I did. On the first morning, he entered my tiny office to wish me well. Only he couldn't look at me. Instead, he turned his back to me and rested his forehead against the wall to collect himself.

My promotion took effect two days after my 32nd birthday, eight days after I moved into a new apartment with Teresa, who'd left home in desperation after she could no longer tolerate endless fighting caused by Ricky's bad behaviour. It grew intolerable.

She gave Mamma an ultimatum: him or me, and Mamma chose her son: She couldn't evict her crazy, chronically jobless 24-year-old boy, could she? "I brought him into the world and I'm responsible for him. I know you'll be alright, Teresa. You're capable. You'll be able to take care of yourself," she told Teresa.

Teresa took it hard, took it as rejection by her mother in favour of a brother who had only ever exploited and used the woman, the same way her husband had.

Teresa and I rented a two-bedroom flat in a new duplex in Ville Emard, a few blocks from where I'd lived the four years. It didn't require much of an adjustment. Teresa had an easygoing nature, someone who preferred to swallow her anger and walk away rather than argue. I didn't blame her; she'd had seen fighting enough to last a lifetime. I was the one who had the complicated personality, the one whose moods could sometimes make me short-tempered or irritable. Teresa understood me and acted accordingly: she didn't engage.

The arrangement was working well, and we'd expected to live together for a long time since neither of us had our sights set on marriage. However, yet again the universe threw a hot potato into my lap and forced me to make a decision after my employer announced plans to transfer its head office to Ottawa. The non-profit business association had been founded in 1925 when Montreal was Canada's business, financial and manufacturing capital and the hub for transcontinental and international trade. But by the 1970s Québec's independence movement had provoked a steady migration of anglophone companies to other provinces and the city was losing its once-predominant place. My employers also reasoned that as a *national* lobby for Canadian business, it made sense to put its headquarters in the nation's capital.

Should I leave behind my sister, my cousins and my few friends for a life in Ottawa, a dull city of bureaucrats? To my own surprise, I realized how much they meant to me and how I'd taken them for granted. I had thought myself a loner, needless of people and yet I was no hermit. I needed a degree of solitude even during good periods when depression didn't have its jaws clamped on me, but I loved and needed those few people. They tethered me to Earth, kept me from losing myself in the labyrinths of my own mind.

Or should I jump at the opportunity and use it as an incentive to breathe new life into my weary soul?

CHAPTER SIXTY-ONE

The move was set for July 1, 1983. The Chamber gave us almost a year's notice to consider a relocation. Instinct told me this decision would determine the course of my future but for me a whole year to think, meant a whole year of worry and vacillation.

My reasoning got caught in a tangle of conflicting emotions.

Living in Ottawa didn't appeal to me. It was a capital city, a tight-knit world of civil servants and businesses and organizations that dealt with the government. To make a name for myself in that sort of milieu, I'd have to network, to socialize, and I had neither the personality for it nor the interest.

On the other hand, staying put in Montreal would solve my obsession with Roger. He had opted to make the move and once he was out of my life, his absence would gradually starve my infatuation. But if I stayed, I likely wouldn't find a job as satisfying as the one I had—and also work in English.

Québec's economy had taken a serious tumble after the election of the Partie Québecois in 1976 and economic uncertainty run by a separatist government was bound to continue. Add to that ongoing affirmative action to hire *pure laine* Québecers, and my chances got slimmer still. I might speak French like a francophone but my name pegged me as an immigrant, and I'd been educated in English.

I went over the situation over and over with anyone who'd listen but especially Teresa. They were reluctant to push me in either direction, and Daniele no longer was around to say, "Take a chance, kiddo! What's the worst that can happen?"

Everybody promised they'd come to see me often, after all, Ottawa was a mere two-hour drive from Montreal. But could I count on them? Once I took myself out of the flow of their lives, wouldn't they tire of making the effort?

I sought out Roger for advice. Maybe I'd hoped he'd say, "Come! I· need you. I can't imagine going without you."

But true to form, he said, "I want you to come with us, of course, but far be it from me to try to talk you into it. You have to do what's best for you."

I lost weight during that year. Until then, it was typical of people to see the world in black and white, I'd known where I stood about things and made decisions quickly, impulsively. Now with three months left and still no closer to making up my mind, the universe got fed up with me and staged an intervention.

The incident occurred outside our Beaver Hall Hill with Helen—the woman who had replaced me as Roger's admin assistant—and I at the end of a long day's work at the end of a long week. We were heading to a nearby restaurant for a quick bite and then to a movie and engaged in animated talk about something that had happened at work that day when a young man wearing wire-framed glasses—maybe a university student— accosted us.

"*On est au Québec, crisse. Parlez francais!* We're in Québec, Christ. Speak French!" he yelled, his face white with anger.

Guilt was my first reaction, as though Helen and I had done something illegal by speaking English on a public street. But in a heartbeat, a geyser of rage shot from the soles of my feet through the top of my head and chased away every vestige of wrongdoing.

The bullet of rage had penetrated my skin the day my father had tried to force Mamma to put a noose around her own neck, and it had flourished within me ever since, slithering along my blood vessels. Fed by unreasonable strictures and prohibitions at home, and unfairness and misogyny at work and punished when I tried to advocate for myself, it had corroded my spirit, had sickened my heart and soul.

That day, when yet another arrogant man stepped in my path to bar my way, to shut me up, it lanced the boil of my long silence and had I had a weapon, I would have used it to kill him. "*Va te faire foutre, espèce de niaiseux.!* Fuck off, you stupid idiot!" My hands throbbed, fat with blood, swollen from the need to hit him. If Helen hadn't grabbed me and pulled me away, I would have jumped on him no matter the consequences.

I looked over my shoulder and kept yelling at him as Helen dragged me away from him: "*Je m'en coliss de ce que tu veux. Je parlerai la langue qui me plais.* I don't give a fuck what you want. I'll speak whatever language I like."

"*Maudit têtes carrées!* Damned square heads!" The term was a slur used against English-speaking Québecers perceived as anti-French.

It felt wonderful to speak out. Why hadn't I done it before? But I knew why: outspoken girls and women were punished for speaking out. Non-compliant women faced endless confrontations in their personal and professional lives, and few had little to show for it in the end except maybe self satisfaction.

Women understood that if we chose to play craps alongside the men that the die were loaded.

"It's not worth getting a black eye over it," Helen said, the daughter of Ukrainian immigrants. "Let's face it, we don't belong here anymore."

For days I fumed. I'd walked the streets of Paris, Rome and Madrid and not once had looked at me askance for speaking English. But here in Montreal, the city I'd called home for more than thirty years, speaking English had made me a target. Helen had been right. We didn't belong there anymore.

Along with majority of my colleagues, including Helen, I left Montreal in 1983, knowing that leaving Quebec was the right decision. And if things didn't work out for me in Ottawa, well, Canada was a big country.

ACKNOWLEDGEMENTS

I met Lisa Meekison and Francine Volker during a mystery writing course we attended at the University of Toronto more than twelve years ago. We've been meeting regularly ever since. Without these two brilliant women with whom to bat around ideas, to challenge me and to encourage me to keep going when the task seemed impossible, this book would not exist. I owe them profound and heartfelt thanks.

My cousin Pasquale Biondi, with his prodigious memory, gave of his time unstintingly to help me fill in some of the blanks as to what happened when. He also provided chapter and verse on what life was like in Campochiaro, Italy, in the 1950s.

My cousin Liliana Stellato recalled details of unsettling things she had witnessed my father do and got stirred up all over again in retelling them.

My thanks to yet another cousin, Lydia Girardello, who picked her father's brain about the past on my behalf.

My friend and former colleague, Don Sellar, did heavy lifting on the final manuscript. Ever the gentleman, any suggestion he put forward came wrapped in great delicacy.

My thanks to Barbara Marks for her impeccable line by line reading.

And my gratitude to the people who read the manuscript and offered encouragement: Celine Gauthier, Daniele Dubois, Angie Biondi, Carmie Guidabrio, and Carla Blackmore.

Photo by Peter Rehak

ABOUT THE AUTHOR

Elvira Cordileone got on a ship with her mother in sunny Naples, Italy, in 1952, at the age of 3. She landed in Halifax, Nova Scotia, and got on a train to Montreal to join her father. She learned French on the city's poorer east-end streets with neighbourhood children. However, like most Italian immigrants at the time, her formal education was entirely in English.

She graduated from Sir George Williams University (since renamed Concordia) with a bachelor's degree in English literature in 1972. The degree equipped her for little other than teaching, but teaching didn't appeal to her sense of adventure, so instead, she took on and left or got fired from a long series of jobs: an invoice clerk in a jewelry factory; a child care worker in a prison for adolescent girls; a magazine production coordinator; a cost accounting clerk; an administrative assistant in a public affairs department, and a publications manager for a national business association, among others.

She moved to Toronto in 1983; six years later, after more dead-end jobs, she found her berth when the Toronto Star hired her as an editorial assistant. Another decade went before the Star promoted her to the job she had longed for: full-fledged reporter. She relished the work and kept at it for the next twelve years, leaving the Star in 2011 to devote herself to writing full-time.

She lives in Toronto's Riverdale area with her dog, Jojo.

*If you enjoyed this title,
you will also enjoy these other Renaissance titles!*

BALLET IS NOT FOR

MUSLIM GIRLS

by MARIAM S. PAL

Mariam wanted to be a Canadian girl.

A "normal" first name would have been a good start. At school they called her Marilyn, Marian - anything but Mariam. Hers was the only house for miles that didn't hand out Halloween candy or put up Christmas lights. When Mariam came home from Grade 1 bawling because she was the only kid who didn't have a turkey sandwich the day after Thanksgiving, her parents started a roasting a bird each year.

From biryani to borscht, the food was always fabulous in Canada's only Polish-Pakistani family. Mariam S. Pal's memoir, *Ballet is not for Muslim Girls*, is set in this remarkable Victoria B.C. household in the 60s and 70s. Growing up, Mariam struggled to navigate three cultures: her Pakistani father's, her Polish-Canadian mother's and Canada's, where Mariam was born and raised.

NOTHING WIHTOUT US

EDITED BY CRIT GORDON AND TALIA C. JOHNSON

"Can you recommend fiction that has main characters who are like us?" This is a question we who are disabled, Deaf, neurodiverse, Spoonie, and/or who manage mental illness ask way too often. Typically, we're faced with stories about us crafted by people who really don't get us. From hospital halls to jungle villages, from within the fantastical plane to deep into outer space, our heroes take us on a journey, make us think, and prompt us to cheer them on. These are bold tales, told in our voices, which are important for everyone to experience.